Revised Knight Templarism Illustrated

by

Charles A Blanchard

ISBN: 978-1930097360

Revised Knight Templarism Illustrated

All Rights reserved. No part of this book may be reproduced without written permission from the publishers, except by a reviewer who may quote brief passages in a review to be printed in a newspaper or magazine.

Printed June, 2014

Published and Distributed By:

Lushena Books, Inc
607 Country
Club Drive,
Unit E
Bensenville, IL 60106

www.lushenabks.com

ISBN: 978-1930097360

Printed in the United States of America

REVISED
Knight Templarism Illustrated.

A FULL AND COMPLETE

ILLUSTRATED RITUAL

OF THE SIX DEGREES OF THE

Council and Commandery,

COMPRISING THE DEGREES OF

Royal Master, Select Master, Super Excellent Master, Knight of the Red Cross, Knight Templar and Knight of Malta.

WITH A SKETCH OF THEIR ORIGIN AND CHARACTER

ONE HUNDRED AND FIFTY MONITORIAL AND FOOT NOTE QUOTATIONS FROM STANDARD MASONIC AUTHORS CONFIRM THE TRUTHFULLNESS OF THIS REVELATION AND SHOW THE CHARACTER OF THESE DEGREES.

Printed In Canada

ORIGINAL PREFACE.

This volume is designed as a companion to "Freemasonry Illustrated," issued in July, 1879, the third edition of which has just been issued. In the preface of that work the following language is used: "To strengthen the testimony of these godly men, [seceders who had testified against the lodge and exposed its so-called secrets] and by a most rigid examination and cross-examination of the witnesses of the defendant in this struggle against the powers of darkness to prove that the published revelations of Freemasonry are correct, and that the doctrines inculcated in its ritual and ceremonies, as stated by the highest Masonic authorities, are more damning than any one would dream from the mere perusal of the ritual and its horrible oaths, is the object of this volume. To accomplish this the monitorial part which is inserted in the body of the degrees, is quoted from standard Masonic monitors, and nearly four hundred foot notes, which consist of extracts from standard Masonic publications, confirm the exposition in every important particular, even to the oaths and murderous penalties. We thus put on the witness stand Dr. Albert G. Mackey, Daniel Sickels, Robert Morris and A. T. C. Pierson, each of whom is a supreme ruler of the order, 33d degree, with the title of *Sovereign Grand Inspector General*. We shall see whether any attempt will be made to impeach their testimony, which is terribly damaging to the order."

Sixteen months have passed since that work was issued and our fondest hopes have been realized. Not only has no champion of the order been foolhardy enough to assail this book, but so overwhelming is the mass of *Masonic* testimony quoted, that to our knowledge lodges in some localities where the book has been circulated have not only ceased making Masons, but rarely hold a lodge meeting, and the Worshipful Master of one of these suspended lodges recently being rallied upon the fact that the lodge so rarely met, answered "The fact is, Mr. ———, you can make Masons cheaper than we can." Mr. ——— had been zealously circulating "Freemasonry Illustrated" in his neighborhood.

Before issuing the work referred to, our plan included another volume giving the Council and Encampment degrees, and we had hoped that "President Blanchard's pen like a trenchant broadsword" might be employed on this work also, but God has ordered otherwise. Whether the spirit of this Elijah of the reform against the lodge has in *any* measure come upon the writer the reader must judge. Certain it is that our work has been accompanied by much prayer to God for divine wisdom.

Though the issue of this volume was planned some time ago, other duties had so crowded upon us that not until the *"Great Knights Templar Triennial Conclave"* in this city was close at hand were we aroused to the importance of the *immediate* issue of this work.

As public attention has, in an unusual degree, been called to the higher Masonic degrees by the Chicago Knights Templar Conclave we are hopeful that the character of Knight Templarism may receive such an investigation as it deserves, and since this volume contains not only the most complete and accurate ritual of these degrees extant, but nearly two hundred different quotations from standard Masonic authors, it does not seem presumptuous to hope that this book may prove of great value as a sort of encyclopedia of Knight Templarism. It is true that the first three degrees of the volume form no part of the Commandery degrees, and some Knights Templar have never taken them, but no careful observer will fail to see that Satanic ingenuity could scarce have contrived ceremonies better calculated to completely terrorize and enslave souls and prepare them to do his bidding. Nor are we dependent upon the ritual and ceremonies themselves for this conclusion; Dr. Albert G. Mackey, Daniel Sickels and Robert Morris, each *"Sovereign Grand Inspector General"* of the order give such overwhelmingly damaging testimony against the order as quoted in the foot notes and monitorial part, that to read their testimony alone must convince every patriot and particularly every Christian that Freemasonry is utterly incompatible with republican institutions and in the highest degree antagonistic to Christianity. In reference to the Council degrees the attention of the reader is particularly called to pages 121-123, where the testimony of Mackey ought to settle the question of the character and design of Freemasonry beyond all dispute. Thus far we have called attention particularly to the Council degrees, not because they are worse than those of the Commandery, for the reverse is true, but they are first in regular order.

The reader will observe that the three Commandery degrees are all knightly or military orders, yet professedly religious. Were it not that Freemasonry from first to last is a system of deception and falsehood, there would be reason for surprise at the conflicting testimony of Mackey and Morris as to the connection of the modern order with the Templars of the Crusades. Some will be not a little astonished to see that with reference to this order Dr. Morris frankly admits the historic fact (note 119) that "wealth and prosperity naturally led to licentiousness, neglect of Templar law and in the end destruction."

As soon as the Christian public realize what a hideously blasphemous, heaven-defying order is in their midst, professedly a defense of Christianity, nay more, professing to be "intensely Christian" (Morris Dict., Art. Christian Masonry), we believe as certain destruction awaits the order of modern Knights Templar.

For overwhelming *Masonic* evidence that the deception and blasphemy practiced in these degrees and orders can not be painted in too dark colors, the reader is referred to Chapters I. and II., pages 121-123 and pages 282-285, and to notes 3, 6, 8, 9, 11, 13, 14, 16, 18, 21, 22, 25, 26, 27, 32, 35, 36, 38, 44, 46, 55, 58, 59, 60, 61, 62, 63, 64, 65, 66, 67, 69, 70, 71, 72, 74, 81, 84, 85, 86, 88, 89, 92, 93, 94, 95, 97, 98, 101, 110, 111, 131, 132 and 134. The monitorial quotations all through the degrees prove conclusively the blasphemous use of the Word of God, and the impious representation even of the life, sufferings, resurrection and ascension of the Lord Jesus.

Ezra A. Cook.

Chicago, Nov. 1, 1880.

REVISER'S PREFACE

Free Masonry Illustrated has been for about twenty-five years before the public, the last edition having been published in 1904. This edition being exhausted, I have been desired by the publisher to go over the book, making such suggestions as seem to me helpful. I hesitate somewhat to do so. Those who knew President Jonathan Blanchard do not need to be told of the powerful manner in which he wrote concerning the evils of secret societies, and all other institutions which seemed to him hostile to the teachings of the Holy Scripture and the interests of mankind. I have, therefore, done this work as well as I might and with some diffidence, and the sincere prayer that God may bless the work committed to the public which must read and judge.

It is not improper in this connection to say a single word respecting the contribution which the publisher has made to the great discussion of the secret society movement in our country and age. He was associated with President Jonathan Blanchard from the beginning of the movement. Personally he was a quiet, earnest man, but devoted himself with prayer and self-forgetfulness to the proclamation of unpopular truths. It is a pleasure, as well as a duty, to testify to the earnestness, the charity and the self-sacrifice with which he has done his work. No man who knew him well is likely to question the propriety of the adjectives just used, and the many who have rejoiced in his testimony, and who have been delivered from the traps, snares and pitfalls which the secret society system has placed for the feet of the unwary, will sympathize with him in these days of his weakness and affliction; and will pray that all Divine blessing may rest upon him and his household.

CHARLES A. BLANCHARD.

Chicago, July 22, 1911.

CONTENTS

Original Preface.. 3
Reviser's Preface.. 7
History of the Council and Commandery Degrees............ 18
    Secret Societies, Parasites, High Wages and Leisure Favorable to them.. 18
    Secret Societies Flourish where Prosperity Abounds.... 19
    Council Degrees introduced in Charleston, S. C......... 19
    The Antiquity of the Secret Orders a Pretense......... 19
    Royal, Select and Superexcellent Masters are Modern Degrees 19
    "Out of Darkness Dark Deeds Grow"....................... 20
    Knights a Cruel, Licentious, Unprincipled Class of Men. 20
    Modern Knight Templarism not the Knight Templarism of the Middle Ages... 21
    Aim to Gratify Vanity, Secure Power, and Immunity from Crime.. 21
Character of the Council and Commandery Degrees......... 22
    The Character of Secret Societies Essentially the same. 22
    A Pretense of some Valuable End to be Secured......... 23
    The Masonic Stone of Foundation a Symbol of Divine Truth 24
    The Order Seeks to Supply Man's Need of Christ in the Soul 24
    "I Will Obey"; "I Will Obey"; "I Will Obey".......... 25
    Penalties of the Knight Templar Degrees call for Murder 26
    Eyes Torn from Sockets, Hands Chopped Off, Body Quartered 26
    The Five Libations.. 27
    "I Think any Man who Breaks his Masonic Oath ought to be Killed".. 27
    Members must Yield Private Judgment.................... 28
    Pray for Double Damnation upon His Soul................ 28
    Why are Good Men in the Lodges............................ 29
    If any man Walk not by this Rule it is because there is no Light in them.. 27
    The Unpardonable Crime of Masonry is Disobedience.. 30
    God does not Allow man to Trust in man. He requires Man to trust in Him... 30

CONTENTS.

Diagram of Royal Master's Council	32
CHAPTER III.—**Royal Master's Degree—Opening Ceremonies**	33
Calling the Council to Order	33
Purging and Tyling the Council	33
Attainment of Truth Design of Masonic Labor. Note 3.	34
Principal Conductor Represents Hiram Abif. Note 5	34
E. A. Due Guard and Sign, and Fellow Craft Due Guard	35
Fellow Craft Sign, Master Mason's Due Guard and Sign	36
Mark Master's Due Guard and Sign	37
Past Master's Due Guard and Sign	38
Most Excellent Master's Due Guard and Sign	38
Royal Arch Due Guard and Sign	39
Royal Master's Due Guard	40
Royal Master's Opening Prayer	40
CHAPTER IV.—**Royal Master's Degree—Initiation**	41
Preparation of Candidate, Royal Master's Degree	41
Monitorial	41
Form Cherubim	42
Prayer by Principal Conductor	42
Royal Master Seeking for the True Word. Note 8	42
Royal Master must be Content with a Substitute for Truth. Note 8	42
Rite of Circumambulation	43
Royal Master's Degree Represents the Imminence of Death. Note 9	43
Monitorial Lessons about Death	43
Symbolic Colors show Grief at Loss of Operative Grand Master. Note 10	45
Initiate under Wings of Cherubim Symbolizes Divine Protection. Note 11	46
Scripture Reading about the Cherubim	47
Divine Truth Concealed under Symbol of Ineffable Name. Note 13	47
The Masonic Steps of Eight Degrees	48
Preparation for Obligation	49
Royal Master's Obligation	49
Royal Master's Grip, or Grip of the Broken Triangle	50
Legend of a Violent Death in Ancient Mysteries. Note 14	50
Coincidence between Ancient Mysteries and Masonry. Note 14	50
Means of Recognition the Practical Value of the Degree. Note 15	50
Blasphemous Use of Alpha and Omega, a Title of Christ. Note 16	50
Scripture Quotation—"Behold I Come Quickly," etc.	52
History, or Narrative Lecture, Royal Master's Degree	52
Legend Refers to Combination to Extort Masonic Secrets. Note 17	52
Investiture of Candidate Represents Instruction in Divine Truth. Note 18	54
Monitorial—Description of the Sanctum Sanctorum	55
CHAPTER V.—**Royal Master's Degree—Lecture**	56
CHAPTER VI.—**Royal Master's Degree—Closing Ceremonies**	60
Closing Prayer, Royal Master's Degree	60
Benediction, Royal Master's Degree	60
Diagram of Select Master's Council	61
Explanation of Select Master's Degree	62
CHAPTER VII.—**Select Master's Degree—Opening Ceremonies**	63

CONTENTS.

This Degree the Summit of Ancient Masonry. Note 20..	63
Accounts for Concealment of Essentials of Craft for 470 Years. Note 20	63
Ancient Mysteries Performed in Subterranean Edifices. Note 21	63
Mysteries Taught the Resurrection. Death and Initiation Synonymous. Note 21	63
The Vault Symbolic of Death. Note 22	64
Initiation Symbolic of Death, where alone is Divine Truth. Note 22	64
Must Descend into Secret Vault of Death to Find Truth. Note 22	64
No less than 9 or more than 27 can Confer this Degree. Note 23	64
Nine a Sacred Masonic Number because Sacred in the Mysteries. Note 24	64
Opening Prayer. Select Master's Degree	65
Due Guard or First Sign, Select Master's Degree	65
Second, Third and Fourth Select Master's Signs	66
Other Select Master's Signs	67
Secrecy, Silence and Darkness the "Words" of the Degree	67
CHAPTER VIII.—Select Master's Degree—Initiation	68
The Tragedy of the Degree Begins—Candidate as Izabud..	68
"O my Unfortunate Friend Izabud!"	69
Izabud and Achishar Historical Personages—Events Legendary. Note 25	69
Laws of Masonry Inviolable, its Penalties Inexorable. Note 26	69
Candidate as Izabud Set Free. Achishar the Grand Steward Executed	71
Oath to Conceal Knowledge of the Secret Vault	71
The Legend about Achishar a Mythical Symbol. Note 27	71
Mercy to Izabud—Zealous Love for Masonry Led him to Disobey. Note 28	71
Obligation of a Select Master	72
Select Master's Sign, Grip and Word	73
Select Master's Pass, Izabud or Ish Sodi, Explained. Note 29	73
History or Lecture in Narrative Form	74
Manner of Concealing Masonic Secrets the Basis of the Degree. Note 30	75
Emblems of the Degree the Trowel and Nine Arches. Note 31	75
Masonry more like the Mysteries of Adonis than any other. Note 32	75
Based on a Beautiful Legend—The Nine Arches not Improbable. Note 33	76
The Ark of the Covenant Necessarily Part of the Paraphernalia. Note 34	79
"The Great Object of all Masonic Labor is Divine Truth." Note 35	79
Divine, Synonym for God—Ineffable Name a Symbol of Truth. Note 35	79
The Masonic Stone of Foundation a Symbol of Divine Truth. Note 36	80
Masonic Legends to Represent the Progress of Truth in the Soul. Note 36	81
Monitorial—Pretended History of the Degree	81
In some states this Degree Precedes the M. E. M. and R. A. Note 37	81
Ineffable Name, when Engraved on it, Sanctifies a Stone Idol. Note 38	81

CONTENTS.

The Masonic God only the Grand Architect of the Universe. Note 38.. 81
World Allegorically Erected on Masonic Stone of Foundation. Note 38 81
Lying Statements about the Power of Heathen Gods..... 82
" Name of God Giving Saul Wisdom 82
Lying Statements about the Name of God Giving David Wisdom 83
Lying Tradition about Solomon Finding Immense Treasures 83
Lying Tradition about Marble Pillar and Grand Omnific Word 83
Lying Tradition about Solomon and the Death of Hiram Abif 84
Pretended Rabbinical Tradition about Adam, Seth and Enoch 84
Ineffable Name Pronounced by High Priest but Once a Year 85
Traditional Explanation of the Jewish Teraphim 85
Charge to Candidate, Select Master's Degree 86
Silence and Secrecy, Cardinal Masonic Virtues 86
CHAPTER IX.—Select Master's Degree—Lecture or Examination 88
Name Gebal, afterward called Byblus, Used in this Degree. Note 39 89
CHAPTER X.—Select Master's Degree—Closing Ceremonies 91
Closing charge, Select Master's Degree 93
Diagram of Super-Excellent Master's Council 94
CHAPTER XI.—Super-Excellent Master's Degree—Opening Ceremonies 95
Positions of Gedaliah, 1st, 2d and 3d Keepers of Temple, etc. Note 40 95
Commemoration of Zedekiah's Perfidy and Punishment. Note 41 95
Due Guard or First Sign, Super-Excellent Master 96
Second Sign, Super-Excellent Master 97
The Most Excellent King Represents Zedekiah. Note 42.. 98
Zedekiah Captured, Eyes Put out, and he Carried to Babylon. Note 43 99
Obligation of a Super-Excellent Master 100
The Pretended Enemy Seize the Candidate 101
Scripture Reading—"How doth the City Sit Solitary," etc. 101
Object to Teach the Fatal Effects of Breaking Masonic Oaths. Note 44 101
Monitorial Hymn—"By Babel's Stream we Sit and Weep" 102
Monitorial—Scripture Reading about the Israelitish Camp 102
Monitorial Verse—"Our Walls no more Resound with Praise" 103
Monitorial Scripture Reading—"Judah is Gone into Captivity," etc. 103
Monitorial Verse—"Here Mourning Toil the Captive Bands" 104
Monitorial Scripture Reading—"The Word of Jeremiah to," etc. 105
Monitorial Verse—"But Should the Ever Gracious Power" 105
The Gedaliahs Mentioned in Scripture. Note 45 105
Grand Hailing Sign of a Super-Excellent Master........ 106
Pass Grip of a Super-Excellent Master 106
Real Grip of a Super-Excellent Master 107
Monitorial History of the Degree 107
Mackey Thinks the Legend of the Degree not Improb-

CONTENTS.

able. Note 46	107
The Moral Purpose of the Degree to Inculcate True Devotion	109
Masons to Erect a Perfect Moral and Masonic Temple in the Heavens	110
Monitorial Charge to Candidate, Super-Excellent Master's Degree	110
Second Moral and Masonic Temple Eternal in the Heavens	111
CHAPTER XII.—Super-Excellent Master's Degree—Lecture	112
CHAPTER XIII.—Super-Excellent Master's Degree—Closing	113
Similar Incidents Found in Royal Arch Degree. Note 47	113
Analysis of the Council Degrees	115
Historical Sketch of these Degrees from Mackey's Ritualist	115
Three Different Masonic Bodies Claim the Right to Sell Them	115
Committee Appointed to Investigate the Matter	115
First Conferred in Sublime Grand Lodge of Perfection, Charleston, S. C.	116
Established there by Three Deputy Inspectors General from Prussia	116
These Deputy Inspectors General Peddle these Degrees Elsewhere	117
Copy of Ritual Furnished Supreme Council of Princes of Jerusalem	118
Rev. Dr. Frederick Dalcho Grand Commander of Supreme Council	119
Originally Side Degrees of the A. & A. Scotch Rite	119
They were Peddled over the Country by Adventurers	119
John Barker, Jeremy L. Cross and others Peddle them by Due Authority	120
Blasphemous Use of Alpha and Omega, a Title of Christ	120
Masonic Claim of their Identity with the Heathen Mysteries	120
Ridiculous Legend about the Nine Arches	120
The Puerile and Ludicrous Story about Izabud and Achishar	121
Secrecy and Silence the Cardinal Masonic Virtues	121
The Pagan, and all False Religions Teach Secrecy and Silence	122
Mackey Teaches Secrecy and Silence in Building Temple of Eternal Life	123
The Teachings of Christ vs. Freemasonry	123
Death to those who Break Masonic Obligations	123
Diagram of Red Cross Council Room	124
CHAPTER XIV.—**Knights of the Red Cross—Opening Ceremonies**	125
This Degree same as Prince of Jerusalem in Scotch Rite. Note 48	125
No Analogy to Chivalric Degrees but Conferred in a Commandery. Note 49	125
Military Drill	126
Plan of Council Room; Divisions Formed Inward Face	128
Sword Practice	130
Draw Swords—Carry Swords—Present Swords	130
Salute—Return Swords—Form Cross	131
Sword Cuts Explained	132
Opening Ceremonies Continued—Drill	133
Jewish Pass—Judah—Benjamin	135
Persian Pass—Tatnai—Shethar-bozani	136
Red Cross word—Veritas	137
Red Cross Grand Sign, Grip. and Word (Libertas)	137

CONTENTS.

Knights at Devotions—The Lord's Prayer 138
The Lecture of the Degree 138
The Name Taken from the Red Cross in their Banner.
    Note 52 143
CHAPTER XV.—Knights of the Red Cross—Initiation 145
The Grand Omnific Royal Arch Word 146
Degree Conferred only on Royal Arch Masons. Note 53.. 147
Founded on Difficulties in Building Second Temple.
    Note 53 147
Candidate represents Zerubbabel, Presiding Officer, King
    Darius. Note 54 147
Monitorial Scripture Lesson 148
"The Grand Council Assembled at Jerusalem." Note 55.. 148
New Hopes of Protection from King Darius. Note 56 ... 148
Vow of Darius before Crowned King to Restore the Holy
    Vessels. Note 57 148
Candidate alias Zerubbabel Offers to go to Babylon to see
    Darius. Note 58 148
The Council joyfully Accept his Offer. Note 59 152
Obligation, Knight of the Red Cross 152
Candidate alias Zerubbabel on the Road from Jerusalem
    to Babylon 154
Captured by Persian Guard, put in Chains and Clothed
    as a Slave. Note 60 155
"A Prince of the House of Judah" Demands to See the
    King. Note 60 155
He Consents to Appear before the King as a Captive and
    Slave. Note 61 155
Darius Admits, Recognizes him and Demands his Business. Note 62 156
Trouble in Rebuilding Temple—Asks the Place of a Servant. Note 63 157
Darius Offers Aid if he will Reveal Masonic Secrets.
    Note 64 157
Royal Favor Declined if only Obtained by Sacrifice of Integrity. Note 65 158
"King Struck with Admiration at his Firmness and Discretion." Note 66 158
Banquet by Darius, Questions Asked by him Afterwards.
    Note 67 158
A Purple Robe, Silken Tiara, etc., for Best Answers.
    Note 67 158
Questions about the Strength of Wine, the King and
    Women. Note 68 159
Dramatic Effect of the Discussion from I Esdras 3:4.
    Note 69 159
Zerubbabel says Women are Stronger,—Truth Beareth
    Victory. Note 70 159
King, Struck with Zerubbabel's Answer, Orders a Discussion. Note 71 159
Monitorial—The Strength of Wine 160
Monitorial—The Power of the King 160
Monitorial—The Power of Women and Truth 161
Monitorial—"Zerubbabel, thou art Found Wisest" 162
"The Rulers and Princes Cried Out, 'Great is Truth and
    Mighty.'" Note 74 162
Monitorial—"O King Remember thy Vow which thou Hast
    Vowed" 162
Darius Embraced him, Gave Passports, Restored Holy
    Vessels. Note 75 162
The Green Sash Reminds us Truth is a Divine Attribute.
    Note 76 163
Symbolic Color, Green; Motto, **Magna est Veritas et Pre-**

CONTENTS.

valebit. Note 77	163
CHAPTER XVI.—Knights of the Red Cross—Lecture or Examination	165
CHAPTER XVII.—Knights of the Red Cross—Closing Ceremonies	178
CHAPTER XVIII.—Knights Templar—Opening Ceremonies	182
Knights Templar Declared by Mackey to be Freemasons. Note 78	182
Assembly Called Commandery—Eminent Commander Presides. Note 79	182
Jewel of Generalissimo a Square with Paschal Lamb above it. Note 80	182
Morris Declares the Templars of the Crusades not Freemasons. Note 81	182
The Duties of the Generalissimo. Note 83	185
Pilgrim's Warrior's Pass—Maher-shalal-hash-baz—Definition. Note 84	185
Pilgrim Warrior's Pass Explained	186
Mackey's Definition of Maher-shalal-hash-baz. Note 85	186
Pilgrim Penitent's Pass—Golgotha	187
Morris Says "Golgotha" is Introduced with much Propriety. Note 86	187
Knight Templarism Originally Run by Roman Catholics. Note 87	189
Knights Templar Grip and Word	190
Immaculate word—Immanuel—Morris Says the Word is Used. Note 88	190
Knights Templar Due Guard	191
Lecture of the Degree	191
Modern Knight Templarism Born in France in 1804. Note 89	191
Successor of Jesuit System of Strict Observance. Note 89	191
Original Name "Poor Fellow Soldiers of Jesus Christ." Note 90	192
Banner—Fair to Friends and Terrible to Enemies of Christ. Note 91	193
Triple Triangle—Prelate's Jewel; a very Sacred Symbol of Deity. Note 92	195
Rebold, the Masonic Historian, Praises the Christless Prayer. Note 93	195
Charity and Hospitality Peculiar Characteristics of the Order. Note 94	196
Monitorial Opening Charge, Knights Templar Degree	197
CHAPTER XIX.—Knights Templar—Initiation	199
Freemasons not Successors of Knights Templar. Note 95	199
Commandery Degrees must not be Sold under Twenty Dollars. Note 96	199
"Gloomy Emblems" of Chamber of Reflection. Note 97	199
Questions Answered in Chamber of Reflection. Note 98	200
Fees for Commandery Degrees must be Fully Paid. Note 100	201
Seven years of Pilgrimage Enjoined on Candidate	202
Candidate Dressed as a Pilgrim with Staff and Sandals. Note 101	202
Monitorial Exhortation by First Guard	203
" " " Second Guard	204
" " " Third Guard	205
" " " First Guard (Another Form)	205
" " " Second " " "	206
" " " Third " " "	207
Avenue Formed for Administering Obligation	208
Knights Templar Obligation	208
Irreligion and Unqualified Equality, Genuine Masonic Se-	

CONTENTS. 15

crets. Note 103 209
Organization of the Grand Encampment, U. S. A., in 1816. Note 104 209
Commanderies can Punish Non-affiliated Members. Note 105 209
Scoundrels Managed the Order in France and Mocked Religion. Note 106 210
Lodges in France Hot-beds of Corruption and Immorality. Note 107 211
Commanderies must Punish the Guilty. Note 108 211
Pilgrim Warrior—His Declaration of Intention 212
Commandery Called an Asylum in Reference to Cities of Refuge. Note 109 213
Masonic Libations because there were Heathen Libations. Note 110 215
Monitorial—First Scripture Lesson, the Betrayal of Christ 216
Knights Commend themselves to God by a Pure Life. Note 111 216
Their Rule or System of Regulations Prescribed by the Pope. Note 112 216
The Twelve Tapers—Candidate Extinguishes One 217
Defection of Judas, the Infamous Model of Treachery. Note 113 217
Monitorial—Second Scripture Lesson, the Agony of Christ at Gethsemane 218
Monitorial—Third Scripture Lesson, Christ before Pilate— His Crucifixion 219
Fourth Libation; to the Memory of Simon of Cyrene 220
One Year's Penance Enjoined on Candidate 220
Monitorial—Fourth Lesson, Christ's Resurrection and Ascension 221
Monitorial—Resurrection Ode 222
Caricature of Death, Resurrection and Ascension of Christ. Note 114 223
The Commandery Called an Asylum. Note 115 225
The Fifth or Double Damnation Libation, from a Skull.. 227
The Fifth Libation Enforced 228
Monitorial—Fifth Scripture Lesson, Matthias Chosen an Apostle 229
Candidate Elected to Fill Vacancy in Number of Masonic Apostles 230
Caricature of this Election Admitted. Note 116 230
Candidate Dubbed and Created a Knight 230
Templars Received in Name of St. Peter, the Pope and Mary. Note 117 230
Pilgrim Penitent Entitled to Rewards of a Valiant Templar. Note 118 231
History of the Order Full of Interest—Their Banner. Note 119 231
Great Wealth Led to Licentiousness and Destruction. Note 119 231
Modern Templarism Constituted Nov. 4, 1804. Note 120.. 231
Sword of Valiant Knight Endowed with Sublime Qualities. Note 121 231
Knights Templar Grand Hailing Sign 232
This Sign Proved Correct by Mackey. Note 122 232
Knights Templar Grip 233
CHAPTER XX.—Knights Templar—Lecture or Examination 234
Crusade Knights Members of the Syriac Fraternities. Note 123 234
Knights Templar Due Guard and Pilgrim Penitent's Pass 248
Knights Templar Grand Hailing Sign, Grip and Word ... 249

CONTENTS.

CHAPTER XXI.—Knights Templar—Closing Ceremonies ... 250
CHAPTER XXII.—Knights of Malta—Opening Ceremonies.. 256
  Vows of Chastity, Obedience and Poverty. Note 124 256
  Titles of the Officers of the Order. Note 125 256
  Original Official Title of Chief Officer "Aletezza Eminent-
    issima." Note 126 257
  A Military, Religious Order Established at Time of Cru-
    saders. Note 127 260
  Knight of Malta Sign 260
  Monitorial—Knight of Malta Opening Prayer 261
CHAPTER XXIII.—Knights of Malta—Initiation 262
  An Appendant Order to the Knights Templar. Note 128.. 262
  Order Abolished in 1856 as Unnecessary; Restored in 1862.
    Note 129 265
  Order must be Conferred after Knights Templar. Note
    130 265
  Knight of Malta Obligation 266
  Paul's Visit to the Island of Malta. Note 131 266
  Monitorial, about Paul's Shipwreck on Island of Malta.... 267
  Grand Sign and Grip of a Knight of Malta 267
  Monitorial about the Unbelief of Thomas 268
  Grand Word INRI 269
  Motto—"Jesus Nazarenus Rex Judaorum" 269
  The grand Word and Motto Proved by Mackey. Note 132 269
  Knights of St. John, Knights of Rhodes, Knights of
    Malta. Note 133 269
  Connection of Modern with Ancient Knights Templar
    Denied. Note 134 270
  Monitorial—Knight of Malta Charge to Candidate 273
CHAPTER XXIV.—Knights of Malta—Lecture or Examina-
  tion 277
CHAPTER XXV.—Knights of Malta—Closing Ceremonies... 280
Analysis Commandery Degrees............................... 282
  Truthful Masons have ceased to Affirm that Non-Masons
    cannot Know Masonry..................................... 282
  Ceremonies of the Council and Commandery Degrees
    may be Known from this Ritual....................... 283
  Knight Templars break the Lord's Day.................... 284
  Churches are Innocent of Wholesale Sabbath Desecration
    which Lodges Practice................................... 284
  Triennial Conclaves attract Loose Women................. 285
  The Bible speaks of Idolatry as Adultery................. 285
  The Order promotes Lewdness among Members and a
    Disregard of God's Laws................................. 285
  Mormons and Mohammedans have nothing that corre-
    sponds to Christian commands.......................... 286
  Our Lord's Friends do His commandments............... 286
  Templarism tends to Destroy Marriage.................... 287
  Not every one that saith to me Lord, Lord shall enter
    into the Kingdom... 287
  Knight Templarism Counterfeits the Teachings of Christ 288
  Burned his Knight Templar Uniform in the Stove........ 288
  Ignores Regeneration by Repentance and Faith.......... 289
  Sin must be Realized and Acknowledged; after Pardon
    comes Cleansing 289
  Newspapers on the Conclave................................ 290
  Prominent dealer Estimated that a Round Million of Dol-
    lars spent for Liquor..................................... 291
  From the Chicago Interocean, Times, the Religious
    Press 292
  Significance of the Emblems................................. 293
  Professions of the Order are Baits, Lures and Snares... 294
  Come out from among them and be ye separate......... 295

CONTENTS.

CHAPTER XXVI.—Secrets of Thirteen Masonic Degrees Illustrated 296
   Secrets and Doctrines of the First Degree Illustrated 296-302
   Secrets and Doctrines of the Second Degree Illustrated 302-304
   Secrets and Doctrines of the Third Degree Illustrated 306-315
   Secrets and Doctrines of the Fourth Degree Illustrated 315-319
   Secrets and Doctrines of the Fifth Degree Illustrated 319-320
   Secrets and Doctrines of the Sixth Degree Illustrated 320-321
   Secrets and Doctrines of the Seventh Degree Illustrated 322-328
   Secrets and Doctrines of the Eighth Degree Illustrated 329
   Secrets and Doctrines of the Ninth Degree Illustrated 329-331
   Secrets and Doctrines of the Tenth Degree Illustrated 331-332
   Secrets and Doctrines of the Eleventh Degree Illustrated 333-337
   Secrets and Doctrines of the Twelfth Degree Illustrated 338-340
   Secrets and Doctrines of the Thirteenth Degree Illustrated 340 341

CHAPTER 1.

HISTORY OF THE COUNCIL AND COMMANDERY DEGREES

Secret Societies Flourish Where Prosperity Abounds.—The Antiquity of the Secret Orders, a Pretense.—Out of Darkness Dark Deeds Grow.—Modern Knight Templarism; not the Knight Templarism of the Middle Ages.—Modern Secret Societies Essentially One with Those of Greece, Rome and Africa.

The United States of America is the great secret society nation of the world. Secret societies being parasites and living upon institutions which are able to furnish them with sustenance, have comparatively small place in savage, semi-civilized and aristocratic countries. The Christian religion makes men free, and increases their leisure and their property. A man who earns from three to ten cents a day as in India, China or Africa, will not have a great deal of time or money to spend upon lodges. A hard working German peasant who earns forty dollars a year by long days of hard labor, does not furnish a very favorable object for secret society plunderers. Where wages are high and hours of labor are comparatively short, and where opinion, speech and assemblage are free, secret societies find their most fertile soil. Thus it has been that the country which was settled by Puritans, Covenanters, by Hollanders, by Huguenots and Lutherans, all of whom by teaching and example condemn secret associations, is a country where secret associations most flourish. A new generation arises which does not know Joseph. The sons of the Pilgrims glorify their fathers with words, and turn their backs upon their examples.

It is also natural that in the United States secret

THE ANTIQUITY OF THE SECRET ORDERS A PRETENCE. 19

societies should find their strongest adherents in the South, where for two hundred years and more white men lived on the unrequited toil of black men, thus having money and time to spend on secret societies. Masonic historians teach us that the Council Degrees were introduced into America in Charleston, South Carolina. Albert G. Mackey gives the names of the Grand Council of Princes of Jerusalem which received through a certain Brother Myers from Frederick II, King of Prussia, certified copies of the Council Degrees. "Although these degrees were once exclusively under the control of the Supreme 'Council of the Ancient and Accepted Scottish Rite," we are assured by Mackey that "the first of the three Council degrees is not ancient, so it is fair to presume that the rest are not." The pretense of antiquity, which is so common among lodge men, is one of the strange things connected with these Orders. Organizations which are formed in our own time, and which are confessedly of the most modern origin, frequently assume the title "ancient" as the badge of their organizations. Why they should do this is a mystery. That they do it, all moderately well informed persons know. We may therefore conclude this section by saying that the degrees of Royal, Select and Superexcellent Masters are modern degrees, probably invented among the infidels of Germany, introduced into this country in Charleston, South Carolina, and now conferred in Councils of Royal and Select Masters throughout the bounds of the Nation

THE HISTORY OF THE COMMANDERY DEGREES

The Commandery degrees, Knights of the Red Cross, Knights Templar and Knights of Malta, are also modern creations. There is a strange inconsistency in the Masonic historians as they write respecting them. We are at one moment given to understand that the Knights of our time are lineally descended from the Knights Templar of the middle ages; at other times Masonic writers tell us plainly that the Knight Templarism of our time has no connection whatever with that of the crusades. Some of these writers speak of the Knights in terms of highest praise (Mackey's Lexicon of Free Masonry, article, Knight Templary); others of them tell us plainly that they were a cruel, licentious, unprincipled class of men. What little honor they had was expended among themselves. Regarding the masses of the people they were an unmitigated shame and curse. (Note 114, page 231, Morris.) In this confusion and discord of Masonic writers, we are thrown back upon our own reason and observation.

Secrecy naturally leads to evil. "Out of the darkness dark deeds grow." No fairly intelligent man doubts that all helpful, wholesome enterprises are open, and that all shameful and malevolent organizations are naturally secret in character. The slightest reflection makes this perfectly plain. Homes are open. Houses of shame are concealed. Men come and go from the one freely and in the light; men come and go from the others secretly and in the dark. Of course there are cases where shame is lost and this latter remark does not apply to, but generally speaking it is absolutely true. The same thing may be said respecting a manufactory of goods for the needs of men, and a manufactory for the coining of counterfeit currency. The same thing can be said about an assemblage for the worship of God in a church, and an assemblage of men for the purpose of stealing horses or cattle. Honest things naturally seek the light; dishonest and evil things naturally seek the cover of secrecy; and the secrecy in many instances produces the evil which it afterward seeks to hide. So here we find that provisions which are needless for any good purpose will always be devoted to some evil one. Reason declares that this must be done; experience shows that it is.

We may conclude here, as in respect to the degrees of Royal, Select and Superexcellent Masters, by saying that the degrees of the Red Cross, the Knights Templar and the Knights of Malta are modern degrees invented for various purposes, e. g., to gratify the vanity of men, to secure power, to secure immunity from crime. We are compelled to affirm that they have no connection whatever with the Knight Templarism of the middle ages. It would be no particular credit to them if they were, but they have no such relation, and their pretense to antiquity must be set down as another falsehood used by the advocates of Templarism as a recommendation for the institution, which thoroughly understood, must be universally condemned.

CHAPTER II

CHARACTER OF THE COUNCIL AND COMMANDERY DEGREES

A Pretense of Some Valuable End to Be Secured.—Characteristics of Knight Templarism Secrecy, and Obedience.—The Order Seeks to Meet Man's Need of Christ in the Soul.—Penalties of the Knight Templar Degrees Call for Murder.—The Lodge a Continuous Education for Murder.—The Five Libations.—Members Must Yield Private Judgment.—Why Are Good Men in Lodges?—The Unpardonable Crime of Masonry Is Disobedience.—Follow Christ's Commands Rather Than the Instructions of the Lodge.—If Any Man Have Not the Spirit of Christ He is None of His.

There is a very wearisome similarity in the Rituals of all secret societies. The character of such orders is essentially the same. If you know one, you in fact know them all. This is true both of the ancient and of the modern secret societies. The mysteries of India, Greece, Rome and Africa did not essentially differ. The secret societies of our own time are also the same in their fundamental principles. There are different names, regalias, and forms of words, but the underlying principles are everywhere identical. For example: There is always a pretense of some good to be gained. This is of course unavoidable. Mackey, speaking of the degree Royal Master, says that "the ceremonies of this degree present one great idea, the truly Masonic one of the laborer seeking for his reward. Through all the symbolism of Masonry from the first to the last degree the search for the word has been considered as a symbolic expression for the search for truth. The attaining of this truth has always been counted to be the great object and design of all Masonic labor."—*Mackey's Ritualist*, page 507.

Why one who is seeking to attain truth should band himself with other men in a secret society he does not even pretend to say. In like manner men tell us that patriotism and brotherhood, relief of suffering and growth in knowledge, are the purposes of one secret society and another; and in all these cases there is no explanation even attempted of the relation between secrecy and the object which is to be secured; but always a pretense of some valuable end to be secured.

SECRET SOCIETIES RELIGIOUS

Another universal fact in secret societies which is very clearly exemplified in the degrees of Royal, Select and Superexcellent Masters is that all these organizations, first or last, in some way or other, deal with the religious needs of man. God has so constructed the human soul that it reaches out for superhuman help. The sense of weakness, the sense of sin, an intimation of immorality, a dread of what it may bring, and the desire for happiness in it, are the common inheritance of the race. At times the religious sense is dulled, pushed into the background, dwarfed, perhaps occasionally seems dead; but in every instance there is a terrible awakening, and in some way or other men seek to satisfy the religious longings of their souls. Christian faith is intended to do two things: first, to help men to live comfortably and well in this world, and in the second place to help men to go into the coming life with hope and joy and blessedness. In some form or other, to some degree or other, lodges seek to meet these two needs, and the degrees of the Council of Royal and Select Masters are like all the rest. For example: Mackey, in his Ritualist, page 549, speaking of the Select Master's degree, says: "The Masonic stone of foundation so conspicuous in the degree of Select Master, is a symbol of Divine Truth, upon which all speculative Masonry is built, and the legends and traditions which refer to it are intended to describe in an allegorical way the progress of truth in the soul, the search for which is a Mason's labor, and the discovery of which is to be his reward."

Truth practised becomes virtue. That is, virtuous action is action according to the facts of the case. When we treat men and things according to their real nature we live virtuously. If we really attain to truth in our hearts we shall live wisely and well in our lives. This is the practical end which all secret societies profess. Temperance, Brotherly Kindness, Faith, Courage, Perseverance; all these are professed objects in the various lodges of our time. If the lodges could really produce the virtues which they profess, they would be as truly religious as the Christian system, which has actually brought about these virtues of which the lodges lyingly boast.

THE KNIGHTS TEMPLAR DEGREE

These degrees, our remarks are especially suggested by the fifth of the Knights Templar degree, are professedly Christian. Ignorant men who know nothing about Christianity and very little about Templary, frequently declare that a faithful member of one of these Templar lodges must be a Christian man. Let us dwell for a moment upon the characteristics of these degrees; and in the first place we remark that their members are introduced in every case by a slave's oath. With a painful iteration that would be ridiculous if it were not tragic, time after time, degree after degree, the candidate is sworn to obey. "I will keep secret," "I will keep secret," "I will keep secret," "I will obey," "I will obey," "I will obey." It would be strange were it not for the fact that evil like good is progressive in character, to know that the assurance of the Master that the lodge oath is not to interfere with the duties of the lodge man is omitted in these higher, or lower, degrees. In the Blue Lodge the candidate has the assurance of the Master that nothing in the ob"gation which he is about to assume shall interfere with the exalted duties which he owes to himself, his family, his country or his God. There is no such statement made in Council or Commandery degrees, but time after time the candidate is simply sworn that he will conceal and that he will obey.

Another characteristic of all these degrees is in the constant repetition of the signs of the degrees. These signs refer either to the destruction of life or the mutilation of the body. The sign of the Entered Apprentice degree is a motion that indicates the cutting of the throat; the sign of the Fellow Craft degree is a motion which indicates the tearing out of the heart; the sign of the Master Mason indicates the cutting in two of the body; the sign of the Mark Master represents the cutting off of the hand. The sign of the Past Master refers to the penalties of the first three degrees, throat cutting, heart tearing out and cutting of the body in two. The sign of the most Excellent Master degree refers to the tearing open of the breast; the sign of the Royal Arch Mason refers to the cutting off of the top of the head. The penalty of the Royal Master is that a candidate be burned alive; of the Select Master that his eyes should be torn from their sockets, his hands chopped off and his body quartered. The penalty of the Superexcellent degree is that his thumbs should be cut off, his eyes put out and his body bound in chains of brass and carried away to a distant land. The penalty of the Knight of the Red Cross is that his house should be torn down, the timbers set up and he hanged thereon. The penalty of the Knight Templar degree is that his head should be smitten off and placed upon the highest spire of Christendom. There is a Satanic perseverance in the way in which these penalties, which call for murder, are constantly kept before the mind of the candidate. In all the Council and Commandery degrees in opening and closing, every one of the signs which refer to these mutilating or murderous penalties has to be given. Every time a man takes a new degree he gets a new sign which reminds him that if he does not stay by the Order, he is likely to lose his life. There are probably twenty-five or thirty well known cases in which Masons have been murdered by their fellow lodge men for failing to maintain their secret society oaths: but instead of wondering at this, one who reads the Rituals and sees how degree after degree a man must not only give the sign which calls for the penalty of that degree, but the signs of the penalties of all the preceding degrees,—I say, when one thinks of this, he is astonished that the murders are not a hundred fold more frequent than they are. I remember well to have been asked at one time by a Knight Templar Mason what the trouble with Masonry was. He said that he tried to be a decent man, and he could not see what the objection to the lodge could be. I replied, well, there are many objections; one of them is that the lodge is a continuous education for murder. He said: "That is nonsense; there is not a word of truth in it." I said, well, let me ask you a question; do you think that a man could be in a Masonic lodge room once a week, and hear the oath administered and see the signs given, without coming to believe that it would be right to kill a man who should break his Masonic oath? "Why," he replied, "I think any man who breaks a Masonic oath ought to be killed." Well, I said, then you have in yourself evidence for the truth of what I say; killing a man for breaking a Masonic oath in this country is murder, and you are ready for it now.

The third characteristic of these degrees is that they are blasphemous. For example: To have drunken, profane, Godless men forming the Cherubim, which they do repeatedly in the Council of the Royal and Select Masters, is one instance. Then to have the same sort of men kneeling on one knee, or on the other knee, or on both knees, and putting their hands on the Bible,—not the Bible as a sacred book, but on the Bible with the square and compass above it, three "articles of furniture" as they are called. Then to have men, such as we all know to be in the Councils of Royal and Select Masters, and in the Commanderies of Knights Templar, repeating such words as these:

"And behold I come quickly and my reward is with me to give every man according as his work shall be." "I am Alpha and Omega, the beginning and the end, the first and the last." Words which seem perfectly appropriate in the mouth of our Lord and Savior, but horribly blasphemous in the mouths of men who in Councils and Commanderies are repeating them.

I heard a seceding Mason once say: "I have not gone so far in Masonry as some men have, but I went far enough to see a drunken, profane wretch sitting behind a burning bush saying, 'I am the God of thy fathers,' and that was far enough for me."

The way in which the lodge in the Select Master's degree speaks of the Word of God is another instance of the same sort; the name of God is spoken of as used among the Jews, as used among the fire worshipers, then as among the Trojans and Canaanites, then among the Egyptians, and one receives the impression that one of these words is about as good as another, that they all mean substantially the same thing, so that God or Baal may be used indifferently. In the Commandery perhaps the most horrible instance of this kind is in the Chamber of Reflection, where a skull is placed on the Bible and where the five libations are taken: one to the honor of Solomon, one to the honor of Hiram of Tyre, one to the honor of Hiram the architect, a fourth in honor of Simon the Cyrenian and the fifth is declared to be a testimony to belief in immortality of the soul and the candidate says: "As the sins of the whole world were laid upon the head of my Savior, so may the sins of him whose skull this was (speaking of the skull bowl out of which he drinks) be laid upon me in addition to my own, should I prove untrue to this, my solemn obligation of a Knight Templar." What a wretched mixup there is of truth and falsehood, and what a horrible thing for a human being, a sinner who must be saved by the blood of Jesus, or die eternally, to pray double damnation upon his soul in this fashion.

FREE MASONRY AN ABSOLUTE CHRISTLESS DESPOTISM

This is evident on every page of the Masonic Law. Low degrees and high degrees alike bear their testimony to this tremendous fact. General A. T. C. Pierson says: "We may not call in question the propriety of this organization. If we would be Masons we must yield private judgment; to the law and to the testimony, if any man walk not by this rule, it is because there is no light in him." (*Pierson's Traditions, page* 30). Albert G. Mackey says in his Lexicon article, "Master of the Lodge": "The power of the Master in his lodge is absolute." He says again in an article "obedience": "The Mason is obedient to the Master, the Master to the lodge and the lodge to the Grand Lodge." Robert Morris, on page 195 of Webb's Monitor, edition with the synopsis of Masonic law, says: "The first duty of the reader of this synopsis of Masonic law is to obey the edicts of his Grand Lodge, right or wrong. His very existence as a Mason hangs upon obedience to the powers immediately set above him. Failure in this must invariably bring down expulsion, which as a Masonic death, ends all. The one unpardonable crime in a Mason is contumacy or disobedience."

What is here stated in plain terms is implied throughout the whole work of lodge, chapter, council and commandery. There is no provision in the whole system for the exercise of conscience on the part of the Mason. Secrecy and obedience are declared to be the cardinal virtues of the Mason. He may be a drunkard and an adulterer, a thief, and be a worthy Mason. That is to say, he will not by the commission of any of these offenses necessarily deprive himself of membership in the Order, but he must obey, and if he does not obey, then he becomes a Masonic outcast. He must conceal the proceedings of his lodge, chapter, council or commandery from his wife, from his neighbors and friends who are not Masons, from his brethren in the Church, if he professes to be a Christian; and if he does this, keeps the secrets of the Order and obeys the commands, signs, summons and tokens sent to him, he then may be a good and satisfactory member of the Order. Is it possible to conceive of any Satanic institution more clearly and evidently devilish than this?

MASONIC PREACHERS AND CHURCH MEMBERS

We are continually asked how it is possible that Free Masonry should be such a system as a study of these degrees shows it to be, and that at the same time ministers, members and other officers of churches should be connected with the Order. It is undoubtedly a great mystery, but it is not the only one. Anyone who reads the New Testament knows that Jesus would have his brethren clean, and yet all know that many of them are not so. How can professed Christians accumulate money, as they do, neglecting the cry of the suffering, and the needs of a thousand million heathen? How can professed Christians bribe legislators or judges, and how can professed Christians who are judges or legislators, accept bribes, and do the unlawful things which many of them do? How was it possible for ministers, bishops and members of churches to own slaves, and buy them and sell them, and work them without wages, and educate, clothe and feed their own children by selling slave children? How was it possible that professed Christian people should do such things as these? Everybody who knows the facts at all, knows that they did just such things, and it is not any more difficult to understand how professed Christians should be lodge men, should consent to the shameful and degrading ceremonies, should incur heathenish obligations, and the murderous, devilish penalties of lodge, chapter, council and commandery, than it is to understand how they should do these other things which all men know they have done, some of which they are still doing. The fact is, God does not allow man to trust in man. He requires man to trust in Him. Jesus never told us to follow the example of pastors, elders, bishops or deacons: He told us to follow Him. If we fail to do this we fail to live Christian lives; and every reader, if he is a professing Christian, should seriously ask himself this question: "Am I leading the Christlike life? Am I speaking and acting as Jesus did?" If not, then so far as he fails of thus living, he fails of the Christian life, and if he is not in will and purpose devoted thus to live, he is not a Christian at all. "If any man have not the spirit of Christ, he is none of His."

32   DIAGRAM OF ROYAL MASTER'S COUNCIL.

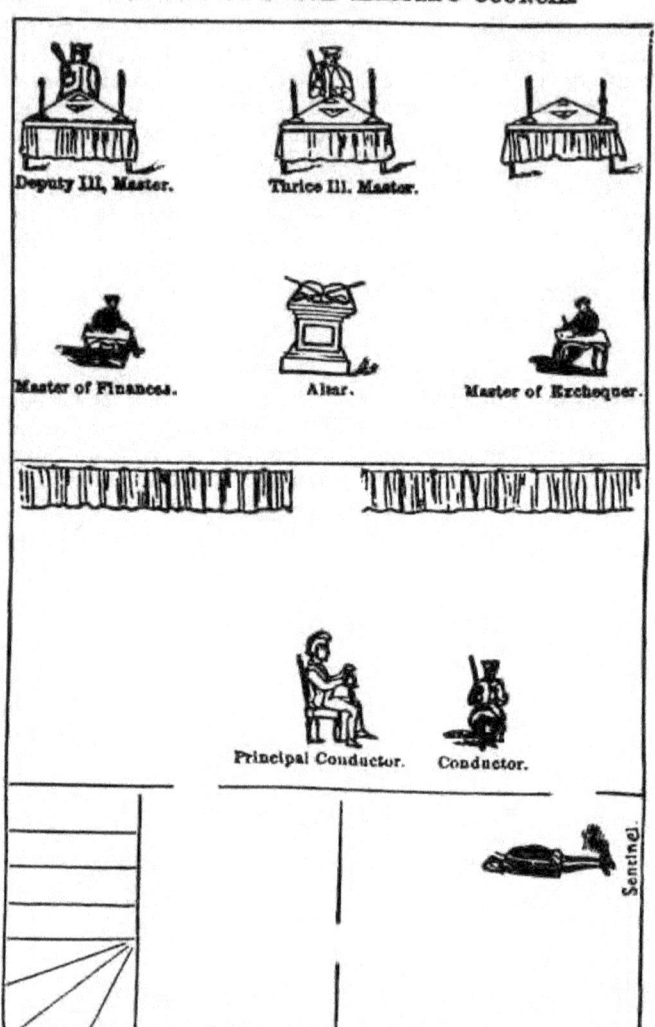

KNIGHT TEMPLARISM ILLUSTRATED.

CHAPTER III.

EIGHTH, OR ROYAL MASTER'S DEGREE.

OPENING CEREMONIES.

Thrice Illustrious Master'(one rap, calling to order)—Companion Captain of the Guard proceed to satisfy yourself that all present are Royal Masters.

Captain of the Guard (having looked around)—Thrice Illustrious, all present are Royal Masters.

Thrice Illustrious Master—Is the Sentinel at his post and the sanctuary securely guarded?

Captain of Guard—I will ascertain and report. Companion Steward see that the Sentinel is at his post and the sanctuary securely guarded, and inform him that the Thrice Illustrious Master is about to open —— Council' —— of Royal Masters, and direct him to guard accordingly. (Steward gives eight raps, three three and two, 000-000-00 on the door, Sentinel answers with the same when Steward opens the door, communicates the order, returns and reports:)

Steward—Companion Captain of the Guard, the Sentinel is at his post and the sanctuary securely guarded.

Captain of Guard—Thrice Illustrious Master, the sanctuary is secure.

Thrice Illustrious Master—Are you a Royal Master?

Captain of Guard—I have visited the *sanctum sanctorum* and seen the glory of Israel.

NOTE 1.—"THRICE ILLUSTRIOUS GRAND MASTER, as King Solomon, seated in the East, dressed in purple robes, a crown on his head and a sceptre in his hand. His jewel is a square and trowel, within a triangle."—*Sickels' Monitor, Part 3, page* 3.

NOTE 2.—"The assembly of Royal and Select Masters is called a Council."—*Sickels' Monitor, Part* 3, *page* 3.

ROYAL MASTER'S DEGREE.

Thrice Illustrious Master—Where were you received as a Royal Master?

Captain of Guard—In a legally constituted Council of Royal Masters,² assembled in a place representing the *sanctum sanctorum* of King Solomon's Temple.

Thrice Illustrious Master—How many compose such a Council?

Captain of Guard—Nine⁴ or more.

Thrice Illustrious Master—When composed of nine of whom does it consist?

Captain of Guard—Thrice Illustrious Master, Deputy Illustrious Master, Illustrious Principal Conductor,⁵ Captain of the Guard, Companions Treasurer, Recorder, Conductor, Steward and Sentinel.

Thrice Illustrious Master—Companion Captain of the Guard, it is my order that —— Council —— of Royal Masters be now opened for work.

Captain of Guard—Companions, it is the order of the Thrice Illustrious Master that —— Council —— be be now opened for work; take due notice and govern yourselves accordingly.

[Led by the Master, the signs and due guards from Entered Apprentice to Royal Master are now given:]

NOTE 3.—"The ceremonies of the degree of Royal Master are very brief and simple—briefer and simpler, indeed, than those of any of the preceding degrees. Symbolically, however, they present one great idea—the truly Masonic one—of the laborer seeking for his reward. Throughout all the symbolism of Masonry, from the first to the last degree, the search for the WORD has been considered but as a symbolic expression for the search after Truth. The attainment of this Truth has always been acknowledged to be the great object and design of all Masonic labor."—*Mackey's Ritualist, page 507.*

NOTE 4.—"No less than nine nor more than twenty-seven Royal Masters can work together in a council; if more are present they refrain from taking part in the proceedings."—*Morris' Dict., Art. Royal Master.*

NOTE 5.—"PRINCIPAL CONDUCTOR OF THE WORK, as Hiram Abif, on the left of Solomon, dressed in scarlet and yellow robes. His jewel is the plumb and trowel, within a triangle."—*Sickels' Monitor, Part 2, page 2.*

OPENING CEREMONIES.

Due-Guard, Entered Apprentice.

DUE-GUARD OF AN ENTERED APPRENTICE.

Hold out left hand, with palm up, a little in front of the body, height of hips; next place right hand horizontally over the left, two or three inches above it. [See cut.]

SIGN OF AN ENTERED APPRENTICE.

Made from due-guard by dropping left hand to side, and at same time raise right arm, with hand still open, and draw hand quickly across the throat, the thumb being next to the throat, then hand drops to side. [See cut.]

Sign of Entered Apprentice.

Due-Guard, Fellow Craft.

DUE-GUARD OF A FELLOW CRAFT.

Hold out right hand, palm down, height of hips, and raise left hand to point perpendicularly upward, forearm forming a right angle with arm. [See cut.]

36   ROYAL MASTER'S DEGREE.

SIGN OF A FELLOW CRAFT.

Made from due-guard by dropping left hand carelessly to side while raising right hand to left breast, fingers crooked a little; then draw hand quickly across the breast; then drop hand to side. [See cut.]

Sign of Fellow Craft.

Due-Guard, Master Mason.

DUE-GUARD OF A MASTER MASON.

Extend both hands, in front of the body, height of hips, palms down, thumbs nearly touching each other. [See cut.]

SIGN OF A MASTER MASON.

Made from due-guard, by dropping left hand and drawing right hand across the bowels to the right, thumb toward the body, height of hips. [See cut.]

Sign of a Master Mason.

OPENING CEREMONIES. 37

Due-Guard, Mark Master.

DUE-GUARD, OR SIGN OF SMITING OFF RIGHT EAR.

Third and fourth fingers of right hand closed; thumb and first and second fingers extended; position of carrying the keystone; then bring right hand up to right ear and move it back and forth as if brushing back a lock of hair, ear passing between thumb and fingers each time. [See cut.] This refers to the penalty of having right ear smote off.

SIGN OF A MARK MASTER.

Made from due-guard by dropping right hand and arm to a horizontal position, extended in front on a line with the hips, and at same time raise left hand about the height of your chin, and bring it down edgewise on right wrist, as if to chop off right hand. [See cut.] This refers to last part of penalty of the obligation of this degree.

Sign, Mark Master.

88 ROYAL MASTER'S DEGREE.

PAST MASTER'S DUE-GUARD.

Fingers of right hand closed, end of thumb between closed lips, as if ready to split open the tongue with thumb nail.

P. M. SIGN.

Raise right hand to left shoulder, hand open, and draw it diagonally down across body to right hip, thus crossing the penalties of the first three degrees

Step and Due-Guard of Past Master.

Sign of a Past Master.

DUE-GUARD, OR PENAL SIGN, MOST EX. MASTER.

Hands on center of breast, fingers just touching each other, crossed as if to tear open breast, which is the penalty of this degree. [See Cut.]

SIGN, OR SIGN OF ASTONISHMENT.

Hands and arms extended forwards and upwards, eyes rolled back. [See cut.]

Due-Guard or Penal Sign M. E. Master.

Sign of Astonishment, Most Excellent Master.

OPENING CEREMONIES.   39

R. A. Due-Guard—First Position.

ROYAL ARCH DUE-GUARD.

Turning to the left and looking up, raise left hand and arm, as shown in cut, first position, palm of hand out; then bring up right hand, with a slight slap on back of left; then turn to the right, and raise right hand, and bring up left hand with a slap on right hand.

R. A. Due-Guard—Second Position.

ROYAL ARCH SIGN.

Right hand held with edge against forehead, thumb next to forehead; then draw hand across to the right. This refers to the penalty of the degree—skull smote off.

Royal Arch Sign.

ROYAL MASTER'S DEGREE.

DUE GUARD OF A ROYAL MASTER.
Place forefinger of right hand on lips.

Due-guard.

Thrice Illustrious Master (eight raps, 000 000 00.)
Deputy Illustrious Master (eight raps 000 000 00.)
Principal Conductor (eight raps 000 000 00.)

PRAYER ON OPENING A COUNCIL OF ROYAL MASTERS.

"Almighty God thou art from everlasting to everlasting; unchangeable in thy being; unbounded and incomprehensible. Thou didst speak into being this vast fabric of the Universe. We adore and bow before thee with reverential awe, and acknowledge our sins and misdeeds for thou hast promised to heal our backslidings and to love us freely. Look down from thy holy habitation and bless us with thy approbation. Teach us to praise thy holy Name aright, for thou art the God whom we fear, and to whom we bow with humble submission. Lord, hear our prayer, and accept our sacrifice of thanksgiving."—*Mackey's Ritualist*, page 513.

All—So mote it be.

Thrice Illustrious Master—I declare —— Council —— of Royal Masters opened. Companion Captain of the Guard, inform the Tyler, (one rap all seated. Tyler is informed in same manner as before.)

NOTE 6.—"This prayer, and the one for closing, were in use by the Supreme Council of Sovereign Grand Inspectors General, from the first introduction of the degree into this country by that body. The ritual in my possession, which contains these prayers, was copied by the Grand Commander, about the year 1822, from the authorized ritual in the archives. Their beauty and antiquity justify their retention in every manual of Cryptic Masonry."—*Mackey's Ritualist, page* 13.

CHAPTER IV.

EIGHTH, OR ROYAL MASTER'S DEGREE.

INITIATION.

Thrice Illustrious Master—Companion Captain of the Guard, you will see that the candidate is prepared and presented. (Captain of the Guard goes to the preparation room, takes off candidate's coat and hands him a golden bowl or basin (imitation gold) when they enter the council room, pass to the northeast corner and then to the east in front of the Principal Conductor, who, representing Hiram Abif, stands at a table where there are or should be other golden (?) vessels. See diagram.)

Captain of Guard—I have a piece of work for your inspection.

Principal Conductor (as Hiram Abif, taking the vessel from candidate)—This is a beautiful piece of work indeed and the companion who wrought it is worthy of the confidence of the craft and in due time shall receive his reward. (Principal Conductor turns to his table, examines the vessels and then reads from a monitor:

"And Solomon made all the vessels that pertained unto the house of the Lord: the altar of gold, and the table of gold, whereupon the shew-bread was; and the candlesticks of pure gold; five on the right side and five on the left, before the oracle; with the flowers, and the lamps, and the tongs of gold; and the bowls, and the snuffers, and the basins, and the spoons, and the censers of pure gold: and the hinges of gold, both for the doors of the inner house, the most holy place, and for the doors of the house, to wit, of the Temple. So Hiram made an end of doing all the work that he

---

NOTE 7—"GRAND CAPTAIN OF THE GUARD, as Adoniram, in the West, dressed like the Royal Arch Captain. His jewel is battle-ax and trowel, within a triangle."—*Sickels' Monitor, Part 5, page 4.*

made King Solomon for the house of the Lord.—1 Ki. 7: 48,-5), 40."—*Sickels' Monitor, Part 3, page 4.*

Thrice Illustrious Master—Illustrious Companion Principal Conductor, how goes the hour?

Principal Conductor—High twelve, Thrice Illustrious.

Thrice Illustrious Master—It being high twelve you will call the craft from labor to refreshment.

Principal Conductor (three raps)—Companions, it is the will and pleasure of Thrice Illustrious King Solomon, that the craft be now called from labor to refreshment. You are so called (one rap). (The Companions now form a "cherubim" about the altar; that is, form so as to represent the outstretched wings; the Principal Conductor, leaving his table, goes to the south side of the cherubim, enters, goes to the altar and repeats:)

PRAYER BY PRINCIPAL CONDUCTOR.

"Remove far from me vanity and lies; give me neither poverty nor riches; feed me with food convenient for me; lest I be full and deny thee and say, Who is the Lord? or lest I be poor and steal and take the name of my God in vain."—*Chase's Council Monitor, page 11.*

(At the conclusion of his prayer the Principal Conductor approaches the west, when the Captain of the Guard, who had remained south of the cherubim follows the Principal Conductor, and the Captain of the Guard says:)

Captain of Guard—Grand Master Hiram Abif, when shall I receive the Master's Word?

Principal Conductor—My worthy friend Adoniram,*

NOTE 8.—"The reward had been promised, and the time had now come, as Adoniram thought, when the promise was to be redeemed, and the True Word—divine Truth—was to be imparted. Hence, in the person of Adoniram, or the Royal Master, we see symbolized the Speculative Mason, who, having labored to complete his spiritual temple, comes to the Divine Master that he may receive his reward, and that his labor may be consummated by the acquisition of Truth. But the temple that he has been building is the temple of this life; that first temple which must be destroyed by death, that the second temple of the future life may be built on its foundations. And in this first temple the truth can not be found. We must be content with its substitute. This, then, is the symbolism of the Royal Master's degree."—*Mackey's Ritualist, page 208.*

it is uncertain whether you will ever receive it, for by the solemn obligation assumed by Solomon, King of Israel, Hiram, King of Tyre and myself, it can not be communicated until the Temple is completed and we three are present and agreed. Then, and not till then, all those who shall prove themselves worthy, by their industry, skill and fidelity, shall receive the secrets of a Master Mason. [The Principal Conductor turns to pass on towards the west, when the Captain of the Guard again stops him with a question:]

Captain of Guard—Grand Master Hiram, this being so, suppose one of you three, even you, yourself, should be removed hence by death, prior to the completion of the Temple, what then would become of the Master's Word? (Principal Conductor stands meditating a moment, then taking candidate by the left arm, moves slowly about the altar, moving with the sun, as in all the degrees in the rite of circumambulation. As they pass along, he says:)

Principal Conductor—"Companion Adoniram, death is a subject that admits of no levity, when mentioned by mortal man. The young *may* die, the old *must* die, the wisest knoweth not how soon.

"The youngest Entered Apprentice upon the checkered pavement below, dwells even in the shadow of death," while the invisible hand extends equally above King Solomon on his ivory throne. We walk upon the ashes of the generations who have gone this way before us, and our bodies must soon crumble into dust. It is not for me, Companion Adoniram, to hope that I shall escape the common doom of man, but when [I die they will bury it here.]

NOTE 9.—"Its ritual is ingeniously arranged. The imminence of death and the confusion that our temporal affairs experience by its sudden approach, are eloquently wrought into it."—*Morris' Dict., Art. Royal Master.*

"Death terminates the labor of a man. There is no work, nor device, nor knowledge, nor wisdom in the grave. The most gifted of mortal k.ngs thus meditates: 'Brief life is here our portion.' Speedily do we hasten to the end of these cares and labors. What an incentive is this to an industrious use of our faculties, that we should labor diligently to complete that inner temple for God's eternal praise and be ready to sleep in peace, as the night cometh when no man can work. My work, Companion Adoniram, is not finished though I have labored faithfully and long, but when [I die they will bury it here.]

Companion Adoniram, it is through the gate of death that we find an entrance to the place of wages, refreshment and rest. The Supreme Master of the universe, before whom we bow in adoration, and whose All-seeing Eye has marked our labors in the lodge below, promises to spread before us in the stupendous lodge above all the joys and glories of his Eternal Sabbath. After the strong hand of death has leveled all in the humiliation of the grave, the Almghty hand of the Supreme Master shall prevail and exalt every brother to the glorious companionship of that undissolving lodge. There the designs upon the trestle-board will be seen completed. There the adoration of the twelfth hour will be the everlasting joy. There the noontide of bliss will eternally shine. There the scales of doubt and darkness shall fall from my eyes and the wise purposes of the Divine Architect be displayed in all their splendor. With this light of faith beaming upon me, O death where is thy sting!

'My hope, Companion Adoniram, rests in the higher

INITIATION. 45

lodge to which I am advancing, and when [I die they will bury it here]."—*Chase's Council Monitor, page 11.*

[The Principal Conductor passes around to the east, and the Captain of the Guard and candidate mingle with the companions who "break cherubim.")

Thrice Illustrious Master—Illustrious Companion Principal Conductor, how goes the hour?

Principal Conductor—It is one hour past high twelve, Thrice Illustrious.

Thrice Illustrious Master—It being one hour past high twelve you will call the craft from refreshment to labor.

Principal Conductor (three raps)—Companions it is the will and pleasure of Thrice Illustrious King Solomon, that the craft be now called from refreshment to labor. You are so called (one rap).

Captain of Guard—The craft being called from refreshment to labor we will repair to the clay grounds between Succoth and Zarthan and there resume our labors. [Captain of the Guard retires to the preparation room with the candidate. The jewel and gavel of the Principal Conductor (Hiram Abif") are placed on his table clothed in mourning and his seat is vacant in preparation for the initiatory ceremonies.]

Conductor of Candidate (in preparation room, eight raps).

Captain of Guard—Thrice Illustrious, there is an alarm at the door of the preparation room.

NOTE 10.—"The symbolic colors of a Royal Master are black and red. The black is significant of the grief of the craft for the loss of their Operative Grand Master, and the red, of his blood, which was shed in defense of his integrity. Hence the apron and collar of a Royal Master should be black, lined and edged in red. The apron must be triangular in form, in allusion to the sacred Delta."—*Mackey's Ritualist, page 512.*

Thrice Illustrious Master—Attend to the alarm.

Captain of Guard (stepping to the door and giving eight raps)—Who comes here?

Principal Conductor—A companion Royal Arch Mason, who wishes to receive further light in Masonry by being admitted to the rights and honors of a Royal Master.

Captain of Guard—Is it of your own free will and accord?

Candidate—It is.

Captain of Guard—Companion Conductor, is he worthy and well qualified?

Conductor—He is.

Captain of Guard—Is he duly and truly prepared?

Conductor—He is.

Captain of Guard—Has he made suitable proficiency in the preceding degrees?

Conductor—He has.

[The same dialogue occurs between the Captain of the Guard and Thrice Illustrious Master.]

Captain of Guard (to Council)—You will form cherubim" from wall to wall for the reception of candidate, and it is the will and pleasure of the Thrice Illustrious that the candidate enter this Council of Royal Masters and be received in due and ancient form. [They enter and pass eight times under the cherubim, the Thrice Illustrious Master reading from a monitor:]

NOTE 11.—"The cherubim were eminently and purely symbolical. But although there is great diversity of opinion as to their exact signification, yet there is a very general agreement that, under some one manifestation or another, they allude to and symbolize the protecting and overshadowing power of the Deity. When, therefore, the initiate is received beneath the extended wings of the cherubim, we are taught by this symbolism how appropriate it is, that he who comes to ask and to seek Truth, symbolized by the True Word, should begin by placing himself under the protection of that Divine Power who alone is Truth, and from whom alone Truth can be obtained."—*Mackey's Ritualist*, page 515.

INITIATION.
SCRIPTURE READING.

"And he set the cherubim within the inner house: and they stretched forth the wings of the cherubim, so that the wing of the one touched the one wall, and the wing of the other cherub touched the other wall; and their wings touched one another in the midst of the house.— Kings."—*Sickels' Monitor, Part 3, page 5.*

[As they pass the station of the Thrice Illustrious Master the first time he gives one rap; and two the second time, etc. When they reach the west the eighth time the Thrice Illustrious dissolves the cherubim" by one rap, when the Captain of the Guard with candidate approaches the east.]

Captain of Guard (eight raps in front of Thrice Illustrious Master.)

Thrice Illustrious Master—Who comes here?

Captain of Guard—A companion Royal Arch Mason who wishes to receive further light" in Masonry by being admitted to the rights and honors of a Royal Master.

[The candidate is required to give the signs and due guards from Entered Apprentice to Royal Arch, as given pages 33 to 39.]

Thrice Illustrious Master (to Captain of the Guard)—You will conduct the brother to the west and teach him how to approach the east by eight upright, regular steps, his feet forming two sides of an equilateral tri-

---

NOTE 12.—"The principal emblem of this degree is the cherubim. The name of Adoniram is introduced with much effect."—*Morris' Dict., Art. Royal Master.*

NOTE 13.—"Divine Truth—the knowledge of God—concealed in the old Cabalistic doctrine, under the symbol of his Ineffable Name, and typified in the Masonic system, under the mystical expression of the True Word, is the reward proposed to every Mason who has faithfully wrought his task. It is, in short, the 'Master's wages.' Now, all this is beautifully symbolized in the degree of Royal Master."—*Mackey's Ritualist, page 508.*

angle. (Candidate is conducted to the west and faced around to the east.)

Captain of Guard (to candidate)—Step off with your left foot as an Entered Apprentice; (he steps off with *left* foot, bringing heel of right to hollow of *left* foot) with your right foot as a Fellow Craft; (he steps off with *right* foot and brings heel of left to hollow of *right* foot) with your left foot as a Master Mason; (he steps off with the left foot bringing the heel of the right to the heel of the left) with your right foot as a M rk Master; (he steps off with the right foot bringing the heel of the left to the toe of the right foot) with your left foot as a Past Master; (he steps off with the left foot bringing the right heel to the toe of the left foot) with your right foot as a Most Excellent Master; (he steps off with the right foot bringing the heel of the left to the heel of the right foot) with your left foot as a Royal Arch Mason; (he steps off with the left foot bringing the heel of the right to the hollow of the left).

Captain of Guard (to candidate)—Take one additional step with your right foot and bring both heels together; your feet forming two sides of an equilateral triangle.

Captain of Guard (to Thrice Illustrious Master)—Your orders have been obeyed Thrice Illustrious.

Thrice Illustrious Master (to candidate)—Companion you are again before the altar of Freemasonry.

Thrice Illustrious Master—Companion Captain of the Guard, place the candidate in due form to be made a Royal Master.

Captain of Guard (to candidate)—Advance, kneel on both knees, your body erect and both hands resting on the Holy Bible, square and compass.

INITIATION.

Captain of the Guard—Thrice Illustrious, the candidate is in due form.

OBLIGATION.

Thrice Illustrious Master (three raps, all rise)—You will repeat your name and say after me: "I, ———, of my own free will and accord, and in the presence of Almighty God and this Council of Royal Masters erected to him and dedicated to Hiram Abif, do hereby and hereon most solemnly and sincerely promise and swear that I will not communicate the secrets belonging to this degree to any one of an inferior degree, nor to any person or persons whomsoever, except it be to a true and lawful Companion Royal Master or in a regularly constituted Council of such, nor unto him or them until by strict trial, due examination or legal information, I shall have found him or them as lawfully entitled to the same as I am myself.

"I furthermore promise and swear that I will stand to and abide by all the laws, rules and regulations of any Council of Royal Masters of which I may become a member, and the constitution and laws of the Grand Council under whose jurisdiction the same may work.

"I furthermore promise and swear that I will answer and obey all due signs and summons sent me from a Council of Royal Masters, or handed me by a companion Royal Master, if within the length of my cable-tow.

"I furthermore promise and swear that I will not cheat, wrong or defraud, a Council of Royal Masters, or a companion Royal Master, knowingly.

"All this I promise and swear with a firm and steadfast resolution to perform the same, binding myself under no less a penalty than that of being burned alive."

Thrice Illustrious Master (to candidate)—Companion,

you now discover me approaching you on the step and under the due guard of a Royal Master. (Turns toward the east, to Hiram King of Tyre, who stands near, and they give the "grip of the broken triangle."

Thrice Illustrious Master—What do you see there?

Deputy Master (as Hiram, King of Tyre)—A broken triangle.

Royal Master's Grip.

GRIP OF THE BROKEN TRIANGLE OR ROYAL MASTER'S GRIP.

Right hand hold of each other's right wrist, and left hand hold of each other's left wrist, raise arms as if to begin giving the Royal Arch word, when left hands fall to side and right drop on to each other's shoulders, each looks down and the dialogue begins.

Thrice Illustrious Master—Alas!

Deputy Master—Poor Hiram!

[It takes three to give the Grand Omnific or Royal Arch Word and hands and feet all form triangles.]

Thrice Illustrious Master (turning toward the altar) —Companions! Masonic tradition informs us that this grip of the broken triangle originated in this manner: Shortly after the death of our Grand Master Hiram Abif," Solomon King of Israel and Hiram King of

---

NOTE 14.—"In all the initiations into the mysteries of the ancient world, there was, as it is well known to scholars, a legend of the violent death of some distinguished personage, to whose memory the particular mystery was consecrated; of the concealment of the body and of its subsequent discovery. That part of the initiation which referred to the concealment of the body was called the '*aphanism*,' from a Greek verb which signifies 'to conceal,' and the part which referred to the subsequent finding was called the '*euresis*,' from another Greek verb, which signifies 'to discover.' It is impossible to avoid seeing the coincidences between this system of initiation and that practiced in the Masonry of the third degree."—*Mackey's Ritualist, page* 509.

INITIATION.

Tyre, met in the *sanctum sanctorum* or holy of holies and involuntarily placed themselves in this position to give the Grand Omnific Word, when, quickly remembering that one of their illustrious number was absent never more to return, they sadly placed their hands on each other's shoulders and looking down, King Solomon inquired, "What do you see there?" Hiram, King of Tyre, replied, "A broken triangle." And King Solomon, in the agony of his soul exclaimed, "Alas!" Hiram of Tyre responded. "Poor Hiram!" And this is the grip" of a Royal Master and the word is *Alas! poor Hiram.*

[The Thrice Illustrious Master now gives the lecture and real word with the Deputy Master.]

Thrice Illustrious Master (three taps with his toes on the floor)—Do you know anything about this?

Deputy Master (three taps with his toes)—Yes, I know something about it, and I know the beginning. What do you know about it?

Thrice Illustrious Master—I know the ending. What is the beginning?

Deputy Master—Alpha. And what is the ending?

Thrice Illustrious Master—Omega.

Deputy Master—The beginning.

Thrice Illustrious Master—And the ending.

Deputy Master—The first.

Thrice Illustrious Master—And the last.

Thrice Illustrious Master (turning to the altar)—The real word of a Royal Master is, *Alpha and Omega,*" and

---

NOTE. 15—"The practical value of the degree of Royal Master, lies in the ready means of recognition which it affords to Royal Arch Masons, whose own methods of examination are elaborate and tedious in the extreme."—*Morris' Dict., Art. Royal Master.*

NOTE 16.—"Alpha is the first and Omega is the last letter of the Greek alphabet, equivalent to the beginning and the end or the first and the last of anything. The Jews used the first and last letters of their alphabet, Aleph and Tau, to express the same idea, but St. John, although a Hebrew, used the Grecian letters in the Apocalypse, because he was writing in the Greek language. Alpha and Omega are adopted as a symbol of the Deity."—*Mackey's Ritualist,* page 313.

is never to be given in any other way, form or manner except in that in which you have now received it, by first giving the lecture. They allude to a certain text of Scripture:

"And behold I come quickly; and my reward is with me, to give every man according as his work shall be. I am Alpha and Omega, the beginning and the end, the first and the last. Blessed are they that do his commandments, that they may have a right to the tree of life, and may enter in through the gates into the city.—Rev. 22; 12–14."—*Chase's Council Monitor, page 14.*

Thrice Illustrious Master (one rap, seating Council) —Companion Captain of the Guard, conduct our newly admitted companion to the east.

HISTORY.[17]

Thrice Illustrious Master (to candidate)—My worthy companion, our Grand Masters, Solomon King of Israel, Hiram, King of Tyre and Hiram Abif, at an early period in the construction of the Temple, resolved to reward all those craftsmen who should prove themselves worthy by their industry, skill and fidelity, by communicating to them the Master's Word. This being agreed upon, it became necessary to agree at what time and under what circumstances the secrets of a Master Mason should be communicated to them. Several plans were proposed and discussed at the frequent meetings of our Grand Masters, but all were found objectionable, so that their deliberations on this subject continued until the Temple was approaching its completion, when it was

---

NOTE 17.—"The legend refers to a combination among a few of the Temple-builders to extort by violence, from the principal conductor of the work, the secrets of Speculative Masonry."—*Morris' Dict., Art. Royal Master.*

proposed by Hiram Abif that the Master's Word should not be given until the Temple was completed and then only when they three were present and agreed by three times three. This plan was adopted and they bound themselves by a solemn obligation to a strict observance of the same.

When the *sanctum sanctorum* was nearly completed, King Solomon selected seven of the most expert, true and trusty workmen, from a certain other selection, to fashion and construct all the holy vessels designed for use in the holy of holies. Hiram Abif and Adoniram were two of the seven, and while laboring together they entered into frequent conversations respecting the condition and prospects of the craft. Upon one of these conversations, which took place just before the death of our Grand Master Hiram Abif, this degree was founded.

After the *sanctum sanctorum* was completed, and a portion of the furniture placed therein, on a certain day near high twelve, Adoniram repaired thither to deposit one of the holy vessels and when the craft were called from labor to refreshment, he did not return with the rest of the craftsmen, but lingered behind with Hiram Abif, whose custom it was at high twelve to enter into the *sanctum sanctorum* to offer up his adorations to Deity and draw his designs upon his trestle-board. After our Grand Master had fulfilled his usual custom he was met by Adoniram near the south gate who inquired of him when he should receive the Master's Word. Hiram Abif replied,

"My worthy friend Adoniram, it is uncertain whether you will ever receive it, for by the solemn obligation assumed by Solomon King of Israel, Hiram King of

Tyre and myself, it can not be communicated until the Temple is completed and we three are present and agreed. Then and not till then, all those who shall prove themselves worthy by their industry, skill and fidelity, shall receive the secrets of a Master Mason."

Hiram Abif turned to pass on, when he was again accosted by Adoniram:

"Grand Master Hiram, this being so, suppose one of you three, even you, yourself, should be removed by death prior to the completion of the Temple, what then will become of the Master's Word?"

Hiram Abif being struck with the remark, reflected that in such a case the Master's Word would be lost, meditated for a moment and then giving three gentle taps with his foot said,

"When I die they will bury it here."

As it was then one hour past high twelve, and the craft were returning to their labors, the conversation was broken off and never afterward resumed. After the death of Hiram Abif, this conversation was related by Adoniram to King Solomon and led to the deposit of the Master's Word where it was subsequently found at the rebuilding of the Temple. After the Babylonish captivity two surviving Grand Masters founded this degree in memory of the illustrious Tyrian whose unrivaled skill and unflinching fidelity rendered him worthy to be the companion of kings, and in order to reward the noble Adoniram for his timely suggestion, they admitted him to the rights and honors" of a Royal Master.

NOTE 18.—"But the ancient initiation was not terminated by the eurcals or discovery. Up to that point the ceremonies had been funereal and lugubrious in their character. But now they were changed from wailing to rejoicing. Other ceremonies were performed, by which the restoration of the personage to life or his apotheosis or change to immortality, was represented, and then came the *autopsy* or illumination of the neophyte, when he was invested with a full knowledge of all the religious doctrines which it was the object and design of the ancient mysteries to teach—when, in a word, he was instructed in Divine Truth. Now, a similar course is pursued in Masonry. Here also there is an illumination, a symbolical teaching, or, as we call it, an *investiture* with that which is the representative of Divine Truth."—*Mackey's Ritualist, page 209.*

INITIATION.

MONITORIAL.

"The furniture of the *sanctum sanctorum* consisted of many holy vessels made of pure gold, but the most important there was the Ark of the Covenant, called the glory of Israel, which was seated in the middle of the holy place, under the wings of the cherubim. It was a small chest or coffer, three feet nine inches long and two feet three inches wide and deep. It was made of wood. excepting only the mercy seat, but overlaid with gold both inside and out. It had a ledge of gold surrounding it at the top, into which the cover, called the mercy seat, was let in. The mercy seat was of solid gold, the thickness of an hands breadth; at the two ends were two cherubim, looking inward toward each other, with their wings expanded; which, embracing the whole circumference of the mercy seat, they met on each side, in the middle; all of the Rabbins say it was made out of the same mass, without any soldering of parts.

"Here the Shekinah, or Divine Presence, rested, and was visible in the appearance of a cloud over it. From hence the Bathkoll issued, and gave answers when God was consulted. And hence it is, that God is said in the Scripture, to dwell between the cherubim; that is between the cherubim on the mercy seat, because there was the seat or throne of the visible appearance of his glory among them."—*Chase's Council Monitor, page 16.*

CHAPTER V.

EIGHTH, OR ROYAL MASTER'S DEGREE.

LECTURE.

[At the close of initiation, as given in the last chapter, the Thrice Illustrious Master usually appoints some one to "post" the initiate in the lecture of the degree, but until the candidate wishes to take the next degree he rarely pays any attention whatever to the lecture, except the portion which is always rehearsed in the opening and closing ceremonies.

Having decided to take the next degree, he is obliged to post himself in the lecture, as it is termed as the questions and answers which form the lecture are used in his examination, which usually takes place on the evening of his initiation, but before the ceremonies of initiation begin.

Sometimes this catechetical form is all given before the candidate at the close of his initiation, when the Captain of the Guard or some other officer usually answers the questions; but the Thrice Illustrious Master rarely gives anything more than the "History" of the degree or lecture in "narrative" form, as it is termed, and the portion of the lecture used in opening and closing the Council. Hence we give the lecture in the form of an examination.]

Thrice Illustrious Master—Are you a Royal Master?

Candidate—I have visited the *sanctum sanctorum* and seen the glory of Israel.

Thrice Illustrious Master—Where were you received as a Royal Master?

Candidate—In a legally constituted Council of Royal Masters assembled in a place representing the *sanctum sanctorum* of King Solomon's Temple.

Thrice Illustrious Master—How many compose a Council of Royal Masters?

Candidate—Two or more.

Thrice Illustrious Master—When composed of nine, of whom does it consist?

Candidate—Thrice Illustrious Master, Deputy Illustrious Master, Illustrious Principal Conductor, Captain of the Guard and Companions, Treasurer, Recorder, Conductor, Steward and Sentinel.

Thrice Illustrious Master—Have you a sign belonging to this degree?

Candidate—I have.

Thrice Illustrious Master—Advance and give it.

(Candidate gives due guard same as on page 40.)

Thrice Illustrious Master—What is that called?

Candidate—The due guard of a Royal Master.

Thrice Illustrious Master—Have you another sign and grip?

Candidate—I have.

Thrice Illustrious Master—Give it.

(Candidate with Thrice Illustrious Master gives the grip of the broken triangle, as on page 50.)

Thrice Illustrious Master—What is that called?

Candidate—The grip of the broken triangle.

Thrice Illustrious Master—To what does it allude?

Candidate—To the death of our ancient Grand Master, Hiram Abif.

Thrice Illustrious Master—Explain the circumstance.

Candidate—Masonic tradition informs us that this grip of the broken triangle originated in this manner:

Shortly after the death of our Grand Master Hiram Abif, Solomon, King of Israel, and Hiram, King of Tyre, met in the *sanctum sanctorum* or holy of holies, and involuntarily placed themselves in this position to give the Grand Omnific Word, when, quickly remembering that one of their illustrious number was absent never more to return, they sadly placed their hands on each other's shoulders, and looking down, King Solomon inquired, " What do you see there?" Hiram, King of Tyre, replied, " A broken triangle." And King Solomon in the agony of his soul exclaimed, " Alas!" Hiram of Tyre responded, " Poor Hiram!" And this is the grip of a Royal Master, and the word is, '*Alas! Poor Hiram.*"

Thrice Illustrious Master (three taps with his toes on floor.)—Do you know anything about this?

Candidate (three taps with toes.)—Yes, I know something about it, and I know the beginning. What do you know about it?

Thrice Illustrious Master—I know the ending. What is the beginning?

Candidate—Alpha. And what is the ending?

Thrice Illustrious Master—Omega.

Candidate—The beginning.

Thrice Illustrious Master—And the ending.

Candidate—The first.

Thrice Illustrious Master—And the last.

Thrice Illustrious Master—What are they called?

Candidate—The real word of a Royal Master.

Thrice Illustrious Master—To what do they allude?

Candidate—To a certain text of Scripture: " And behold I come quickly; and my reward is with me, to give every man according as his work shall be. I am Alpha and Omega, the beginning and the end, the first and the last. Blessed are they that do his commandments, that they may have a right to the tree of life, and may enter in through the gates into the city."—*Chase's Council Monitor, page 14.*

[Sometimes a lot of questions about the history of the degree here follow.]

CHAPTER VI.

EIGHTH, OR ROYAL MASTER'S DEGREE.

CLOSING CEREMONIES.

[The closing ceremonies, with trifling variations are the same as in opening. Usually there is a prayer or benediction after the catechetical exercise (lecture) when the Master declares the Council closed.]

ROYAL MASTER'S CLOSING PRAYER".

"Incomprehensibly holy, supremely good and All-wise God, thou art our Father and our Friend; we are thy people and the sheep of thy pasture. Prostrating ourselves before thee, we acknowledge our unworthiness to appear in thy presence. But thou hast said that thou art the Lord God, mercifully forgiving sin and transgression. Pardon, we beseech thee, what thou hast seen amiss in us at this time. Confirm and strengthen us in every good work, and take us henceforth under thy holy protection. For thine is the power and the glory, forever and ever."—*Mackey's Ritualist, page 521.*

All—So mote it be.

BENEDICTION.

"Let brotherly love continue. Be ye careful to entertain strangers. And may the God of peace and love, be with us always."—*Mackey's Ritualist, page 522.*

NOTE 14.—"This prayer and the benediction, as well as the opening prayer, are very old and of high authority."—*Mackey's Ritualist page 521.*

DIAGRAM OF SELECT MASTER'S COUNCIL.

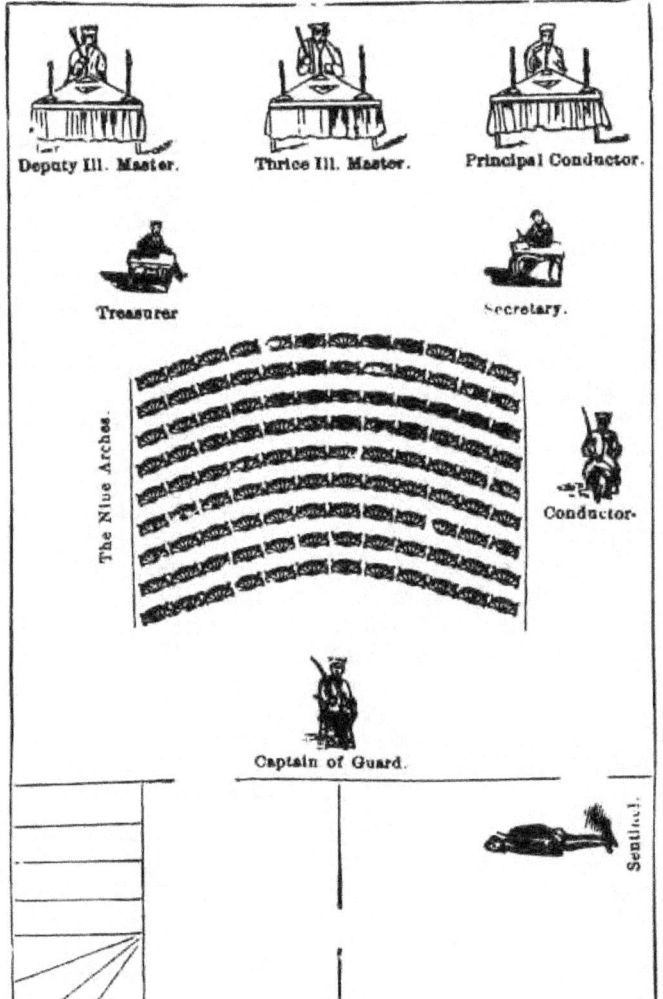

NINTH, OR SELECT MASTER'S DEGREE

EXPLANATORY.

Unlike the Blue Lodge and Chapter degrees where the highest or last is the governing degree, the Select Master's degree is the governing degree of the Council, and the same is true of the Commandery degrees: the degree of Knight Templar, though the middle degree, is the ruling degree. This comes from the fact that the Knight of Malta degree, though following that of Knight Templar, is considered appendant thereto, and as will be seen by note 129, page 265, "the Grand Encampment of the United States in 1856 abolished the order of Knights of Malta, as being unnecessary and embarrassing, but in 862 restored it to the anomolous place it had previously occupied."

Although Mackey does not inform us that the Super-Excellent Master's degree has ever been abolished, he does state in very forcible language his opinion that it does not belong among the Council degrees. He says: "The degree of Super-Excellent Master certainly has no onnection in its history or its symbolism, with the Royal and Select degrees, nor was it ever, until it was very recently introduced, by a few Councils in some of the Northern and Western States, considered as forming any part of the work of a Council. I do not myself acknowledge its legitimacy as a degree of Cryptic Masonry."—*Mackey's Ritualist, page 553.*

The main object of the degree is undoubtedly to so excite the fear of the vengeance of the order as to ensure the keeping of its "secrets," and thus prepare the mind for the horrible blasphemy of the Knights Templar degree. That this is the object of the Super-Excellent Master's Degree is unmistakably set forth by Mackey as quoted in note 44, page 101.

CHAPTER VII.

NINTH, OR SELECT MASTER'S DEGREE.

OPENING CEREMONIES.

Thrice Illustrious Master (one rap, calling to order)—Companion Captain of the Guard, proceed to satisfy yourself that all present are Select Masters".

Captain of Guard (having scanned the room)—Thrice Illustrious, all present are Select Masters.

Thrice Illustrious Master——Companion Captain of the Guard, you will see that the secret vault is made secure and inform the Sentinel that I am about to open a Council of Select Masters and direct him to guard accordingly. (He obeys the order and reports:)

Captain of Guard— Thrice Illustrious the secret vault" is made secure and the Council is securely guarded.

Thrice Illustrious Master- (one rap)—Most Illustrious Companion of Tyre, shall we now resume our labors and complete the sacred work which we have so happily begun?

NOTE 20.—"This degree is the summit and perfection of ancient Masonry, and without it the history of the Royal Arch degree can hardly be said to be complete. It rationally accounts for the concealment and preservation of those essentials of the craft which were brought to light at the creation of the Second Temple; and which lay concealed from the Masonic eye for four hundred and seventy years."—*Macoy's True Masonic Guide, page* 167.

NOTE 21.—"The initiation into the ancient mysteries was almost always performed in subterranean edifices; and when the place of initiation, as in some of the Egyptian temples, was really above ground, it was so constructed as to give to the neophyte the appearance, in its approaches and its internal structure, of a vault. As the great doctrine taught in the mysteries was the resurrection from the dead, as *to die* and *to be initiated* were synonymous terms. It was deemed proper that there should be some formal resemblance between a descent into the grave and a descent into the place of initiation. 'Happy is the man,' says the Greek poet Pindar, 'who descends beneath the hollow earth, having beheld these mysteries, for he knows the end as well as the divine origin of life;' and in a like spirit Sophocles exclaims, 'Thrice happy are they that descend to the shades below after having beheld these sacred rites, for they alone have life in Hades, while all others suffer there every kind of evil.'"—*Mackey's Ritualist page*

SELECT MASTER'S DEGREE.

Right Illustrious Master—Thrice Illustrious, it is my most ardent wish to see the secret vault" completed and the sacred treasures therein safely deposited, that I may return to my own country with the satisfaction of having faithfully performed my duties to the craft.

Thrice Illustrious Master—Illustrious Principal Conductor, are our Select Masters all present?

Principal Conductor—I find the number three times nine".

Thrice Illustrious Master—What is the hour?

Principal Conductor—Nine" at night, when all prying eyes are closed in sleep.

Thrice Illustrious Master—Since it is nine at night it is my will and pleasure that —— Council, ——, be now opened for the dispatch of such business as may regularly come before it, under the usual Masonic restrictions.

NOTE 22.—"The vault was, therefore, in the ancient mysteries, symbolic of the grave, for initiation was symbolic of death, where alone Divine Truth is to be found. The Masons have adopted the same idea. They teach that death is but the beginning of life; that if the first or evanescent temple of our transitory life be on the surface, we must descend into the *secret vault* of death before we can find that sacred deposit of truth which is to adorn our second temple of eternal life. Looking, therefore, to this reference of initiation to that subterranean house of our last dwelling, we significantly speak of the place of initiation as 'the secret vault, where reign silence, secrecy and darkness.' It is in this sense of an entrance through the grave into eternal life, that the Select Master is to view the recondite but beautiful symbolism of the secret vault. Like every other myth and allegory of Masonry, the historical relation may be true or it may be false; it may be founded on fact or the invention of imagination; the lesson is still there, and the symbolism teaches it exclusive of the history."—*Mackey's Ritualist, page* 536.

NOTE 23.—"No less than nine nor more than twenty-seven must associate together in working it; if more are present they refrain from taking part in the proceedings."—*Morris' Dict., Art. Select Master.*

NOTE 24.—"The number *nine* is the sacred number of the Select degree, which, however, also refers to *twenty-seven*, simply because that is the product of *nine* multiplied by *three*. *Nine* was called by the Pythagoreans *teleios*, or the number of completion, and as such it is appropriate to that degree which professes to complete the circle of Masonic science."—*Mackey's Ritualist, page* 543.

OPENING CEREMONIES.

Principal Conductor (to Council)—Companions it is the will and pleasure of the Thrice Illustrious Master that ——— Council, ———, of Select Masons be now opened for the dispatch of such business as may regularly come before it, under the usual Masonic restrictions. You will therefore take your proper stations, and after the regular alarm is given, commence your labors. agreeably to the instructions you have received. (Companions assemble in their respective arches, and stand facing the east.)

Captain of Guard—Thrice Illustrious, the companions are at their stations.

OPENING PRAYER.

"May the Supreme Grand Master graciously preside over all our counsels, and direct, approve, and bless all our labors. May our professions as Masons be the rule of our conduct as men. May our secret retreat ever be the resort of the *just* and *merciful*, the seat of the moral virtues, and the home of the *select*." Mackey's Ritualist, page 529.

All—So mote it be.

Captain of Guard—Look to the east. (All, led by the Thrice Illustrious Master, make the signs and due guards from Entered Apprentice to Select Master. See pages 33 to 40 for the signs of the first eight degrees.)

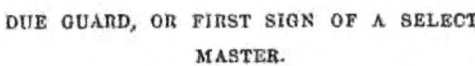

DUE GUARD, OR FIRST SIGN OF A SELECT MASTER.

Arms held similar to second position in Master Mason's sign of distress, with hands clenched in allusion to the penalty of the obligation; to have both hands chopped off to the stumps. See cut.

SECOND SELECT MASTER'S SIGN.

Crossing hands and arms as in engraving quickly draw the hands edgewise across the body, downwards, as though in the act of quartering your body; then hands drop to side. This refers to the penalty in obligation, to have the body quartered.

2d S. M. Sign.

3d S. M. Sign.

THIRD SELECT MASTER'S SIGN.

Place the hands over eyes as shown in engraving, and quickly jerk arms downwards, as though tearing out your eyes and throwing them on the ground; then hands drop to side. This also refers to the penalty in obligation.

FOURTH SELECT MASTER'S SIGN.

Place left hand on upper part of forehead, palm down and right hand over it, heels together and body erect as in cut first position. Then take a long, *vigorous* step with right foot, throwing out hands and arms as in cut, second position.

1st position.   2d position.
4th Select Master's Sign.

OPENING CEREMONIES.   67

OTHER SELECT MASTER'S SIGNS.

Forefinger of left hand on upper lip, hand open, palm inward and forearm horizontal; say, SILENCE

Right hand on bowels and say, SECRECY.

Other Select Master's Signs.

Left forefinger to lips and right hand over eyes and say, SILENCE AND DARKNESS.

Thrice Illustrious Master (nine raps in triplets, or in some Councils eight raps and one rap.)

Right Illustrious Master (nine raps.)

Principal Conductor (nine raps.)

Thrice Illustrious Master—I now declare this Council of Select Masters, opened in due form.

CHAPTER VIII.

NINTH, OR SELECT MASTER'S DEGREE.
INITIATION.

[The preparation room is supposed to represent King Solomon's most retired room, and the Steward's station is just inside the door. In the Council room, nine arches extend across the room from west to east, so that entering from the preparation room the arch first entered is the first arch. The preparation room and first arch are very dimly lighted. The candidate is instructed to enter alone and without knocking, at the open door, supposed to be guarded by the Steward, who is instructed to feign himself asleep and let the candidate pass. Candidate enters.]

Captain of Guard—Who comes here?

Candidate (previously instructed)—A zealous brother, wishing to participate in your labors.

Captain of Guard—Give me the sign, word and token of your entrance!

Candidate—I can not.

Captain of Guard (three raps, all rise)—An intruder! An intruder!

Thrice Illustrious Master—Companion Captain of the Guard, what is the cause of all this confusion?

Captain of Guard—An intruder has penetrated the secret vault.

Thrice Illustrious Master—Then put him to death

immediately!

Captain of Guard (to candidate)—Kneel, and prepare for instant death!

Captain of Guard—Thrice Illustrious King Solomon, are you aware upon whom I am about to inflict this awful penalty? This is none other than your particular friend and favorite, Izabud.[25]

Thrice Illustrious Master—Izabud! Is it possible? Then bind him fast in chains and have him forthcoming when called for, or your life shall answer for his escape! Let us retire and consult!

(Candidate is securely bound, when they withdraw and are supposed to go to the ninth arch to consult. They soon return.)

Thrice Illustrious Master—Bring forth the intruder!

Thrice Illustrious Master (to candidate)—O my unfortunate friend Izabud! your curiosity and disobedience have cost you your life. I have consulted with my colleagues and find them inflexible. The nature of our obligation is such that you can not be pardoned;[26] you must therefore prepare for instant death. (Captain of the Guard and candidate kneel).

Candidate (as Izabud)—Thrice Illustrious King Solomon, you well know my long and sincere attachment to your sacred person, your secrets and your service. Having been several times of late denied admission to your most retired room, I feared that I had lost your royal favor and for a long time grieved in silence.

Note 25.—"Izabud. This, like Achishar, is an historical personage, although the events recorded of him as peculiar to this degree are altogether legendary. The word is one of those corruptions of Hebrew names unfortunately too common in Masonry. The true name is Zabud; and he is mentioned in the First Book of Kings, 4:5, where it is said, 'Zabud, the son of Nathan, was principal officer and the king's friend.'"—Mackey's Ritualist, page 537.

Note 26.—"An excess of honest zeal may lead to forfeiture of life. The laws of Masonry are inviolable, its penalties inexorable."—Morris Dict. Art. Select Master.

Unable to endure it longer I humbly mentioned my fears to your majesty, and received for answer: "Be content, my friend Izabud, the time will soon come when the door will be left open for your reception as heretofore." This satisfied me. This evening having some particular business with your majesty, I came to your most retired room as usual; not finding you there, and finding the door open and not guarded by Achishar, the Grand Steward, as before, I took it for granted that it was left open for my reception, in fulfillment of your promise, and accordingly entered; but I beg your majesty to believe that it was neither curiosity nor disobedience that caused me to enter, but fervency of zeal for your majesty's service.

Deputy Illustrious Master—Thrice Illustrious King Solomon, if this be true, Izabud is not guilty of the charge alleged against him; his intrusion was owing to some unguarded expression of yours; he ought to be pardoned and admitted one of our select number.

Thrice Illustrious Master—My illustrious companion of Tyre, I acknowledge this to be true, but it can not be, since our select number is already full, and he can not be admitted.

Principal Conductor—Thrice Illustrious King Solomon, let Achishar, the Grand Steward, be discharged and executed, for he is no longer worthy of our confidence. He has betrayed his trust and forfeited his life by falling asleep at his post, and let Izabud be pardoned and admitted in his stead.

Thrice Illustrious Master—I thank you, my illustrious companion, for your good and timely counsel; it shall be done.

Thrice Illustrious Master—Captain of the Guard, let

INITIATION. 71

Achishar[27] be put to death instantly.

Captain of Guard (to Steward, who still feigns slumber)—Achishar, awake and hear thy doom! Thou art condemned to die!

Achishar—Mercy! mercy! is there no mercy?

Captain of Guard—None for you; it has been extended to another. Do you hear?

Achishar—Alas! I die. I deem it just.

Captain of Guard (pretending to kill him)—Then die!

Captain of Guard—Thrice Illustrious, your orders have been obeyed.

Thrice Illustrious Master—Izabud, are you willing to take a solemn obligation to keep it an inviolable secret that there is such a place as the secret vault?

Izabud—I am.

Thrice Illustrious Master—Companion Captain of the Guard, free[28] Izabud from his shackles and let him advance to our sacred altar, there to take upon himself the solemn obligation of a Select Master. [The candidate is placed at the altar, kneels on both knees, with his hands on the Bible, square, compass and trowel.]

Captain of Guard—Thrice Illustrious, the candidate is in due form.

Note 27.—"Achishar. This is the person named in the First Book of Kings, 4:6. under the name of Ahishar, and there described as being 'over the household' of King Solomon. Achishar is therefore properly described in this degree as the steward of the household. As to the legend of his conduct and his punishment, it has no known foundation in history, and may be considered simply as a mythical symbol."—**Mackey's Ritualist**, page 536.

Note 28.—"And here, too, is exemplified an instance of justice and mercy by our ancient patron, towards one of the craft who was led to disobey his commands by an over-zealous attachment for the institution. It ends with a description of a particular circumstance, which characterizes the degree."—**Sickel's Monitor**, Part 3, page 6.

SELECT MASTER'S DEGREE.

OBLIGATION OF A SELECT MASTER.

Thrice Illustrious Master (three raps)—You will repeat your name, and say after me: I, ———, of my own free will and accord, and in the presence of the Grand Architect of the Universe, and this Council of Select Masters, erected to Him and dedicated to Hiram Abif, do solemnly swear that I will never discover the secret signs, tokens and words belonging to this degree to any one of an inferior degree, nor to any person or persons whomsoever, except it be to a true and lawful Companion Select Master or in a regularly constituted Council of Select Masters, nor unto him or them until by strict trial, due examination, or legal information, I shall have found him or them as lawfully entitled to the same as I am myself.

I furthermore promise and swear that I will stand to and abide by all the laws, rules and regulations of any Council of Select Masters of which I may become a members, and the constitution, laws and edicts of the Grand Council under whose jurisdiction the same may work, so far as they shall come to my knowledge.

I furthermore promise and swear that I will answer and obey all due signs and summons sent to me from a Council of Select Masters or handed me by a Companion Select Master, if within the length of my cable-tow.

I furthermore promise and swear that I will not be present at the opening of a Council of Select Masters, except there shall be present at least nine Select Masters, myself included.

I furthermore promise and swear not to be present at the conferring of this degree upon any one except he shall have taken all of the necessary preceding degrees from Entered Apprentice to Royal Master inclusive.

I furthermore promise and swear that I will not penetrate into the ninth arch without the express permission of the three Grand Masters, nor reveal to any one the existence of such a place as the secret vault.

All this I promise and swear, with a firm and steadfast resolution to perform the same, without any hesitation, mental reservation, or secret evasion of mind. whatever; binding myself under no less a penalty than that of having my eyes torn from their sockets, my hands chopped off and my body quartered, and then thrown among the rubbish of the Temple, should I in the least violate this my Select Master's obligation. So help me God, and keep me steadfast in the due performance of the same.

Thrice Illustrious Master (to candidate)—I will now explain to you the signs, grip and word of this degree: [Master makes signs one to four, as on pages 61 and 62.]

Thrice Illustrious Master (to candidate)—These allude to the penalty of your obligation. We have other signs also. [Thrice Illustrious Master gives the other signs as explained on page 63, and adds:]

Thrice Illustrious Master—These signs allude to that silence and darkness in which you should always keep the world without, with reference to the existence of this secret vault. (Puts his left hand on candidate's right breast, then grasps the right lapel of his coat just below the collar, saying,) Rise, Izabud! be voluntarily deaf, dumb and blind to all you may hear and see in the ninth arch. This (the grip of the lapel of the coat) is the grip of a Select Master and the word is IZABUD or ISH SODI,[29] which signifies, man of my choice, or

Note 29.—"Ish Sodi, therefore, in this degree, very clearly means, a man of my intimate counsel, a man of my choice, one selected to share with me a secret task or labor. Such was the position of every Select Master to King Solomon, and in this view those are not wrong who have interpreted Ish Sodi as meaning a Select Master."—Mackey's Ritualist, page 559.

Select Master. Izabud, you have now our permission to enter the ninth arch. (The officers retire to the ninth arch or "East," followed by the candidate in charge of the Captain of the Guard.)

Captain of Guard (at ninth arch; nine raps.)

Principal Conductor—Who comes here?

Captain of Guard—Izabud, the king's friend, who has the express permission of the three Grand Masters to enter the ninth arch.

Principal Conductor—You will enter. (They enter and stop near the "Ark of the Covenant" in front of the Thrice Illustrious Master, when he proceeds to rehearse the "history" of the degree:)

HISTORY.

Thrice Illustrious Master—My companion, our three ancient Grand Masters by their wisdom and knowledge of the writings of Moses and the prophets, held firmly in the belief that the children of Israel would in the process of time continue not in the belief of the Supreme Judge to obey his laws and commandments, and that in consequence thereof their enemies would be let loose upon them, their city and Temple be sacked and destroyed, and they themselves be carried away into captivity, where many of them would fall away into idolatry; and that the worship of the one true God would cease for a time among them, and all the forms and ceremonies he had enjoined upon them to pursue would all be forgotten. They further foresaw that in the destruction of the Temple would also perish all those sacred treasures contained in the secret vault. To avert so dreadful a calamity, and to provide for the future prosperity of the craft they agreed to erect a secret vault,[30] beginning at King Solomon's most retired room, leading a due westerly course, and ending under the *sanctum sanctorum,* or holy of holies. It was divided into nine[31] apartments or arches. The ninth arch was erected by our three Grand Masters themselves, as a place in which to meet in Grand Council to confer the Master Mason's degree, when the Temple should be completed, and also as a safe and secure place in which to deposit exact imitations of the sacred treasures contained in the *sanctum sanctorum* above, and also a true copy of the book of the Law and Testament as given by the Lord unto Moses; for God had revealed unto them by the writings of his prophets, that after three score and ten years his people should be released from their captivity and restored to their native country; that he would put it into the heart of a prince of the house of Judah to rebuild the city and house of the Lord, and that he would give unto him a sign to reward his perseverance and encourage his faith, and that the sign should be the discovery of these valuable treasures.

There were selected to erect the other eight arches, twenty-two from Gebal, a city in Phœnicia, who were called Giblemites[32] or stone squarers, together with Achishar, the Grand Steward, and Adoniram, the Cap-

Note 30.—"The practical character of this degree refers to the manner of deposit and concealment of the essential secrets of Masonry, which form the basis of so many Masonic traditions."—**Morris' Dict., Art. Select Master.**

Note 31.—"Its emblems are the trowel and a series of nine arches arranged horizontally, alluding to the vast excavations beneath the Temple of Solomon."—**Morris' Dict., Art. Select Master.**

Note 32.—"The Giblemites, or Inhabitants of Gebal, were subject to the king of Tyre, and were distinguished for their skill as builders. The town of Gebal was called Byblos by the Greeks and was celebrated as the principal seat of the worship of Adonis, whose mysteries, and the initiation accompanying it, more nearly resembled, in its symbolism and allegorical teaching the initiation into Masonry than any other of the ancient rites. It is not, therefore, unnatural to suppose that the Giblemites held a higher place in the confidence of King Solomon than any other of the Temple builders."—**Mackey's Ritualist, page 541.**

76   SELECT MASTER'S DEGREE.

tain of the Guard. These were all skilled in the arts
and sciences, particularly in that of sculpture. Their
hours of labor were from nine at night until twelve,
when they were called from labor to refreshment.

During the erection of this secret vault a circumstance occurred which characterizes this degree and upon which the principal ceremonies are founded.[33] One of King Solomon's particular friends and favorites, named Izabud, having been several times denied admission to King Solomon's most retired room, feared that he had lost the favor of the king, and for a long time grieved in silence, until at length, unable to endure it longer, he humbly mentioned his fears to King Solomon and received for answer: "Be contented, my friend Izabud, the time will soon come when the door will be left open for your reception as heretofore." This satisfied him, but one evening, having some particular business with King Solomon, he retired to his most retired room in search of him. Finding the door open, and not being hindered as before by Achishar, the Grand Steward (he having fallen asleep at his post), he took it for granted it was left open for his reception in fulfillment of King Solomon's promise, and accordingly entered, and not finding King Solomon there, and observing an open passage, he followed it in search of him, and upon entering was accosted by Adoniram, the Captain of the Guard, who demanded the sign, token and word of his entrance. Not being able to give them, an alarm was made which brought our three Grand Masters from their apartments in the ninth arch. On being informed that an intruder had entered the secret vault, King Solomon ordered him to be put to death instantly.

Note 33.—"The entire legend is beautiful, and in the light of recent discoveries under Mount Moriah, not irrational."—Morris' Dict., Art. Select Master.

The Captain of the Guard, as he was about to execute the order, discovered who the intruder was, and thus addressed King Solomon:

"Thrice Illustrious King Solomon, are you aware upon whom I am about to execute this sentence? This is none other than your particular friend and favorite, Izabud."

At this King Solomon exclaimed: "Izabud! Is it possible!" and then ordered him to be securely bound and had forthcoming when called for. Our Grand Masters then retired to their apartments in the ninth arch for consultation, and on returning King Solomon ordered the intruder to be brought forth, and thus addressed him:

"O my unfortunate friend Izabud! Your curiosity and disobedience have cost you your life. I have consulted with my colleagues and find them inflexible. The nature of our obligation is such that I can not pardon you; you must therefore prepare for instant death."

Izabud fell upon his knees and thus addressed King Solomon:

"Thrice Illustrious King Solomon, you well know my long and faithful attachment to your sacred person, your secrets and your service. Having been several times of late denied admission to your most retired room, I feared that I had lost your royal favor and for a long time grieved in silence, until at length, unable to endure it longer, I humbly mentioned my fears to you, when I received for answer, 'Be contented, my friend Izabud, the time will soon come when the door will be left open for your reception as heretofore.' This satisfied me. This evening, having some particular business with your sacred person, I came to your most retired room in search of you, and finding the door open and not being hindered as before by Achishar, the Grand Steward, I took it for granted that it was left open for my reception in fulfillment of your promise, and accordingly entered. Not finding you there and observing an open passage leading hither, I followed it in search of you. Far be it from me that either curiosity or disobedience should have tempted me hither, but rather impute my intrusion to my fervency and zeal in your royal service."

Upon this our Grand Master Hiram, King of Tyre, observed, "Thrice Illustrious King Solomon, if this be true, Izabud is not guilty of the charge alleged against him. His intrusion was owing to an unguarded expression of your own; he ought to be pardoned and admitted one of our select number."

King Solomon replied, "My illustrious companion of Tyre, I acknowledge this to be true, but how can it be, since our select number is already full, and he can not be admitted?"

At this Hiram Abif interposed and said, "Thrice Illustrious King Solomon, let Achishar, the Grand Steward, be discharged and executed, for he is no longer worthy of our confidence; he has betrayed his trust and forfeited his life by falling asleep at his post. Let Izabud be pardoned and admitted in his stead."

King Solomon thanked him for his good and timely counsel and ordered Achishar to be put to death instantly. Achishar was accordingly discharged and executed, and Izabud, after taking a solemn obligation to keep it an inviolable secret that there was such a place as the secret vault, was admitted among the select number.

INITIATION. 79

When the ninth arch was completed our three ancient Grand Masters deposited therein an exact imitation of the Ark[34] of the Covenant, within which they also placed imitations of the Pot of Manna, Aaron's Rod, a true copy of the Book of the Law, with the writings of Moses and the Prophets up to that time, and that these things should be duly appreciated if ever brought to light, they placed their names on three sides of the ark, on the fourth side the time when, by whom and for what purpose deposited. It was deposited in the year of the world three thousand, by Solomon King of Israel, Hiram King of Tyre, and Hiram Abif, for the good of the craft in general and the Jewish nation in particular.

Ark of the Covenant.
Aaron's Rod.
Pot of Manna

After the completion of the secret vault and this deposit had been made in the ninth arch, but before the completion of the Temple, our Grand Master, Hiram Abif, was assassinated, as we have had an account in the Master Mason's degree, and it was then supposed that the Master's Word[35] was forever lost; but

Note 34.—"The Substitute Ark. The Ark or Coffer, which necessarily constitutes a part of the paraphernalia of a Council of Select Masters, is the same as that which forms a part of the furniture of a Chapter of Royal Arch. But it must be distinctly understood that neither of these represents that Ark of the Covenant which had been constructed in the wilderness by Moses, Aholiab and Bezaleel, which had been placed in the tabernacle, and afterward, at the dedication of the Temple of Solomon, was removed to the holy of holies."—Mackey's Ritualist, page 539.

Note 35.—"The great object of all Masonic labor is divine truth. The search for the lost word is the search for truth. But divine truth is a term synonymous with God. The Ineffable Name is a symbol of truth, because God, and God alone, is truth. It is properly a Scriptural idea. The Book of Psalms abounds with this sentiment. Thus it is said that the truth of the Lord 'reacheth unto the clouds,' and that 'His truth endureth unto all generations.' If, then, God is truth, and the Stone of Foundation is the Masonic symbol of God, it follows that it must also be the symbol of divine truth."—Mackey's Ritualist, page 548.

80   SELECT MASTER'S DEGREE.

by a communication from Adoniram it was ascertained that Hiram Abif had expressed a wish that in case of his death the Master's Word[36] should be deposited in the ninth arch, as we have seen represented in the Royal Master's degree. The two surviving Grand Masters agreed to this and accordingly placed upon the top of the ark in the center an equilateral triangle, on the three sides of which they placed the name of Deity in three languages, Syriac, Chaldean and Egyptian. This last precaution was taken by our Grand Masters, so that in case the children of Israel should be held so long in captivity as to lose the use of the Hebrew tongue and forget the true pronunciation of the grand and sacred Name, yet by the use of the Syrian, Chaldean and Egyptian languages in which the Grand Omnific Word was inscribed, they might be able to pronounce the Master's Word; and, that it might be known and distinguished if ever brought to light, they placed the three Grand Masters' jewels on the same, one in each language, knowing that a description of these jewels would be handed down to the latest Masonic posterity. Thus was preserved and brought to light the long lost ancient Master's Word or Great and Sacred Name.[37] Masonic tradition informs us that this Word was communicated by God himself to Moses at the Burning Bush, and was in use until the death of Hiram Abif, after which it lay buried in darkness for the space of four hundred and seventy years, until the building of the Second Temple when it was discovered and

Note 36.—"The Masonic Stone of Foundation, so conspicuous in the degree of Select Master, is a symbol of divine truth, upon which all Speculative Masonry is built; and the legends and traditions which refer to it are intended to describe in an allegorical way, the progress of truth in the soul, the search for which is a Mason's labor; and the discovery of which is to be his reward."—Mackey's Ritualist, page 549.

INITIATION. 81

brought to light as represented in the Royal Arch[37] degree, and it has continued in use from that time till the present and will so continue until the sun shall cease to rule the day and the moon to govern the night.

MONITORIAL.

"There may be an inquiry in your mind what was the nature of the word that rendered the Jews so anxious to keep possession; how came it in their possession, and of what importance was it to them—this part Solomon has allusion to when the Master's Word was lost.

"Zoraster (who flourished about 800 years before the building of the Temple) in the Zendavesta writes; 'There are names given by God himself to every nation of unspeakable efficacy in the mysteries.' Therefore, this word in the minds of the Jews was of unspeakable efficacy, preserving them as a nation and conferring upon them a mighty power. We find the Trojans, 200 years before the building of the Temple, having possession of a Palladium which fell from heaven, and only by its loss could their city be destroyed. The Chaldeans wore triangular pieces of metal, sometimes stones,[38] on which were engraven certain characters called talismans, the possession of which they imagined gave them power over the spirits and mortals.

Note 37.—"In the United States, the Royal Arch is considered as the seventh degree, those of Mark, Past and Most Excellent Master being interposed between it and the third. In one or two of the States, however, the Royal and Select Masters have been inserted after the Past and before the Most Excellent."—Mackey's Lexicon, Art. Select Master.

Note 38.—"This Ineffable Name sanctifies the stone upon which it is engraved as the symbol of the Grand Architect. It takes from it its heathen signification as an idol, and consecrates it to the worship of the true God.

"The prominent idea of the Deity in the Masonic system, connects him with his creative and formative power. God is to the Freemason Al-Gabil, as the Arabians call him, that is, The Builder; or, as expressed in his Masonic title, the Grand Architect of the Universe, by common consent abbreviated in the formula G. A. O. T. U. Now, it is evident that no symbol could so appropriately suit him in this character as the Stone of Foundation, upon which he is allegorically supposed to have erected his world."—Mackey's Ritualist, page 246.

The principal was named Bel or Baal. In confirmation we find the Jews saying to Christ, 'You cast out devils by the aid of Beelzebub.' The Hindoos have a word of such tremendous efficacy that the simple utterance of the word by a holy Brahmin would shake the paradise of Swerga to its center, convulse the earth to its foundation, restore the dead to life, destroy the living, transport himself where he pleased, and fill him with the wisdom of the gods. This word is Aun or On, and belongs to the triad. The word On is Egyptian and was esteemed the most ancient of the gods, for Plato, who derived much information from the Egyptians, writes, 'Tell me of the god On, which was and is and never knew beginning.' They ascribe the same powers to 'On' that the Jews did to Jehovah. But the affinity of certain words between Hindoos, Chaldeans and Egyptians is so close that we may presume they came from the same source. The Jews believed by the power of the name. It cured them of evils, warned them of danger, restored the dead to life, brought fire from heaven, rent buildings asunder, maimed and destroyed their enemies, and filled them with great wisdom; the pronunciation shakes heaven and earth, and inspires the very angels with astonishment. The Rabbins call it 'Shem Hamphorish,' the unutterable name. That the word inspired the possessor with great wisdom, the sacred records testify in many instances. The first place where we find it in its proper name is in Samuel, who was inspired with so great wisdom as to be judge of the Jews. We find also, the word had the same power when communicated. Samuel gave the word to Saul, and the possession filled him with wisdom and understanding far above his compeers, and, in the allegorical language of the East, gave him another heart and so surprised those who knew him as to make them exclaim, 'Is this Saul the son of Kish?' But we find on the loss of the word he was greatly troubled and endeavored to regain it in various ways; at last summoned the spirit of Samuel to give it. Samuel gave the word to David, and the Lord was with David from that day forward, for he says expressly, 'For thy word's sake has thy servant known these great things.' And we find David triumphing over all his enemies by the power vested in him.

"When God refused David to build a temple to his name, Solomon was appointed in his stead, and tradition states, that on commencing the foundation he struck on a cavern in which were immense treasures of gold, silver and precious stones. Believing it to be the remains of some temple built before the flood, and fearing that it had been in the service of idolatry, he was informed by a dream that this place had been thrice devoted to God. It was the place whence Enoch was translated, where Abraham was about to offer up his son Isaac, and it was the place of the threshing-floor of Ornan the Jebusite, where David met and appeased the destroying angel. The treasures were collected and used in building the Temple. On exploring the lowest recesses of the cavern they came upon an arched vault, in which they found a white marble pillar, on which, encrusted with precious stones, was a delta, and on which was engraved the Grand Omnific Word, the possession of which filled him with such wisdom and understanding that his name resounded throughout the earth, and has so continued to the present day. It was this that enabled our three Grand Masters to erect such a magnificent structure, the like of which has not been before or since.

"The Arabians have the tradition that the Word was engraved on a seal, and gave them power over the Dives, Afreets, Ghouls and other evil spirits, imprisoning them and confining them at the bottom of the sea by impressing on them the signet. By them it was called a talisman or conferrer of power. By the Egyptians they were worn as amulets or averters of danger, and are still worn at the present day. We now see by the inspiration it gave its possessor what struck Solomon with such consternation and anxiety on the death of Hiram Abif. The key was probably a triangular plate on which was engraved the Omnific Name, this being worn constantly on the breast, would, by lying on it continually, give a faint impression of the Word; * * *. It was the possession of the Word * * * Having mentioned that all nations possessed a word we will inquire how it first came in possession of the Jews. The Rabbinical tradition is, that it was given by God to Adam, who, foreseeing the deluge, enjoined on the sons of Seth to preserve it for future generations, when the flood would have swept all but Noah's family away. Enoch, the son of Seth, while deliberating upon the best means of preserving for future generations the Ineffable Name of Deity, was favored by a mystical vision; he seemed to be transported to the top of a high mountain. On looking up, he discovered in the heavens a triangular plate brilliantly illuminated, on which appeared certain mystic characters which he received a strict injunction never to pronounce; he then appeared to descend to the bowels of the earth; looking beneath him he discovered the same triangle. Instructed by this vision he built

INITIATION. 85

two pillars, on which was engraven the knowledge of the antediluvian world, and beneath he formed a cavern, and in it he deposited the triangle on which was engraved the Ineffable Word. He left a key to the name, as our Grand Masters have done, so those who had this key could pronounce the name. The Eastern nations have the tradition that the key left was composed of small squares joined together, called a Zuarga, which they consult at the present day, as to matters of health and business. It is possible that the key to the Royal Arch Word is the Zuarga of the East.

The Ineffable Name was pronounced once a year by the High-Priest, amid the clang of cymbals and sound of trumpets, at the Feast of Expiation. It was not lawful to pronounce it at any other time. * * * * *

After the loss of the Word, the Jews endeavored to find a substitute by an idol, called by the Rabbins a Teraphim. According to tradition it was constructed in this wise, and occasioned the Jews much trouble in after periods: A head of a child first born and dead born, was placed on a golden plate on whose rim was engraved mystic characters. Under the tongue they placed a laminar of gold, on which was engraved characters and inscriptions of certain planets. After performing invocations before it, it was endowed with speech to foretell events. This is the idol that is so bitterly inveighed against by Isaiah, Jeremiah and Ezekiel. This is following after the abomination of the heathen instead of seeking the Word.

The Babylonians practiced divinations and sorcery, and the Jews copied largely from them, and were in full force from their return from Babylon till the destruction of the Temple by Titus, and thus has been transmitted down to us the various rites, mystic ceremonies and charms yet practiced among the ignorant and uneducated of the present day.

"Thus, Companion, have I endeavored to give a brief epitome and slight explanation of such parts of our work as may stimulate your zeal and energies to further inquiries in penetrating the darkness and bringing to light the long lost Word in all its effulgent splendor.— *Chase's Council Monitor, page 25.*

CHARGE TO CANDIDATE, SELECT MASTER'S DEGREE.

COMPANION—Having attained to this degree, you have passed the *circle of perfection* in ancient Masonry. In the capacity of Select Master you must be sensible that your obligations are increased in proportion to your privileges. Let it be your constant care to prove yourself worthy of the confidence reposed in you, and of the high honor conferred, in admitting you to this select degree. Let uprightness and integrity attend your steps; let *justice* and *mercy* mark your conduct; let *fervency* and *zeal* stimulate you in the discharge of the various duties incumbent upon you; but suffer not an idle or impertinent *curiosity* to lead you astray, or betray you into danger. Be *deaf* to every insinuation which would have a tendency to weaken your resolution or tempt you to an act of *disobedience*. Be voluntarily *dumb* and *blind*, when the exercise of those faculties would endanger the peace of your mind or the probity of your conduct; and let *silence* and *secrecy*, those cardinal virtues of a Select Master, on all necessary occasions, be scrupulously observed. By a steady adherence to the important instructions contained in this degree, you will merit the approbation of the select number with whom you are associated, and will enjoy the high satisfaction of having acted well your part in the important enterprise in which you are engaged; and, after having *wrought your regular hours*, may be admitted to participate in all the privileges of a *Select Master. Sickles' Monitor, Part 3; p. 9.*

CHAPTER IX.
NINTH, OR SELECT MASTER'S DEGREE.
LECTURE OR EXAMINATION.

Thrice Illustrious Master—Are you a Select Master?

Candidate—I am acknowledged as such, and have wrought my regular hours in the secret vault.

Thrice Illustrious Master—What are they?

Candidate—From nine till twelve.

Thrice Illustrious Master—How gained you admission?

Candidate—Through fervency and zeal, which were mistaken for curiosity and disobedience and well nigh cost me my life; but justice and mercy prevailed, and I was admitted.

Thrice Illustrious Master—What is meant by Select Master?

Candidate—One of those who for their skill was selected to work in the secret vault?

Thrice Illustrious Master—How many were selected to work in the secret vault?

Candidate—Twenty-two from Gebal, with Achishar, Adoniram and the three ancient Grand Masters, making in all but twenty-seven, and no more.

Thrice Illustrious Master—Why but twenty-seven and no more?

Candidate—Because there were but nine arches, and three only were permitted to work in each arch.

Thrice Illustrious Master—Where did the secret

Vault begin?

Candidate—At King Solomon's most retired room.

Thrice Illustrious Master—Where did it end?

Candidate—Under the *sanctum sanctorum* or holy of holies.

Thrice Illustrious Master—When were you to be admitted to the ninth arch?

Candidate—When the Temple was completed and the three Grand Masters were present and agreed; but owing to the untimely death of our Grand Master Hiram Abif, it was closed from all eyes.

Thrice Illustrious Master—What countryman are you?

Candidate—A Phœnecian.

Thrice Illustrious Master—In what city were you born?

Candidate—Gebal.[39]

Thrice Illustrious Master—What is your name?

Candidate—Giblim, or Stone-Squarer.

Thrice Illustrious Master—Have you any signs belonging to this degree?

Candidate—I have, several.

Thrice Illustrious Master—Give me a sign.

(Candidate gives due guard or first Select Master's sign, as on page 65.)

Thrice Illustrious Master—Has that an allusion?

Candidate—It has to a portion of the penalty of my obligation (hands chopped off at the stumps).

Thrice Illustrious Master—Give me another sign.

(Candidate gives second sign, as on page 66.)

Thrice Illustrious Master—Has that an allusion?

Note 39.—"The name Gebal, which was one of the maritime towns of Phoenecia, and whose inhabitants were termed Giblites, is introduced into the degree of Select Master. The place afterward called Byblus is on the frontier of that country, near the mouth of the Adonis."—Morris' Dict., Art. Gebal.

SELECT MASTER'S DEGREE.

Candidate—It has, to another portion of the penalty of my obligation (body quartered, see page 73).

Thrice Illustrious Master—Give me another sign.

(Candidate gives third sign, as on page 66.)

Thrice Illustrious Master—Has that an allusion?

Candidate—It has, to another portion of my obligation (eyes torn from their sockets).

Thrice Illustrious Master—Give me another sign.

(Candidate gives fourth Select Master's sign, as on page 66.)

Thrice Illustrious Master—Has that an allusion?

Candidate—It has, to another portion of the penalty of my obligation (body thrown into the rubbish of the Temple after being quartered; see page 73).

Thrice Illustrious Master—Give me the other signs.

(Candidate gives the three Select Master's signs, as explained on page 67.)

Thrice Illustrious Master—Have these an allusion?

Candidate—They have, to the silence and darkness in which we should always keep the world without with reference to the secret vault.

Thrice Illustrious Master—Give me a token.

(Candidate gives Select Master's grip, as on page 73.)

Thrice Illustrious Master—What is that called?

Candidate—The grip of a Select Master.

Thrice Illustrious Master—Has it a name?

Candidate—It has.

Thrice Illustrious Master—Give it.

Candidate—Izabud, or *Ish Sodi*.

Thrice Illustrious Master—What does it signify?

Candidate—Man of my choice, or Select Master.

[Sometimes a long list of questions, as to the history of the degree and the tradition upon which it is founded, follows. See history, page 74.]

CHAPTER X.

NINTH, OR SELECT MASTER'S DEGREE.

CLOSING CEREMONIES.

Thrice Illustrious Master (one rap)—Companion Captain of the Guard, you will see that the secret vault is made secure and inform the Sentinel that I am about to close this Council of Select Masters and direct him to guard accordingly.

Captain of Guard—Thrice Illustrious, the secret vault is made secure and the Council is duly guarded.

Thrice Illustrious Master (one rap)—Illustrious Companion Principal Conductor, are you a Select Master?

Principal Conductor—I am acknowledged as such, and have wrought my regular hours in the secret vault.

Thrice Illustrious Master—What are they?

Principal Conductor—From nine till twelve.

Thrice Illustrious Master—How gained you admission?

Principal Conductor—Through fervency and zeal, which were mistaken for curiosity and disobedience and well nigh cost me my life; but justice and mercy prevailed, and I was admitted.

Thrice Illustrious Master—What is meant by Select Master?

Principal Conductor—One of those who for their skill was selected to work in the secret vault.

Thrice Illustrious Master How many were selected to work in the secret vault?

Principal Conductor—Twenty-two from Gebal, with Achishar, Adoniram and the three ancient Grand Masters, making in all but twenty-seven, and no more.

Thrice Illustrious Master—Why but twenty-seven and no more?

Principal Conductor—Because there were but nine arches, and three only were permitted to work in each arch.

Thrice Illustrious Master—Where did the secret Vault begin?

Principal Conductor—At King Solomon's most retired room.

Thrice Illustrious Master—Where did it end?

Principal Conductor—Under the *sanctum sanctorum* or holy of holies.

Thrice Illustrious Master—When were you to be admitted to the ninth arch?

Principal Conductor—When the Temple was completed and the three Grand Masters were present and agreed; but owing to the untimely death of our Grand Master Hiram Abif, it was closed from all eyes.

Thrice Illustrious Master—What countryman are you?

Principal Conductor—A Phœnician.

Thrice Illustrious Master—In what city were you born?

Principal Conductor—Gebal.

Thrice Illustrious Master—What is your name?

Principal Conductor—Giblim, or Stone-Squarer.

Thrice Illustrious Master—What is the hour?

Principal Conductor—Low twelve; the usual time

to call the craft from labor to refreshment.

Thrice Illustrious Master—What remains to be done?

Principal Conductor—Retire in peace, practice virtue and remain in silence.

Thrice Illustrious Master—(Three raps, all rise and a closing prayer or the following charge is next in order.)

CLOSING CHARGE SELECT MASTER'S DEGREE.

"COMPANIONS: Being about to quit this sacred retreat to mix again with the world, let us not forget, amid the cares and vicissitudes of active life, the bright example of sincere friendship so beautifully illustrated in the lives of the founders of this degree. Let us take the lesson home with us, and may it strengthen the bands of fraternal love between us, unite our hearts to duty, and our desires to wisdom. Let us exercise Charity, cherish Hope, and walk in Faith. And may that moral principle which is the mystic cement of our fellowship remain with and bless us."—*Mackey's Ritualist, page 551.*

Thrice Illustrious Master—Illustrious Companion Principal Conductor, it is my will and pleasure that —————— Council —————— be now closed; communicate this order to the craft for their government.

Principal Conductor—Companions, it is the will and pleasure of the Thrice Illustrious Master that —————— Council —————— be now closed. Take due notice and govern yourselves accordingly.

[The signs and due-guards from Entered Apprentice up are then given, see pages 35-40, 65, 66 and 67. Then the three principal officers in turn each give nine raps, when the Council is closed.]

94. DIAGRAM OF SUPER EXCELLENT MASTER'S COUNCIL.

*During initiation Gedaliah presides in front of the M E King's Station

CHAPTER XI.

TENTH OR SUPER-EXCELLENT MASTER'S DEGREE.

[The King is supposed to be absent, so Gedaliah takes his seat in front of the throne and calls the Council to order.]

Gedaliah[40] (one rap)—Companion First Keeper of the Temple, proceed to satisfy yourself that all present are Super-Excellent Masters.[41]

First Keeper of Temple—All present are Super-Excellent Masters except the candidate. [The candidate is hoodwinked and taken into the hall before opening the Council.]

Gedaliah—As a Super-Excellent Master, let it be your first duty and last care to see the Sanctuary duly guarded.

First Keeper of Temple—Companion Third Keeper of the Temple, are we duly guarded?

(Third Keeper goes to the door and gives seven raps

Note 40.—"Gedaliah is seated in the West, except during a reception, when he assumes a station in front of the King. The First Keeper of the Temple is seated in front of the West. The Second and Third on the left of the West, and near the door of preparation. The Captain of the Guards is seated on the right hand of the King; the Three Heralds are on the outside of the door, and the Treasurer and Secretary occupy the usual positions of those officers in other Masonic bodies."—Mackey's Ritualist, page 555.

Note 41.—"The Masonic legend of the degree of Super-Excellent Master refers to circumstances which occurred on the last day of the siege of Jerusalem by Nebuzaradan, the captain of the Chaldean army, who had been sent by Nebuchadnezzar to destroy the city and Temple, as a just punishment of the Jewish king Zedekiah, for his perfidy and rebellion. It occupies, therefore, precisely that point of time which is embraced in that part of the Royal Arch degree which represents the destruction of the Temple, and the carrying of the Jews in captivity to Babylon. It is, in fact, an exemplification and extension of that part of the Royal Arch degree."—Mackey's Ritualist, page 554.

SUPER-EXCELLENT MASTER'S DEGREE.

—six and one; is answered by the same, returns and reports:)

Third Keeper of Temple—Companion First Keeper of the Temple, we are duly guarded and the Sanctuary is secure.

First Keeper of Temple—Companion Gedaliah, the Sanctuary is duly guarded.

Gedaliah—Where is the King?

First Keeper of Temple—In one of the apartments of the Temple.

Gedaliah—What is the hour?

First Keeper of Temple—It is the time of the second watch.

Gedaliah (three raps, all rise)—Since it is the time of the second watch, let us repair to the Holy Altar and there offer up our fervent aspirations to the Deity that he may be pleased to vouchsafe to us, as heretofore, his protecting care and favor. (They form around the altar, kneeling on the left knee, right elbow on right knee and head resting on right hand, where they remain a moment.)

Gedalih—Let us arise!

Gedaliah—Look to the east. [Led by Gedaliah, the signs and due guards from Entered Apprentice up are now given.]

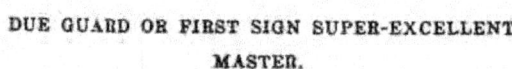

DUE GUARD OR FIRST SIGN SUPER-EXCELLENT MASTER.

Cross arms, as shown in cut, fingers clinched, thumbs pointing upward.

Due Guard.
S. E. Master.

INITIATION.   97

SECOND SIGN SUPER-EXCELLENT MASTER.

Right hand and elbow height of the eyes, two first fingers extended like a fork, thumb and other fingers clinched; then draw arm back, as shown in cut, and dart hand and arm forward horizontally. This alludes to the penalty of S. E. Master's obligation —eyes gouged out.

Gedaliah—Let each repair to his station.
First Herald (blows trumpet on outside of door.)
Third Keeper of Temple—A Herald!
Second Keeper of Temple—A Herald!
First Keeper of Temple—A Herald appears!
(Herald enters.)
First Herald—Nebuchadnezzar approaches with innumerable forces, and fills the city.
Second Herald (sounds his trumpet.)
Third Keeper of Temple—A Herald!
Second Keeper of Temple—A Herald!
First Keeper of Temple—A Herald approaches.
(Herald enters.)
Second Herald—The enemy are formidable and victorious, approaching the King's palace and within a few furlongs of the Temple, and everywhere is unheralded carnage and devastation.
Third Herald (sounds trumpet.)
Third Keeper of Temple—A Herald!
Second Keeper of Temple—A Herald!
First Keeper of Temple—The King approaches.
(King enters with three royal guards, one on each side and one in front.)

98   SUPER-EXCELLENT MASTER'S DEGREE.

Gedaliah (three raps, all rise and face the King, who takes his station in the east.)—Most Excellent King,⁴² the Council is assembled, the officers stationed, and we await your orders.

King (rising)—I proclaim this Council of Super-Excellent Masters organized (one rap, all are seated).

King—Companion Recorder, is there any business before the Council?

Recorder—A candidate, ———, is desirous of taking the degree of Super-Excellent Master.

King Companion Gedaliah, what report brought the Herald?

Gedaliah—That Nebuchadnezzar, King of Babylon, approaches with innumerable forces, and fills the city.

King—How did he report the enemy?

Gedaliah—That they were formidable and victorious, approaching the King's palace and within a few furlongs of the Temple, and everywhere is unheralded carnage and devastation.

First Herald (sounds his trumpet.)
Third Keeper of Temple—A Herald!
Second Keeper of Temple—A Herald!
First Keeper of Temple—A Herald approaches.
(Herald enters.)

First Herald—Nebuchadnezzar, King of Babylon, with battering-rams assaults the Temple, and the courts are filled with carnage. (Much noise is heard outside.)

King—Companion Gedaliah, is there no way of escape?

Geladiah—There is none except by way of the King's

Note 42.—"Its presiding officer is called 'Most Excellent King,' and represents Zedekiah, the last king of Judah."—Mackey's Lexicon, Art. Most Excellent Master.

gardens between the walls, by the private entrance leading out to the plains of Jericho.

King—Let us made our escape in that way.

(The King and guards leave. The noise outside increases.

Second Herald (sounds his trumpet).

Third Keeper of Temple—A Herald!

Second Keeper of Temple—A Herald!

First Keeper of Temple—A Herald approaches.

(Herald enters.)

Gedaliah—What tidings from the King?

Second Herald—The King and all his men of war fled by night by the way of the gate between the walls which is by the King's gardens, and the King went the way toward the plain, and the army of the Chaldeans pursued after the King and overtook him on the plains of Jericho, and all his army was scattered from him; and they took the King and brought him up to the King of Babylon, at Riblah, and they gave judgment upon him. And they slew the sons of Zedekiah[43] before his eyes, and they put out the eyes of Zedekiah and bound him in chains of brass, and carried him to Babylon.

Gedaliah—The sword of the enemy prevails. Our young men are captives and our old men are slain; in this extremity what remains to be done? Let us repair to the Holy Altar and there repledge our faith and renew our vows. (Three raps, all rise, a circle is formed about the altar at which the candidate is caused to kneel, both hands resting on the Holy Bible, square and compass.

Note 43.—"The eyes of Zedekiah were put out, and being loaded with chains of brass he was carried captive to Babylon, where he afterward died."—Mackey's Lexicon, Art. Zedekiah.

100   SUPER-EXCELLENT MASTER'S DEGREE.

Gedaliah (to candidate)—Companion, you are again before the altar of Masonry, where you are about to take the solemn obligation of a Super-Excellent Master.

OBLIGATION OF A SUPER-EXCELLENT MASTER.

Gedaliah—You will repeat your name and say after me: I, ———, of my own free will and accord, and in the presence of the Holy One of Israel and this Council of Super-Excellent Masters, do hereby and hereon most solemnly and sincerely promise and swear that I will not communicate the secrets of this degree to any person or persons, except it be to a true and lawful Companion Super-Excellent Master, or in a legally constituted Council of such, and neither unto him nor them till first by strict trial and due examination, or lawful information, I shall have found him or them as lawfully entitled to the same as I am or shall be myself.

I furthermore promise and swear that I will stand to and abide by all the laws, rules and regulations of any Council of Super-Excellent Masters of which I may become a member, and the constitution, laws and edicts of the Grand Council under whose jurisdiction the same may work, so far as they shall come to my knowledge.

I furthermore promise and swear that I will give meat, drink and lodgings to poor, worthy companions, according to their necessities and my ability, and I will defend them in danger, and vindicate their character so far as truth, honor and justice will warrant.

I furthermore promise and swear that I will not bow down to other gods, nor pay religious adoration to idols, and that I will not worship the sun, moon nor stars of heaven, but in good faith and conscience and to the

INITIATION 101

best of my ability, will serve and worship the only true and living God.

All this I most solemnly and sincerely promise and swear, binding myself under no less a penalty[44] than that of having my thumbs cut off, my eyes put out, my body bound in chains of brass and carried away to a strange and distant land, should I in the least violate this my Super-Excellent Master's obligation. So help me God, and keep me steadfast in the due performance of the same.

[A constantly increasing noise is heard outside during the last part of the obligation, indicating the near approach of the Chaldean army. The Herald sounds the trumpet as the obligation is completed, and a moment after rushes in.]

Herald—The enemy advances!

[Herald is closely pursued by the pretended enemy, who seize the candidate and thrust him out of the room, when the hoodwink is removed and he is conducted into the Council and to the altar. Members are stationed around so as to represent themselves as mourning among the willows in a grove at Babylon.]

SCRIPTURE READING.

"How doth the city sit solitary that was full of people; how is she become as a widow! She that was great among the nations and princess among the provinces, how is she become tributary! She weepeth sore in the night, and her tears are on her cheeks: among

---

Note 44.—"As to the symbolic design of the degree, it is very evident that its legend and ceremonies are intended to inculcate that important Masonic virtue, fidelity to vows. Zedekiah, the wicked king of Judah, is, by the modern ritualists who have symbolized the degree, adopted very appropriately as the symbol of perfidy, and the severe but well deserved punishment which was inflicted on him by the king of Babylon is set forth in the lecture as a great moral lesson, whose object is to warn the recipient of the fatal effects that will ensue from a violation of his sacred obligations."—Mackey's Ritualist, page 854.

all her lovers she hath none to comfort her: all her friends have dealt treacherously with her, they are become her enemies."—Lamentations 1:1, 2.

HYMN.

Air—St. Martin or Balerma.

"By Babel's stream we sit and weep,
Our tears for Zion flow;
Our harps on drooping willows sleep,
Our hearts are filled with woe."

—*Chase's Council Monitor, page 44.*

Gedaliah (strikes his hands together once; all form a square around the altar)—This square represents the encampment of the Israelites, with the ark in the center, three tribes on each side.

MONITORIAL.

"And on the east side toward the rising sun shall they of the standard of the camp of Judah pitch with Issachar and Zebulon."

"On the south side the standard of the camp of Reuben, with Simeon and Gad."

"On the west side the standard of the camp of Ephraim, with Manasseh and Benjamin."

"On the north side the standard of the camp of Dan, with Asher and Naphtali."

"Then the Tabernacle of the congregation shall set forward with the camp of the Levites in the midst of the camp."

INITIATION. 103

"By the rivers of Babylon, there we sat down, yea, we wept, when we remembered Zion. We hanged our harps on the willows in the midst thereof. For there they that carried us away captive required of us a song; and they that wasted us required of us mirth, saying, Sing us one of the songs of Zion."—Psalm 137:1-3.

> "Our walls no more resound with praise,
> Our Temple, foes destroy;
> Judea's courts no more upraise
> Triumphant songs of joy."

—*Chase's Council Monitor, page 48.*

Gedaliah (strikes his hands together twice, when the craft form a triangle about the altar)—This triangle or delta is an emblem of Deity, and represents his omnipotence, omniscience and omnipresence; the links of the chains of the captives also, which were made triangular, the Royal Arch triple triangle and the mystic numbers, etc., of that degree. It also alludes to the triple duty we owe to God, our fellow beings and ourselves.

MONITORIAL.

"Judah is gone into captivity because of affliction, and because of great servitude; she dwelleth among the heathen, she findeth no rest; all her persecutors overtook her between the straits. The ways of Zion do mourn, because none come to the solemn feasts; all her gates are desolate; her priests sigh, her virgins are afflicted, and she is in bitterness."—Lamentations 1: 3, 4.

"How shall we sing the Lord's song in a strange land? If I forget thee, O Jerusalem, let my right hand forget her cunning."—Psalm 137:4, 5.

> "Here, morning, toll the captive bands,
> Our feasts and Sabbaths cease;
> Our tribes dispersed through distant lands,
> Are hopeless of release."

—*Chase's Council Monitor, page 48.*

Gedaliah (strikes his hands together three times, when a circle is formed)—This circle is emblematical of friendship; the ark in the center, as the blazing star in the mosaic pavement, is an emblem of Divine Providence; the radiation from which in direct lines variegates to every part of the circle and we in that. It is also emblematical of the circle of our moral duties, as in the Entered Apprentice degree, and the lesson which the point within the circle embordered by two perpendicular lines, inculcates, I hope you have not forgotten. It is also an emblem of eternity, having neither beginning nor end. The first, the emblem of friendship, may be broken; the second may be changed as the mortal moral agent, but the third, never. This emblem encourages the hope of final immortality, by faith in the Divine promises.

INITIATION. 105

MONITORIAL.

"The word of Jeremiah the prophet, to the captives in Babylon, saying, This captivity is long. Build ye houses and dwell in them; and plant gardens and eat the fruit of them; and seek the peace of the city whither I have caused you to be carried away captives, and pray unto the lord for it; for in the peace thereof shall ye have peace."—Jer. 29:5, 7.

"If I do not remember thee, let my tongue cleave to the roof of my mouth; if I prefer not Jerusalem above my chief joy."—Psalm 137:6.

> "But should the ever gracious Power
> To us propitious be,
> Chaldeans shall our race restore,
> And kings proclaim us free."
>
> —*Chase's Council Monitor, page 49.*

Gedaliah[45] (one rap, seating Council)—I will now explain to you the signs, words and grips of this degree:

This is the due guard of a Super-Excellent Master (makes due guard as on page 96). This alludes to the first portion of the penalty of your obligation.

This is another sign: Raise your right arm as high as your eyes, with the two first fingers extended. First put them to your own eyes, then turn and dart them

---

Note 45.—"There are five persons of the name of Gedaliah who are mentioned in Scripture, but only two of them were contemporary with the destruction of the Temple.

"Gedaliah, the son of Pashur, is mentioned by the prophet Jeremiah (38:1) as a prince of the court of Zedekiah. He was present at its destruction, and is known to have been one of the advisers of the king. It was through his counsels, and those of his colleagues, that Zedekiah was persuaded to deliver up the prophet Jeremiah to death, from which he was rescued only by the intercession of a eunuch of the palace.

"The other Gedaliah was the son of Ahikam. He seems to have been greatly in favor with Nebuchadnezzar, for after the destruction of Jerusalem, and the deportation of Zedekiah, he was appointed by the Chaldean monarch as satrap or governor over Judea."—Mackey's Ritualist, page 563.

toward another's eyes. (See page 97.) Also alludes to the second portion of your obligation. This is the

GRAND HAILING SIGN OF DISTRESS OF A SUPER-EXCELLENT MASTER.

Right hand clinched make sign of a Past Master with a zig-zag motion, and alludes to a portion of your obligation, that of being bound in chains of brass. The word accompanying the last sign is NAHOD ZABOD BONE.

Grand Hailing Sign of S. E. Master.

Gedaliah (continuing)—I will now present you with my hand and with it the pass grip and word and regular grip and word.

PASS GRIP, SUPER-EXCELLENT MASTER.

Pass grip, Super-Excellent Master.

Right hands grasped, as if to pull a person up a steep bank, thumbs touching at ends. See cut.

This is the same as a Mark Master's grip.
WORDS *Siroc, or Mark Well.*

INITIATION. 107

Real grip S. E. Master.

REAL GRIP, SUPER-EXCELLENT MASTER.

Same as pass grip, except grasping each other by both hands, arms crossed. See cut.

1st. (says) *Saul the first king of Israel.*

2nd. (says) *Zedekiah the last king of Judah.*

[The two last sentences are called the "Word" or "Pass."

The grand hailing sign of this degree is like the sign of a Past Master, except that the hand is clenched instead of open and the motion of the hand is zig-zag though drawn in the same direction.

The pass grip is like that of a Mark Master; accompanying "Word" that of the real grip of that degree.]

Gedaliah—Companion Third Keeper of the Temple, conduct our newly admitted companion to the east.

HISTORY.[46]

"The ceremonies through which you have passed have a moral and historic significance.

"The *historic* alludes to the taking of Jerusalem, and

Note 46.—"It is very natural to suppose, that when the enemy were Lost pressing, in their attack upon the devoted city, when the breach which was to give them entrance had been effected, and when perhaps the streets most distant f om the Temple were already filled with Chaldean soldiery, a council of his princes and nobles should have been held by Zedekiah in the Temple, to which they had fled for refuge, and that he should ask their advice as to the most feasible method of escape from the impending dangers. History, it is true, gives no account of any such assembly, but the written record of these important events which is now extant is very brief, and as there is every reason to admit the probability of the occurrence, the original compiler of the degree was authorized to make the meeting of such a council a part of its legendary ceremony."
—Mackey's Ritualist, page 561.

the destruction of the Temple by Nebuchadnezzar, King of Babylon.

"Zedekiah, who reigned at this time in Jerusalem, was the uncle of Jehoiachim, the youthful king placed at eighteen years of age upon the throne.

"The former name of Zedekiah was Mattaniah. The change of name was to indicate that the *justice*, and not the *gift* of the Lord, imparted to him a scepter at the pleasure of the Babylonish monarch.

"Nebuchadnezzar's final and fatal siege of Jerusalem began on Friday, the 30th of December, in the 588th year before the Christian era, being the seventh year of Pharaoh Hophra, King of Egypt.

"The King of Judah besought the aid of Egypt against the Chaldeans. Pharaoh attempted to interpose, but the result was to no purpose, as the prophet had foretold.

"Pharaoh's demonstration only occasioned an intermission of the siege for a period of about one hundred days. The city yielded to the Chaldean power and to famine on Wednesday, the 13th of June.

"Deducting from the 530 days since the forts were built around Jerusalem, the probable interval of 100 days, wherein Pharaoh diverted the attention of the Chaldeans, and we have the 430 days during which Ezekiel was called upon prophetically to bear the iniquities of Israel and Judah.

"Zedekiah, dreading the fury of the monarch to whom he owed his own elevation, had fled from the city, but was pursued by the Chaldeans and captured in the plains of Jericho, about eighteen miles from Jerusalem.

"Northward from this, 100 miles distant, was Riblah,

in the region of Hamath, where Pharaoh Nechi had put in bonds the humiliated Jehoahaz, son of Josiah.

"At this place Nebuchadnezzar now had his quarters and to him the troops conducted the captive Zedekiah: 'And they slew the sons of Zedekiah before his eyes, and put out the eyes of Zedekiah and bound him with fetters of brass and carried him to Babylon.' Thus were verified what had seemed to be the contradictory prophecies of Jeremiah and Ezekiel. The former predicting of Zedekiah: 'Thine eyes shall behold the eyes of the King of Babylon, and he shall speak with thee mouth to mouth, and thou shalt go to Babylon.' And the latter announcing, 'I will bring him to Babylon, to the land of the Chaldeans, yet he shall not see it though he shall die there.'

"Nebuzaradan, the commanding officer of the Chaldean army, presented himself at Jerusalem on Wednesday, the 11th of the succeeding month, and on the following Sabbath, the 14th of July, he completed his cruel and profane ravage in plundering and burning the Temple and city.

"The history prepares us for the thrilling and sacred theme of the pious and wonderful rebuilding of the Lords house. The *moral* purpose of this degree is to inculcate true devotion in spirit and in truth to the Great I AM, in contradistinction to idolatry; to teach traditionally life's vicissitudes; to encourage generous hospitality and friendship; to enlighten the mind and amend the heart, that we may became wiser and purer, brighter and brighter unto the perfect day, and by precept and example to excite our brethren to moral action and the amiable practice of sincere devotion toward God, and of all the social virtues. It also inculcates the faithful fulfillment of our several vows, and the fearless discharge of our respective duties; and teaches us that the violation of our solemn vows, as in the case of Zedekiah, the last king of Judah, will not only cause us to forfeit the respect and friendship of our companions, but will also most surely destroy our own peace of mind.

"Then let us, my companions, labor diligently and fearlessly in the cause of Truth our allotted time, doing with our might whatever our hands find to do, so that, when at the time of the third watch our work is finished, we may be greeted as Super-Excellent Masters, and be released from our captivity in the flesh, to return over the rough and rugged way of the Valley of the Shadow of Death to our abiding-place, eternal in the heavens, there to erect our last and perfect moral and Masonic temple and adore the Holy One of Israel throughout the endless cycles of eternity."—*Chase's Council Monitor, page 50.*

CHARGE TO CANDIDATE, SUPER-EXCELLENT MASTER'S DEGREE.

COMPANION: As Masonry is a science of morality veiled in allegory and illustrated by symbols, it is proper that, as a Super-Excellent Master, you should be instructed in the moral design of the degree into which you have just been initiated. It is intended, in the first place, to inculcate a sincere devotion to the GREAT I AM, in contradistinction to an idolatrous worship, which is, in other words, but a symbolical expression for a reverence of truth and an abhorrence of falsehood.

"It also impresses on us the necessity of a faithful fulfillment of our several vows, and the fearless discharge of our respective duties; and teaches us, by its

INITIATION. 111

legends and its ceremonies, that the violation of our solemn vows, as in the instance of the last king of Judah, will not only cause us to forfeit the respect and friendship of our companions, but will also most surely destroy our own peace of mind.

' 'Let us, then, labor diligently and faithfully in the cause of TRUTH, doing with all our might whatever our hands find to do, so that, when at the time of the third watch our work is finished, we may be greeted as Super-Excellent Masters, and be released from our captivity in the flesh, to return over the rough and rugged way of the Valley of the Shadow of Death to our abiding-place, eternal in the heavens, there to erect our second moral and Masonic temple, that house not made with hands; there to adore the Holy One of Israel throughout the endless circle of eternity."—*Mackey's Ritualist, page 565.*

CHAPTER XII.

Tenth, or Super-Excellent Master's Degree.

LECTURE, OR EXAMINATION.

Gedaliah—Are you a Super-Excellent Master?

Candidate—I have the honor to be.

Gedaliah—Where did you receive that honor?

Candidate—In a duly constituted Council of Super-Excellent Masters.

Gedaliah—Have you any signs belonging to this degree?

Candidate—I have.

Gedaliah—Give me a sign. (Candidate gives due guard, as on page 96.)

Gedaliah—What is that called?

Candidate—The due guard of a Super-Excellent Master.

Gedaliah—Has it an allusion?

Candidate—It has, to a portion of the penalty of my obligation. (Thumbs cut off.)

Gedaliah—Give me another sign. (Candidate gives sign of gouging out eyes, as on page 97.)

Gedaliah—Has that an allusion?

Candidate—It has, to another portion of the penalty of my obligation. (Eyes gouged out.)

Gedaliah—Have these signs any further allusion?

Candidate—They have, to the fate of Zedekiah, King of Judah, who rebelled against Nebuchadnezzar, King of Babylon, who had elevated him to his position. His thumbs were cut off, his eyes put out and his body bound in fetters of brass was carried to Babylon.

CHAPTER XIII.

TENTH, OR SUPER-EXCELLENT MASTER'S DEGREE.

CLOSING CEREMONIES.

Gedaliah (one rap)—Companion First Keeper of the Temple, as a Super-Excellent Master let it be your first duty and last care to see the sanctuary duly guarded.

First Keeper of Temple—Companion Third Keeper of the Temple are we duly guarded? (Third Keeper of the Temple goes to the door, gives seven raps; is answered by same.)

Third Keeper of Temple—We are duly guarded and the sanctuary is secure.

First Keeper of Temple—Companion Gedaliah, the sanctuary is duly guarded.

Gedaliah—Where is the King?[47]

First Keeper of Temple—In the prison at Babylon. His thumbs have been cut off, his eyes put out, his body bound in chains of brass and carried captive to a strange and distant land, as a penalty for perjury.

Gedaliah—The sword of the enemy prevails, our young men are captives and our old men are slain. In this extremity what remaineth to be done? Let us repair to the holy altar and there repledge our faith and renew our vows. (All assemble around the altar and kneel on left knee, right elbow on right knee and head

Note 47.—"The historical incidents, but less in detail, are to be found in the first part of the Royal Arch."—Mackey's Lexicon, Art. Super-Excellent Master.

on right hand, where they remain a moment.)
 Gedaliah—Let us arise. (All rise.)
 Gedaliah—Look to the east. (All, led by Gedaliah make the signs and due guards from Entered Apprentice degree up.)
 Gedaliah—Let each repair to his station.
 Gedaliah (seven raps.)
 First Keeper of Temple (seven raps.)
 Second Keeper of the Temple (seven raps.)
 Gedaliah—I proclaim this Council of Super-Excellent Masters closed.

ANALYSIS OF THE COUNCIL DEGREES.

Established by Adventurers from Prussia—Brief History of their Origin by Mackey—Their Origin in Question—Three Different Grand Masonic Bodies Claim the Right to Sell these Secrets—A Committee Investigates and Reports on their Origin—The Sublime Grand Lodge of Perfection, 33d Degree, Establishes its Claim of Jurisdiction—First Grand Council of Princes of Jerusalem Established at Charleston, S. C.—The Ritual Deposited with them by Joseph Myers. One of the Deputy Inspectors General, from Prussia—These Inspectors General Peddle these Degrees through the Southern and Western States—The Ritual Copied for the Supreme Council, who Send out Jeremy L. Cross and other Rite Peddlers—Blasphemous Use of Alpha and Omega—Silence and Secrecy the Cardinal Masonic Virtues—Other False Religions Teach the Same—The Teachings of Christ vs. Freemasonry—Freemasonry Governs by Terror.

Like the "Holy Royal Arch degree" these Council degrees were established by wandering adventurers, though it is claimed that King Frederick II. of Prussia gave the authority for their establishment to three Deputy Inspectors General. We quote the following brief history of the Council degrees from Mackey's Masonic Ritualist:

"Forty years ago there were very earnest discussions on the subject of the origin and jurisdiction of the degrees of Royal and Select Master. At that time there were three authorities under whom those degrees were conferred in the United States; first, under Grand Councils in some of the States; secondly, under Grand Chapters as in Maryland and Virginia; and thirdly, under the Supreme Council of the thirty-third degree of the Ancient and Accepted Rite, as in South Carolina. This diversity of authority was undoubtedly dependent on an uncertainty of origin. The degrees were here, but few knew whence they came, nor by whom they had been originally introduced.

"But an attempt on the part of the Grand Chapter of Maryland, in the year 1826, 'to assume jurisdiction and authority' over these degrees, led to investigation into their history. In February, 1827, a committee of most able and competent Companions made a report on this subject to the Grand Chapter of South Carolina, in which the history of the origin of these degrees is so fully discussed, that the valuable information it imparts had better be given in the very words of the report itself:

"'The committee appointed at the last stated convocation of the Grand Royal Arch Chapter, in May last, to take into consideration and report upon the propriety and expediency of the different Grand Royal Arch Chapters of the several States respectively assuming jurisdiction and authority over the Royal and Select Master's degrees, and to which committee were referred the proceedings of the Grand Royal Arch Chapter of Maryland upon the subject, respectfully ask leave to state that they have made extensive and careful investigation into the subjects referred to their consideration, and they offer the following statement as the result of their inquiries:

"'They have ascertained that the respectable brothers and companions, Dr. F. Dalcho, Dr. Isaac Auld, Dr. James Moultrie, Sr., and Moses C. Levy, Esq., with many others, received these degrees in Charleston, in February, 1783, in the Sublime Grand Lodge of Perfection, then established in this city (Charleston), of which body three of the above-named brothers are still living, venerable for their years and warm attachment to the glorious cause of Freemasonry, and highly respected and esteemed in the community where they have so long and so honorably sojourned, and they are still members of the same sublime body.

"'Your committee have further ascertained that at the original establishment of the Grand Council of Princes of Jerusalem, in this city, on the 20th of February, 1783, by the Illustrious Brothers Joseph Myers, Barend M. Spitzer and A. Forst, Deputy Inspectors

General, from Frederick II., King of Prussia, Brother Myers then deposited in the archives of the said Grand Council of the Princes of Jerusalem certified copies of the said degrees, from Berlin, in Prussia, which were to be under the future guidance and fostering protection of the government of the above-named presiding body. The above-named three respectable brethren and companions are, and have steadily been, members and officers of the said body of Princes of Jerusalem; their evidence, therefore, must be conclusive upon these points.

" 'Your committee are informed that the above-named Brother Myers, previously to his return to Europe, while pursuing his mercantile concerns, resided some time in several of the cities of Virginia and Maryland, where he communicated a knowledge of the degrees in question.

" 'The committee further state that the Grand Officers and the Sublime Council of Inspectors General have been, since 1783, steadily in the habit of conferring the degrees in question, under their authority, in the Southern and Western States. Your committee have seen and perused the first copy of these degrees that ever came to America, and old copies of charters that have been returned by Councils in States where Grand Councils have been formed, and the bodies surrendering have taken other charters for conferring the degrees from such Grand Councils of Royal and Select Masters thus formed.' * * * *

"As corroborative of these statements, it may be mentioned that in a manuscript record of Brother Peter Snell, who was, in 1827, a member of the Supreme Council, is contained the following memorandum:

" 'Supreme Council Chamber, Charleston, S. C., February 10, 1827. I hereby certify that the detached degrees, called Royal and Select Master, or Select Masters of 27, were regularly given by the Sublime Grand Lodge of Perfection (No. 2, in the U. S. A.), established by Brother Isaac Da Costa, in Charleston, in 1783, one of the original members of which, M. I. Brother Moses C. Levy, is still alive and a member of it to this day, without ceasing to be so for a day. And further, that at the first establishment of a Grand Council of Princes of Jerusalem, in Charleston, in February, 1783, by the Illustrious Deputy Inspectors General, Joseph Myers, B. M. Spitzer and A. Forst, Brother Myers (who succeeded Brother Da Costa, after his decease) deposited a certified copy of the degrees from Berlin, in Prussia, to be under the guidance and fostering protection of the government of the above Grand Council of Princes of Jerusalem.'

"Brother Moses Holbrook, who was Grand Commander of the Supreme Council at Charleston in 1829, has copied this statement of Snell into a manuscript ritual of the degrees, which he deposited in the archives of the Supreme Council, and which is now in the possession of a Past Officer. He has also added in his own hand the following comment:

"'Brother Myers, shortly after this (February 20, 1788), resided some time in Norfolk, Richmond and Baltimore, previous to his removal to Europe, and he communicated a knowledge of these degrees to a number of brethren in those cities. The original copy is still in my keeping; and agreeably to the obligations of the same, and the Grand Constitutions governing those degrees, viz.: Royal and Select Masters of 27, it is correct and lawful to give them either to Sublime Masons, who have arrived to the Knights of the Ninth Arch (13th degree), or to companions of the Third Arch, Royal Arch Masons.'

"The Rev. Frederick Dalcho, who was at one time Grand Commander of the Southern Supreme Council, in the appendix to his 'Masonic Orations,' published in 1803, after giving a list of the regular degrees of the Ancient and Accepted Rite, adds, that 'most of the Inspectors are in possession of a number of detached degrees given in different parts of the world, and which they generally communicate, free of expense, to those brethren who are high enough to understand them. And among these 'detached degrees,' he mentions 'Select Masons of 27,' which is what we now call the Select Master.

"From these statements, then, we gather the following results as to the history of the introduction of these degrees into the United States:

"1. The degrees of Royal and Select Master were originally brought to this country by an Inspector General of the Ancient and Accepted Rite, in the year 1783, deposited by him in the archives, and placed under the control of the Council of Princes of Jerusalem, which was organized in the city of Charleston, South Carolina, in that year.

"2. These degrees were at first conferred in Charleston, by the Council of Princes of Jerusalem, as 'detached degrees,' or what in more modern phrase would be called 'side degrees' of the Ancient and Accepted Rite.

"3. They were disseminated over the whole country by agents or representatives of this Rite, who conferred them on any qualified persons whom they pleased to select, but always with the administration of a pledge of allegiance to the Supreme Council of the Ancient and Accepted Rite.

"4. Charters were granted by these agents of the Supreme Council for the establishment of Councils of Royal and Select Masters, in different States, which councils subsequently united in the formation of State Grand Councils, and threw off their allegiance to the

Supreme Council of the Ancient and Accepted Rite. I do not believe that charters were ever granted immediately and directly by the Supreme Council. I think that they were always issued in its name by its agents, who were empowered so to do by a general warrant. Thus I have been enabled to trace the original Councils of Alabama to the action of John Barker, who was an authorized agent of the Supreme Council. Perhaps more work was done in this way by Jeremy L. Cross, under the same claim, than by any other man in the United States."—*Mackey's Ritualist, pages 606 to 611.*

From this brief sketch the reader will see that there was a fine exemplification of "those truly Masonic virtues, *friendship,* morality and *brotherly love,*" in the wrangle as to who should sell these Masonic secrets. The reader who has carefully noted the ritual of these degrees and the foot notes, particularly notes 3 and 6, and the prayer on same page as note 6; notes 8, 11, 13, 22, 35, 36 and 38 and the charge to candidates, pages 110-111, will need no argument to convince him that these degrees are but a development of the Masonic and Satanic plan of salvation without Christ. The blasphemous use made of one of the chosen titles of the Lord Jesus, *"Alpha and Omega,"* as given on page 51 and the Masonic admission of such use in note 16 on same page, ought to make every true Christian loathe the institution, and the unblushing admission by Mackey in notes 14, 21, 22, 32 and 38, either of the aping of the ancient mysteries, or the actual identity of these degrees with those heathen orders of which Paul says, "it is a shame even to speak of those things which are done of them in secret," (Eph. 5: 12) ought to open the eyes of any person whose mind is not completely blinded by the god of this world (see 2 Cor. 4:4) to the abominable character of this professedly "ancient and honorable institution."

In regard to the design and teaching of these degrees; the "Masonic symbolism," it is doubtless true that many who read the ridiculous story about the nine arches under Solomon's Temple, one of which, the ninth and last, which is pretended was directly under the *sanctum sanctorum*, or holy of holies, and was made alone and entirely by the three Grand Masters, Solomon, King of Israel; Hiram, King of Tyre, and Hiram, Abif, with their own hands, will be simply amused thereby as they would be by some newspaper story about a great sea serpent. As to the puerile and ludicrous story about Izabud, the "particular friend" of Solomon, and Achishar, the unfaithful steward or sentinel, whose pretended condemnation and execution are the basis of the degree, many will see only a meaningless farce. That such a conclusion would be very erroneous is evident from the following:

"The two virtues which it is particularly the symbolic design of the Select Master's degree to inculcate are secrecy and silence. They are, indeed, called the cardinal virtues of a Select Master, because the necessity of their practice is prominently set before the candidate in the legend, as well as in all the ceremonies of the degree. But these virtues constitute the very essence of all Masonic character; they are the safeguards of the institution, giving to it all its security and perpetuity, and are enforced by frequent admonitions in all the degrees, from the lowest to the highest. The Entered Apprentice begins his Masonic career by learning the duty of secrecy and silence. Hence it is appropriate that in that degree which is the consummation of initiation, in which the whole cycle of Masonic science is completed, the abstruse machinery of symbolism should be employed to impress the same important virtues on the mind of the neophyte.

"The same principles of secrecy and silence existed in all the ancient mysteries and systems of worship. When Aristotle was asked what thing appeared to him to be most difficult of performance, he replied, 'To be secret and silent.'

"'If we turn our eyes back to antiquity,' says Calcott, 'we shall find that the old Eygptians had so great a regard for silence and secrecy in the mysteries of their religion that they set up the god Harpocrates, to whom they paid peculiar honor and veneration; who was represented with the right hand placed near the heart, and the left down by his side, covered with a skin before, full of eyes and ears; to signify that of many things to be seen and heard few are to be published.'

"Apuleius, who was an initiate in the mysteries of Isis, says: "By no peril will I ever be compelled to disclose to the uninitiated the things that I have had intrusted to me on condition of silence.'

"Lobeck, in his 'Aglaophamus,' has collected several examples of the reluctance with which the ancients approached a mystical subject, and the manner in which they shrunk from divulging any explanation or fable which had been related to them at the mysteries under the seal or secrecy and silence.

"And lastly, in the school of Pythagoras these lessons were taught by the sage to his diciples. A novitiate of five years was imposed upon each pupil, which period was to be passed in total silence and religious and philosophical contemplation. And at length, when he was admitted to full fellowship in the society, an oath of secrecy was administered to him on the sacred tetractys, which was equivalent to the Jewish tetragrammaton.

"Select Masters therefore work in secrecy and silence, that they may prepare and preserve the sacred deposits of truth until the time shall come for its full revelation. And so should all men do, working *now*, yet not for the present time alone, but that their labor may bring forth fruit in the future; laboring here amid the foundations of the first temple of this transient life, that when their hours of work are finished on earth, the deeds which they have done may be brought to light, and the reward be bestowed in the second temple of eternal life.

"This is the true symbolism of the Select Master's degree."—*Mackey's Ritualist, pages 523-525.*

Such is the character of the Council degrees and of Freemasonry as stated by Dr. Albert G. Mackey, the most prolific writer and generally regarded as the highest Masonic authority in America, and now and for years past a *"Sovereign Grand Inspector General"* of the order. While the Christian religion always and everywhere brings peace and good will to men, and Christ said, "I ever spake openly to the world * * and in secret have I said nothing," (John 18:20) "What ye hear in the ear that preach ye upon the house tops," (Matt. 10:27) the Masonic, like all false religions, of each of whom Satan is the real god, governs its votaries by terror; and, instead of, "Go ye into all the world and preach the Gospel to every creature," secrecy and silence are pronounced "the cardinal virtues."

The teaching and design of the Super-Excellent Master's degree (last of the Council degrees) is stated by the same author still more forcibly and concisely as quoted in note 44, the closing clause of which has an unmistakable ring: "Whose object is to warn the recipient [of the degree] of the fatal effects that will ensue from a violation of his sacred obligations."

124   DIAGRAM OF RED CROSS COUNCIL.

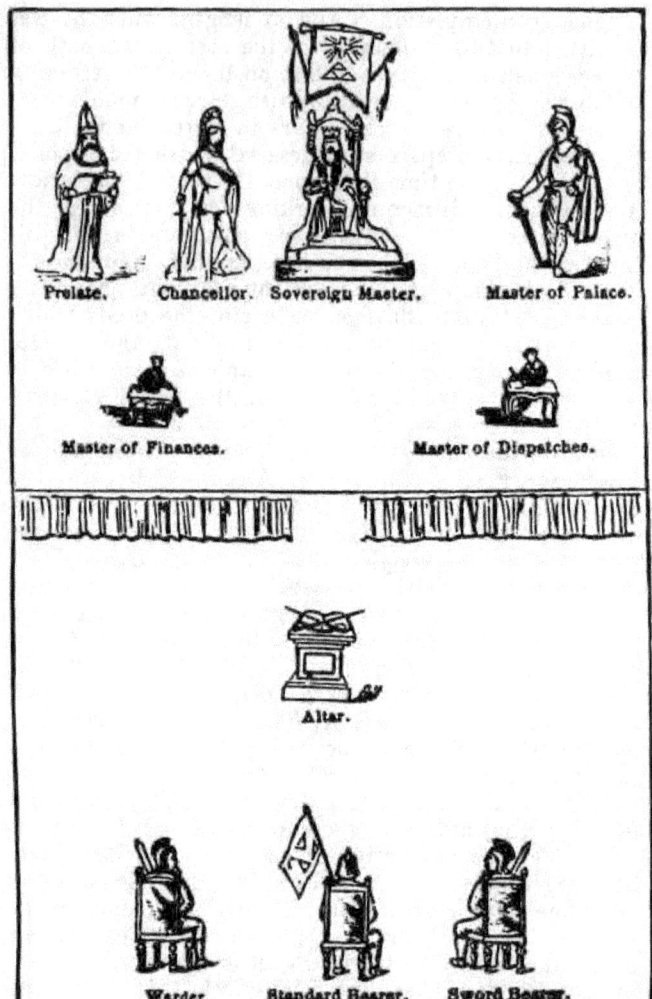

CHAPTER XIV.

KNIGHTS OF THE RED CROSS, OR ELEVENTH DEGREE.

OPENING CEREMONIES.

Sovereign Master—Sir Knight Master of the Palace, it is my will and pleasure that this Council of Knights of the Red Cross[48] be prepared for my reception. Sir Knight Chancellor, accompany me to my apartment. [Sovereign Master, representing King Darius, and Chancellor retire to the king's apartments.]

Master of the Palace (standing at post of Sovereign Master)—Attention, Sir Knights! Clothe and equip yourselves as Knights of the Red Cross! Sir Knight Master of the Cavalry, you will see that this Council of Knights of the Red Cross is in order for the reception of the Sovereign Master!

Master of Cavalry—Sir Knight Warder, satisfy yourself that all present are Knights of the Red Cross.

Warder (after looking around)—All present are Knights of the Red Cross.

Master of Cavalry—When a Council of Knights of the Red Cross[49] is about to be opened, what is the first

Note 48.—"This is the first of the three orders in Encampment Masonry, and corresponds with the degree of Prince of Jerusalem in Scotch Masonry, from which it is borrowed."—Morris' Dict., Art. Red Cross Knight.

Note 49.—"It has no analogy to the degrees of chivalry, dating its existence long before the Crusades, or even the Christian era, as far back indeed, as the reign of Darius, by whom it is said to have been founded. It is, however, always conferred in a commaodery of Knights Templar, and is given preparatory to communicating that degree, though there is no connection whatever between the two."—Mackey's Lexicon, Art. Knight of the Red Cross.

duty?

Warder—To see that the Sentinel is at his post and the council chamber duly guarded.

Master of Cavalry—Perform that duty and inform the Sentinel that a Council of Knights of the Red Cross is about to be opened, and direct him to guard accordingly. (The Warder informs Sentinel as in previous degrees, giving eight raps, 000-000-00, which are answered by the same, and the Sentinel being informed, the Warder returns and reports.)

[As this degree is often conferred on those who have not taken either of the three Council degrees preceding this, it is considered as the eighth Masonic degree, hence but eight raps.]

Warder—The Sentinel is at his post and the council chamber is duly guarded.

Master of Cavalry—Attention, Sir Knights! Fall in! (Knights form in single rank, one behind the other, Indian file, facing the east, and as in other military companies, they stand according to height, the tallest at the right or head.)

Master of Cavalry—Front! (All turning to the left, face the *north*.)

Master of Cavalry—Right—dress! (All turn their eyes to the right and come into lihe, guided by the sword of the Master of Cavalry, which he points down the line, from the head or east.)

Master of Cavalry—Front! (All look to the front.)

Master of Cavalry—From the right—count—twos! (They begin at the right and count, one, two; one, two, down the line, and all those who count *one* form the "First Division," and those counting *two* the "Second Division.")

OPENING CEREMONIES.

Master of Cavalry—Form divisions! Right—face! (All face to the right; the *twos* each step to the right of the one that was on their right, thus forming divisions.)

Master of Cavalry—Officers—posts! (Master of Infantry steps to the right of Second Division, faced to the right, or east; the Standard Bearer, Sword Bearer and Warder form in line facing the east, Standard Bearer in the middle, their right one pace from foot of First Division, of course at right angles with both divisions.)

Master of Cavalry—Form lines for the reception of the Sovereign Master.

Master of Infantry—By file left—march! (The Master of Infantry leading them, turns to the left, and those following, as each comes to the spot where the Master of Infantry turned also turn, and the line after taking four paces receives the command:)

Master of Infantry—By file left—march! (Master of Infantry turns to the left again and is followed as before and they pass along until the head of the division is opposite the left end of the First Division.)

Master of Infantry—Halt! (All stop unless the division has "strung out," when they close up properly.)

Master of Infantry—Front! (All form in line, facing the south and the First Division.)

Master of Infantry—Left—dress! (At the word "left" all turn their *heads* to the left, and at the word "dress" come into exact line.)

Master of Infantry—Front!

DIVISIONS FORMED, INWARD FACE.

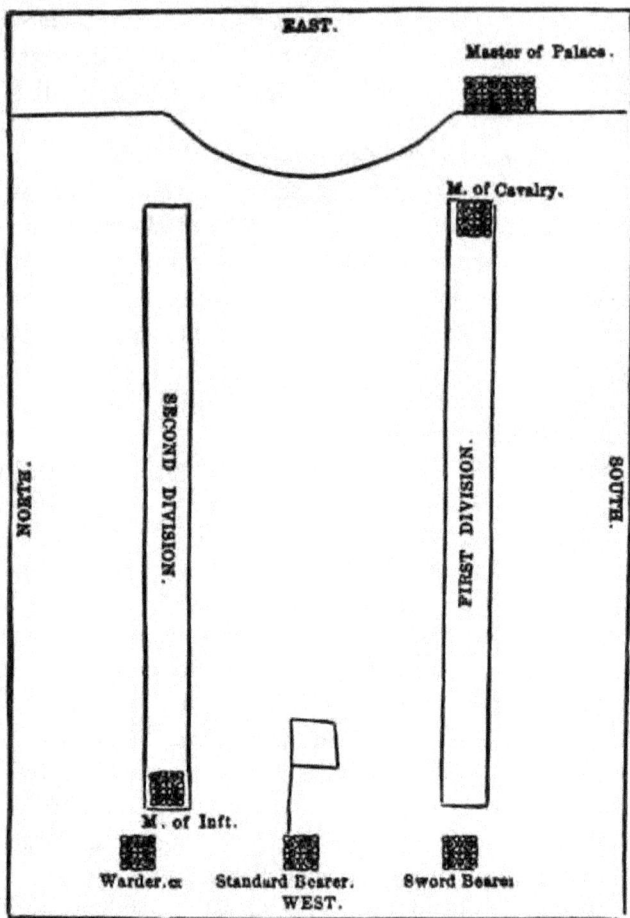

[The lines when formed are as shown in diagram.]

Master of Cavalry—Sir Knight Master of the Palace, the lines are duly formed.

OPENING CEREMONIES.

Master of Palace—Sir Knight Master of Infantry, repair with the Standard Bearer and Sword Bearer to the apartment of the Sovereign Master and inform him that the lines are formed and await his pleasure.

Master of Infantry (facing about)—Sir Knights Standard Bearer and Sword Bearer, left—face! (*he faces to the left.*) By file right—march!

(Master of Infantry leads the way to the quarters of the Sovereign Master.)

Master of Infantry (at apartment of Sovereign Master)—Sovereign Master, the lines are formed and await your pleasure.

Sovereign Master—Sir Knight Chancellor, accompany me to the council chamber.

(Led by the Master of Infantry, Standard Bearer, Sword Bearer and guards, the Sovereign Master and Chancellor approach the council chamber.)

Warder (sounds the trumpet)—They enter.

Master of Palace—Attention, Sir Knights! Present swords!

(Swords are held at "present" while the Sovereign Master and Chancellor pass through the lines from the west and take their stations. The escort, passing along behind the First Division, resume their posts. The Master of Infantry leading and ordering the movement, "By file right—march," as soon as they pass clear of the First Division, "By file right—march," when he reaches the foot of that division and again "By file right—march," to bring them into line with the Warder.)

SWORD PRACTICE.

[Though a detailed description of sword practice seems unnecessary, a few of the more common motions seems desirable.]

DRAW SWORDS.

First Motion. At the word "draw," grasp scabbard with left and sword with right hand, and draw sword about two inches.

Second Motion. At the word "swords," draw sword out, and throwing right hand in front, drop sword in hollow of elbow.

Third Motion. Bring right hand with hilt of sword to right thigh, elbow a little bent, sword perpendicular and held by thumb and forefinger. This is the position of

CARRY SWORDS.

Carry swords.

As this is the usual position of holding a sword, the position is asssumed in executing the order to "Draw—swords," and resumed at the command "Recover," given after a salute or when a cross is formed.

PRESENT SWORDS.

Sword being at "carry," at the word "present" grasp hilt firmly and at the word "swords" raise sword perpendicularly, guard or hilt height of shoulder, arm against the body. See cut.

After "Present—swords," the order "Carry —swords," is executed by extending the hand in front when sword drops in hollow of arm at elbow; then bring hand and hilt to right thigh, sword perpendicular.

Present swords.

OPENING CEREMONIES. 131

SALUTE.

Salute

Bring sword to "present," then extend arm and let point of sword drop as shown in cut, hand on right thigh, back of hand up.

RETURN SWORDS.

First Motion. Bring swords to "present" and at same time grasp scabbard with left hand near the mouth.

Second Motion. Drop point of sword to the mouth of the scabbard and turning the head to the left raise the hand when the sword is pushed in, then, eyes front and hands at side.

FORM CROSS.

This command is given only when lines are formed facing inward, as for reception of Sovereign Master, or Eminent Commander, as he is called in the next degree, or for inspection and review.

Form cross.

Knights facing each other, each throws right foot forward about eighteen inches, throwing the weight of the body forward and right arm extended forward and and upward, when swords of opposite knights are crossed about eight inches from the point.

SWORD CUTS.

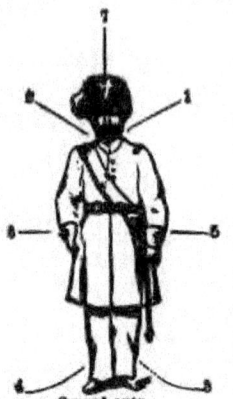
Sword cuts.

There are seven *regular* sword cuts, and when at such practice, the officer in command orders the cuts by the numbers.

The preliminary commands are, first: "*Prepare to guard!*" when sword is brought to the position of "present;" when the second preliminary command, "*Guard!*" is given, and each throws the right foot forward about eighteen inches and at same time extends right arm and cross swords with each other as in "form cross" except that swords are crossed about midway of the blade. Swords are held in this position till the order for the cuts is given.

CUT ONE is a downward cut from the right toward the neck, as shown in engraving, when sword is brought back to position of "prepare to guard," and *after each cut swords are brought to "prepare to guard."*

CUT TWO is same as cut one, except a *left* downward stroke toward the neck.

CUT THREE is made by a sweep of the sword around to the right and then up toward the legs as shown in engraving, and is called a '*right under cut.*"

CUT FOUR is the same as cut three, but from the left and called a "*left under cut.*"

CUT FIVE is a cut from the right toward the body at or near the waist.

CUT SIX is the same as cut five except from the left.

CUT SEVEN is a vertical cut toward the head and is called the "*head cut.*"

OPENING CEREMONIES CONTINUED.

Sovereign Master—Sir Knight Chancellor, it is my will and pleasure that the Sir Knights be displayed by single line, facing the east.

Chancellor—Sir Knight Master of the Palace, it is the will and pleasure of the Sovereign Master that the Sir Knights be displayed in single line, facing the east.

Master of the Palace—Sir Knight Master of Cavalry, display the First Division by single line, facing the east.

Master of Palace—Sir Knight Master of Infantry, display the Second Division by single line, facing the east. (The lines being formed as in diagram, page 128. the Sword Bearer, Standard Bearer and Warder, led by Sword Bearer, march around to the east end of the Second Division, at right angles with the lines, and between the end of the line and Master of Cavalry's station.)

Master of Cavalry—First Division, right—face! (All face to the right.) By file right! (Leader turns half to the right.)

Master of Infantry—Second Division, left face! (All face to the left.) By file left! (Leader turns to the left.)

Master of Palace—March! (Both divisions start together at the word march, the first filing right and the other left, but as the lines were faced inward they really move together. When the end of the two lines has barely passed the line of the Sword Bearer, Standard Bearer and Warder, the Master of the Palace commands:)

Master of Palace—Halt!

Master of Palace—Front! (Each turns to the east, and each one of the Second Division steps to the left of one that was opposite him in the First Division, thus forming one line facing the east.)

Master of Palace—On the center—dress! (All turn their eyes to the center of the line and come into exact line.)

Master of Palace—Front!

Master of Palace—Sir Knight Chancellor, the order of the Sovereign Master has been obeyed.

Chancellor—Sovereign Master, the Sir Knights are displayed by single line, facing the east.

Sovereign Master—Attention, Sir Knights! Return swords! (Knights return swords to scabbard.)

Sovereign Master—Attention to giving the signs!

Sovereign Master—Entered Apprentice! (Led by the Sovereign Master, all give due guard and sign.)

Sovereign Master—Fellow Craft! (All make Fellow Craft due guard, and so on up to the Red Cross degree.)

Sovereign Master—Attention, Sir Knights! Draw swords—carry swords! (Orders are obeyed as given.)

Sovereign Master—It is my will and pleasure that the lines be formed for inspection and review.

Chancellor—Sir Knight Master of the Palace, it is the will and pleasure of the Sovereign Master that the lines be formed for inspection and review. (Master of the Palace repeats the command and the lines are formed facing inward, as in diagram, page 128.)

Master of Cavalry—Sir Knight Master of the Palace, the lines are formed for inspection and review.

Master of Palace—Sir Knight Chancellor, the order of the Sovereign Master has been obeyed.

Chancellor—Sovereign Master, the lines are formed for inspection and review.

Sovereign Master—Sir Knight Chancellor, acccompany me in the inspection and review. (The Sovereign Master and Chancellor approach the lines.)

OPENING CEREMONIES. 135

Master of Palace—Attention, Sir Knights! Present swords! (In passing through the lines they inspect the First Division, and in returning, the Second Division. As they halt before each knight he turns his sword with thumb and forefinger so as to show both sides of the blade. When the Sovereign Master and Chancellor have passed through the lines and resumed their stations, the Sovereign Master orders:)

Sovereign Master—Carry swords! (They bring swords from "present" to "carry.")

Sovereign Master—Sir Knight Master of the Palace, advance and communicate to me the Jewish pass.

JEWISH PASS.

Master of Palace advances to Sovereign Master, brings his sword to "recover," when they give "the word over an arch of steel," as follows: They clash their swords together and then give cuts *one* and *four* [see page 132] as in regular sword practice, the blows being parried. Each then throws forward his left foot and grasps the other's right shoulder with his left hand, when a dialogue takes place.

Giving Jewish Pass.

Master of Palace—JUDAH.
Sovereign Master—BENJAMIN.
Master of Palace—BENJAMIN.
Sovereign Master—JUDAH. (They resume their places.)

Sovereign Master—Receive it from the Sir Knight on your left!

Master of Palace (to knight on his left)—Sir Knight, advance and communicate the Jewish pass! (Given same as explained, when he orders:) Receive it from the Sir Knight on your left!

First Sir Knight (to second)—Sir Knight, advance and communicate the Jewish pass! (Order is obeyed, and he makes same demand of the next knight, and so on till it reaches the Chancellor at the end of the line.)

Chancellor—Sovereign Master, I have the Jewish pass.

Sovereign Master—Advance and communicate it. (Order is obeyed.)

Sovereign Master—The Jewish pass has come correctly through the lines.

Sovereign Master—Sir Knight Chancellor, advance and communicate to me the Persian pass.

PERSIAN PASS.

Sword practice as before, except that there are *four* regular cuts, *two, one, four* and *two* [see page 132] and the word is "given *under* an arch of steel."

Chancellor—TATNAI.[50]

Sovereign Master—SHETH-AR-BOZANI.[51]

Chancellor—SHETHAR-BOZ-ANI.

Sovereign Master—TATNAI.

(They resume their stations.)

Giving Persian Pass.

Sovereign Master—Receive it on your right. (Order is carried down the line as with Jewish password.)

Master of Palace—I have the Persian password.

Sovereign Master—Advance and communicate it. (Order is obeyed.)

Note 50.—"The name of this person is introduced into the order of Red Cross Knights."—Morris' Dict., Art. Tatnai.
Note 51.—"The name of this person is introduced into the order of Red Cross Knights."—Morris' Dict., Art. Shethar-bozani.

OPENING CEREMONIES

Sovereign Master—The Persian password has come up correctly through the lines.

Sovereign Master—Attention, Sir Knights of the First and Second Division Second Division, communicate to the First Division the Red Cross word—charge!

RED CROSS WORD.

Giving Red Cross Word.

The knights opposite each other give cuts *one, two* and *four*, then each draws back his sword in a quick, threatening manner, as if to thrust it into his companion, each of the Second Division whispering, VERITAS, and the First answering, RIGHT.

Sovereign Master—Recover! First Division communicate to the Second Division the grand sign, grip and word of a Knight of the Red Cross!

RED CROSS GRAND SIGN, GRIP AND WORD.

Knights advance to each other; First Division gives cut *three* with swords; then each raises his left hand and places thumb and forefinger against his lips, the others spread open upward as if holding a horn to give a blast, and then with a graceful sweep form a semi-circle around to the left, when hand falls to side. Then give cuts *one, four* and *two* with sword, and throwing left foot forward interlace the fingers of left hands, when knights of First Division whisper to Second Division, LIBERTAS, and Second replies, The word is right. All the way through each knight of the First Division takes the knight opposite him in the Second Division.

138   KNIGHTS OF THE RED CROSS.

Red Cross Sign.   Red Cross Grip.

Sovereign Master—Recover! (Swords are brought to "recover" and each division steps back a pace.)

Sovereign Master—Sir Knight Prelate, repair with me to the lines for the purpose of our devotions.

Sovereign Master—Attention, Sir Knights! Return swords! (Sovereign Master takes his place between the lines at east end, Sword Bearer at west end, Prelate at the altar.)

Sovereign Master—Attention, Sir Knights! To your devotions! (They kneel on left knee, and each crosses his arms and interlaces his fingers with the knight on his right and left, when they repeat the Lord's Prayer in unison.)

Sovereign Master—Attention, Sir Knights! Recover! About—face—to your posts—march! (Order is obeyed and all are seated.)

Sovereign Master—Sir Knight Chancellor, are you a Knight of the Red Cross?

Chancellor—That is my profession.

Sovereign Master—By what will you be tried?

Chancellor—By the test of truth.

Sovereign Master—Why by the test of truth?

OPENING CEREMONIES.

Chancellor—Because none but good men and true are entitled to the honors of our order.

Sovereign Master—Where were you constituted a knight of this order?

Chancellor—In a just and lawfully constituted Council of Knights of the Red Cross.

Sovereign Master—What number composes such a Council?

Chancellor—There is an indispensable number and a constitutional number.

Sovereign Master—What is the indispensable number?

Chancellor—Three.

Sovereign Master—Under what circumstances may three Knights of the Red Cross form and operate a Council of this order?

Chancellor—Three Knights of the Red Cross, being also Knights Templar and hailing from three different commanderies, may, under the sanction of warrant from some Grand Council or from the Grand Encampment of the United States, form and operate a Council of Knights of the Red Cross, for the dispatch of business.

Sovereign Master—What is the constitutional number?

Chancellor—Seven, nine, eleven, or more.

Sovereign Master—When composed of eleven, of whom does it consist?

Chancellor—The Sovereign Master, Chancellor, Master of the Palace, Prelate, Master of Cavalry, Master of Infantry, Master of Finances, Master of Dispatches, Standard Bearer, Sword Bearer, and Warder.

Sovereign Master—What is the Warder's station in

the Council?

Chancellor—On the left of the Standard Bearer, in the west.

Sovereign Master (to Warder)—What are your duties, Sir Knight Warder?

Warder—To announce the approach and departure of the Sovereign Master, to post the Sentinal, and to see that the Council chamber is duly guarded.

Sovereign Master—What is the Sword Bearer's station in the Council?

Warder—On the right of the Standard Bearer, in the west.

Sovereign Master (to Sword Bearer)—What are your duties, Sir Knight Sword Bearer?

Sword Bearer—To assist in the protection of the banners of the order, watch all signals from the Sovereign Master, and see that they are properly obeyed.

Sovereign Master What is the Standard Bearer's station in the Council?

Sword Bearer—In the west.

Sovereign Master (to Standard Bearer)—What are your duties, Sir Knight Standard Bearer?

Standard Bearer—To display, protect and support the banners of the order.

Sovereign Master—Why is your station in the west?

Standard Bearer—That the brilliant rays of the rising sun shedding their luster on the banners of the order may encourage and animate all true and courteous knights and confound and dismay their enemies.

Sovereign Master—What is the Master of Dispatches' station in the Council?

Standard Bearer—On the left in front of the Master of the Palace.

OPENING CEREMONIES.   141

Sovereign Master (to Master of Dispatches)—What are your duties, Sir Knight Master of Dispatches?

Master of Dispatches—Faithfully to record the proceedings of the Council, collect the revenues and pay them over to the Master of Finances.

Sovereign Master—What is the Master of Finances' station in the Council?

Master of Dispatches—On the right, in front of the Chancellor.

Sovereign Master (to Master of Finances)—What are your duties, Sir Knight Master of Finances?

Master of Finances—To receive in charge all the funds and property of the Council, pay all orders drawn on the treasury, and render a just and faithful account of the same when required.

Sovereign Master—What is the Master of Infantry's station in the Council?

Master of Finances—On the right of the Second Division when separately formed, and on the left of the whole when formed in line.

Sovereign Master (to Master of Infantry)—What are your duties, Sir Knight Master of Infantry?

Master of Infantry—To command the Second Division or line of infantry and teach them their duties and exercises; prepare candidates, attend them on their journey, answer all questions for them, and finally introduce them into the Council chamber.

Sovereign Master—What is the Master of Cavalry's station in the Council?

Master of Infantry—On the right of the First Division when separately formed, and on the right of the whole when formed in line.

Sovereign Master (to Master of Cavalry)—What are your duties, Sir Knight Master of Cavalry?

Master of Cavalry—To command the First Division or line of cavalry and teach them their duty and exercises; to form the lines for the approach and departure of the Sovereign Master and to prepare them for inspection and review.

Sovereign Master—What is the Prelate's station in the Council?

Master of Cavalry—On the right of the Chancellor.

Sovereign Master (to Prelate)—What are your duties, Sir Knight Prelate?

Prelate—To preside in the Royal Arch Council, to minister at the altar and offer up prayer and oblations to Deity.

Sovereign Master—What is the Master of the Palace's station in the Council?

Prelate—On the left of the Sovereign Master.

Sovereign Master (to Master of Palace)—What are your duties, Sir Knight Master of the Palace?

Master of Palace—To see that the proper officers make all due preparation for the various meetings of the Council, and that the Council chamber is in suitable array for the introduction of candidates and the dispatch of business, and to receive and communicate all orders of the Sovereign Master issued to the officers of the lines.

Sovereign Master—What is the Chancellor's station in the Council?

Master of Palace—On the right of the Sovereign Master.

Sovereign Master (to Chancellor)—What are your duties, Sir Knight Chancellor?

Chancellor—To receive and communicate all orders, signals and petitions, to assist the Sovereign Master in

OPENING CEREMONIES. 143

his various duties, and in his absence to preside in the Council.

Sovereign Master—What is the Sovereign Master's station in the Council?

Chancellor—In the east.

Sovereign Master—What are his duties?

Chancellor—To preside over and govern his Council; to confer the order of knighthood on those whom his Council may approve; to preserve inviolate the laws and constitutions of the order; to dispense justice, reward merit, encourage truth and diffuse the sublime principles of universal benevolence.

Sovereign Master—Sir Knight Chancellor, it is my will and pleasure that a Council of Knights of the Red Cross[52] be now opened for the dispatch of such business as may regularly come before it; requiring all Sir Knights present to govern themselves according to the sublime principles of our order. Communicate this order to the Master of the Palace, and he to the Sir Knights.

Chancellor—Sir Knight Master of the Palace, it is the will and pleasure of the Sovereign Master that a Council of Knights of the Red Cross be now opened for the dispatch of such business as may regularly come before it; requiring all Sir Knights present to govern themselves according to the sublime principles of our order. Cummunicate this order to the Sir Knights.

Master of Palace—It is the will and pleasure of the Sovereign Master that a Council of Knights of the Red Cross be now opened for the dispatch of such busi-

Note 52.—"They afterward assumed their present name from the Red Cross borne in their banners."—Mackey's Lexicon, Art. Knight of the Red Cross.

ness as may regularly come before it; take notice and govern yourselves according to the sublime principles of the order.

Sovereign Master (eight raps, 000-000-00)—I now declare this Council of Knights of the Red Cross open in form. Sir Knight Warder, inform the Sentinel. (Sentinel is informed same as in previous degrees.)

CHAPTER XV.

KNIGHTS OF THE RED CROSS, OR ELEVENTH DEGREE.

INITIATION.

Master of Infantry (with candidate at door, eight raps.)

Warder—Most Excellent Prelate, there is an alarm.

Prelate—Attend to the alarm. (Warder goes to preparation-room door.)

Warder (eight raps on door)—Who comes here? (Opens the door a little.)

Master of Infantry—A Companion Royal Arch Mason, who, having taken all the necessary preceding degrees, now solicits the honor of being received and constituted a Knight of the Illustrious Order of the Red Cross.

Warder—Is it of your own free will and accord?

Candidate—It is.

Warder—Is he worthy and well qualified?

Master of Infantry—He is.

Warder—Has he made suitable proficiency in the preceding degrees?

Master of Infantry—He has.

Warder—By what further right or benefit does he expect to gain admission?

Master of Infantry—By the benefit of the Royal Arch Word.

Warder—Has he that word?

Master of Infantry—He has, and with your assistance will give it. [The candidate, Warder and Master of Infantry give it.]

146 GRAND OMNIFIC OR ROYAL ARCH WORD.

This must only be given by a group of three. Each with his right hand grasps the right wrist of the companion on the left, and with his left hand the left wrist of his companion on his right, throwing forward his right foot, hollow in front, his toe touching the heel of his companion on the right. This is called three times three, as there are three right hands, three left hands and three feet forming three triangles. They then repeat the verse given on page 500 of *Freemasonry Illustrated*.

They then balance three times three, with a short pause between each three, when they raise their right hands over their heads, as shown in cut, and the Grand Omnific Royal Arch word is given in low breath in syllables, as follows: The first one says *Jah*, second one *buh*, third one *lun;* then the second one says *Jah*, third one *buh*, and first one *lun;* then the third one says *Jah*, first one *buh*, second one *lun*.

Group of Three, Giving Grand Omnific Word.

The word *Je-ho-vah* is treated in the same way, and the word *G-o-d* is given in the same way but letter by letter, thus each of the three being repeated three times, varying each time as explained. In some Chapters only the word Je-ho-vah is given in this way, and in others the word Jah-Bel-On was formerly used.

INITIATION.   147

Warder (after Royal Arch[53] Word is given)—Let him wait with patience until the Most Excellent Prelate is informed of his request and his answer returned.

Warder (in front of Prelate, eight raps on floor.)

Prelate—Who comes here?

[Answer and next five questions same as at the door.]

Prelate—Let him be admitted.

Warder (having returned to the door and opened it without knocking)—Companion, it is the order of the Most Excellent Prelate that you be admitted. (Master of Infantry conducts him to the center of the Council.)

Prelate (to candidate)—Companion, the Council you here see assembled represents the Grand Council convened at Jerusalem in the first year of Darius, King of Persia, to deliberate upon their unhappy situation during the reign of Artaxerxes and Ahasuerus and devise some means whereby they might obtain the favor of their new sovereign and gain his consent to proceed in rebuilding their city and Temple. If you are desirous of joining in our deliberations it is necessary that you assume the name and character of Zerubbabel,[54] a prince of the house of Judah whose hands laid the foundation of the second Temple and whose hands the Lord had promised should finish it.

Candidate (bows assent.)

Prelate—You will attend to a lesson from the records

Note 53.—"This degree is intimately associated with the Royal Arch, and cannot be conferred upon any brother who has not been exalted to that sublime degree.

"It is founded upon incidents which occurred during the reign of Darius, King of Persia; illustrates the difficulties and interruptions encountered by the Jews in rebuilding the house of the Lord at Jerusalem, and rehearses many interesting events that occurred during the sojourn of Prince Zerubbabel at the court of Persia."—Sickels' Monitor, Part 4, page 3.

Note 54.—"The candidate represents Zerubbabel, the presiding officer King Darius."—Morris' Dict., Art. Red Cross Knight.

of our fathers. [All sit in a semi-circle, with uncovered heads, right elbow on right knee and head on hand while the Prelate reads.]

SCRIPTURE LESSON.[55]

"Now in the second year of their coming unto the house of God at Jerusalem, in the second month began Zerubbabel, the son of Shealtiel, and Jeshua, the son of Jozadak, and the remnant of their brethren the priests and the Levites, and all they that were come out of the captivity into Jerusalem; and appointed the Levites, from twenty years old and upward, to set forward the work of the house of the Lord. Then stood Jeshua with his sons and his brethren, Kadmiel and his sons, the sons of Judah, together to set forward the workmen in the house of God; the sons of Henadad, with their sons, and their brethren the Levites. And when the builders laid the foundation of the Temple of the Lord, they set the priests in their apparel with trumpets, and the Levites, the sons of Asaph, with cymbals, to praise the Lord, after the ordinance of David, King of Israel. And they sang together by course, in praising and giving thanks unto the Lord, because he is good, for his mercy endureth forever toward Israel. And all the people shouted with a great shout when they praised the Lord, because the foundation of the house of the Lord was laid.

"When the adversaries of Judah and Benjamin heard that the children of the captivity builded the Temple

---

Note 55.—"Reception. The following passages of Scripture are appropriate to this order, and are rehearsed by the Prelate as the representative of Jeshua, who presided at the Grand Council, assembled at Jerusalem, in the first year of the reign of Darius, King of Persia, to deliberate on the unhappy situation of the Jews, and to devise means whereby they might obtain the favor and assistance of their new sovereign in rebuilding their city and Temple."—Simons' Book of the Commandery, page 6.

unto the Lord God of Israel, then they came to Zerubbabel and the chief of the fathers and said unto them, Let us build with you, for we seek your God as ye do, and we do sacrifice unto him, since the days of Esar-Haddon, King of Assur, which brought us up hither. But Zerubbabel and Jeshua, and the rest of the chief of the fathers of Israel, said unto them, Ye have nothing to do with us to build an house unto our God, but we ourselves together will build unto the Lord God of Israel, as King Cyrus, the King of Persia, hath commanded us. Then the people of the land weakened the hands of the people of Judah, and troubled them in building, and hired counsellors against them to frustrate their purpose, all the days of Cyrus, King of Persia, even until the reign of Darius, King of Persia. And in the reign of Ahasuerus, in the beginning of his reign, wrote they unto him an accusation against the inhabitants of Judah and Jerusalem. And in the days of Artaxerxes, wrote Bishlam, Mithredath, Tabeel, and the rest of their companions, unto Artaxerxes, King of Persia; and the writing of the letter was written in the Syrian tongue, and interpreted in the Syrian tongue. Rehum the chancellor, and Shimshai the scribe, wrote a letter against Jerusalem to Artaxerxes the king, in this sort. This is the copy of the letter that they sent unto him, even unto Artaxerxes, the King: Thy servants, the men on this side the river, and at such a time. Be it known unto the king that the Jews, which came up from thee to us, are come unto Jerusalem, building the rebellious and the bad city, and have set up the walls thereof, and joined the foundations. Be it known now unto the king, that if this city be builded, and the walls set up again, then will they not pay toll, tribute and custom, and so thou shalt endamage the revenue of the kings. Now because we have maintenance from the king's palace, and it was not meet for us to see the king's dishonor, therefore have we sent and certified the king, that search may be made in the book of records of thy fathers; so shalt thou find in the book of the record, and know that this city is a rebellious city, and hurtful unto kings and provinces, and that they have moved sedition within the same of old time, for which cause was this city destroyed. We certify the king, that if this city be builded again, and the walls thereof set up, by this means thou shalt have no portion on this side the river. Then sent the king an answer unto Rehum the chancellor, and to Shimshai the scribe, and to the rest of their companions that dwell in Samaria, and unto the rest beyond the river, Peace, and at such a time. The letter which ye sent unto us hath been plainly read before me and I commanded that search hath been made, and it is found that this city of old time hath made insurrection against kings, and that rebellion and sedition have been made therein. There have been mighty kings also over Jerusalem, which have ruled over all countries beyond the river, and toll, tribute and custom was paid unto them. Give ye now commandment to cause these men to cease, and that this city be not builded until another commandment shall be given from me. Take heed now that ye fail not to do this. Why should damage grow to the hurt of the kings? Now when the copy of King Artaxerxes' letter was read before Rehum, and Shimshai the scribe, and their companions, they went up in haste to Jerusalem unto the Jews, and made them to cease by force and power.

INITIATION.   151

Then ceased the work of the house of God, which is at Jerusalem. So it ceased unto the second year of the reign of Darius, King of Persia.—Ezra 4."—*Simons' Book of the Commandery, page 6.*

[Master of Infantry and candidate arise.]

Master of Infantry—Most Excellent Prelate, our Sovereign Lord Darius[56] having ascended the throne of Persia, new hopes are entertained of his protection and support in the grand and glorious work of rebuilding our city and Temple, for the King when but a private man made a vow[57] to God that should he ever ascend the throne of Persia he would order all the holy vessels now at Babylon back to Jerusalem; and now our most excellent and worthy companion, Zerubbabel[58], offers his valuable services in the hazardous enterprise of traversing the Persian dominions and seeking admission to the King; when the first favorable moment will be seized to remind him of his vow and request a fulfillment of the same; and from his known piety no doubts can be entertained of obtaining his consent, which will remove our enemies far hence and we be no

---

Note 56.—"Darius, the king, having ascended the throne of Persia, the children of the captivity were inspired with new hopes of protection and support in completing their noble and glorious undertaking, which had been so often and so long impeded by their adversaries on the other side of the river."—Sickels' Monitor, Part 4, page 11.

Note 57.—"Darius, whilst he was yet a private man, made a vow to God that if he ever came to the throne he would restore all the holy vessels that were at Babylon, and send them back again to Jerusalem."—Sickels' Monitor, Part 4, page 11.

Note 58.—"Zerubbabel, one of the most excellent and faithful rulers of the Jews, having been formerly distinguished by the favorable notice and friendship of the king, whilst in private life, offered himself to encounter the hazardous enterprise of traversing the Persian dominions, and seeking admission to the royal presence, in order that he might seize the first favorable moment to remind the king of the vow which he had made and to impress upon his mind the almighty force and importance of Truth. From the known piety of the king no doubt was entertained of obtaining his consent, that their enemies might be removed far from thence, and that they might be no longer impeded in the glorious undertaking in which they were engaged."—Sickels' Monitor, Part 4, page 11.

longer hindered or impeded in our grand and glorious work.

Prelate—Zerubbabel, the Council[59] with great joy accepts your noble and generous offer and will immediately invest you with the necessary passwords which will enable you to make yourself known to the friends of our cause wherever you may meet them, and ensure to you their friendship and protection; but before entering upon an undertaking of such vast importance it is necessary that you take upon yourself a solemn obligation to be faithful to the trust reposed in you. I arm you with this sword (hands him a sword) to enable you to defend yourself against your enemies. Advance and kneel at the altar on your left knee, your right hand grasping the hilt of your sword, your left hand resting on the Holy Bible, square and compass and cross swords.

RED CROSS OBLIGATION.

I, ———, of my own free will and accord, in the presence of the Sovereign Architect of the Universe and this Council of Knights of the Red Cross, do hereby and hereon most solemnly and sincerely promise and vow that I will not communicate any of the secrets appertaining to the order of the Knights of the Red Cross, to any person or persons whatsoever, except it be to a true and lawful Sir Knight of the order or within the body of a just and lawfully constituted Council of Knights of the Red Cross, nor unto him or them until by strict trial, due examination or lawful

---

Note 59.—"The Council of rulers accepted, with great joy, this noble sacrifice on the part of Zerubbabel, and invested him with the necessary passports and commendations to enable him to pass through their own dominions in safety."—Sickels' Monitor, Part 4, page 18.

information, I shall have found him or them as lawfully entitled to them as I am myself.

I furthermore promise and vow that I will stand to and abide by all the laws, rules and regulations of a Council of Knights of the Red Cross so far as they shall come to my knowledge.

I furthermore promise and vow that I will vindicate the character of a worthy Sir Knight of the Red Cross when traduced, and will defend him on all lawful occasions.

I furthermore promise and vow that I will not be present at the opening of a Council of Knights of the Red Cross except there shall be present at least seven regular Sir Knights of the order, myself included, or the representatives of three different Councils, working under legal warrants.

I furthermore promise and vow that I will not be present at the conferring of this order upon any one unless he shall have regularly received all the preceding degrees, to the best of my knowledge and belief.

All this I promise and vow, binding myself under no less penalty than that of having my house torn down, the timbers thereof set up and I hung thereon, and when the last trump shall sound I be forever excluded from the society of all true and courteous knights, should I ever willfully or knowingly violate any part of this solemn obligation of Knights of the Red Cross; so help me God and keep me steadfast to keep and perform the same.

[Candidate is directed to kiss the book before him and then to arise.]

Prelate (to candidate)—I now present you with this sash as a mark of our friendship and esteem. (Candidate takes it.) You will wear it as a constant memorial to stimulate you to the practice of every virtue. Its color is green and it is to remind you that the memory of him who falls in a just and righteous cause shall forever flourish like the Green Bay tree.

Prelate—Sir Knight, our Master of Infantry will now invest you with the Jewish pass, which will enable you to make yourself known to the friends of our cause wherever you may meet them and ensure you their friendship and protection. Farewell, companion, and may success attend you. (The Jewish pass is given as explained, page 135.)

Master of Infantry (to candidate)—Follow me. (They now pass through the several apartments of the Council.)

Master of Infantry (eight raps at first door.)

First Guard—Who comes here?

Master of Infantry A friend.

First Guard—Advance and give me the pass. (They give the Jewish pass, and pass to the second apartment where the same is done, when they pass to the third door.)

Master of Infantry (to candidate)—We have now arrived at the confines of the Jewish dominions; further I cannot conduct you. (A small arched frame in imitation of a bridge lies before the next door, which is open.)

Master of Infantry (continuing)—This bridge which separates us from Persian territory, you must pass alone. Farewell! God speed you on your journey! (He passes over the bridge and gives the usual eight raps.)

Master of Cavalry—Who comes here?

Candidate—A friend.

Master of Cavalry—Advance and give me the pass.

Candidate (advancing, gives three cuts with his sword. Guard throws up his sword, when candidate whispers) JUDAH! (Guard seems not to understand him.)

Candidate (louder)—JUDAH!

Master of Cavalry—What?

Candidate (very loud)—JUDAH!

Third Guard—An enemy! A spy! Guards, seize him, disarm him and handcuff him! (Guards seize him, strip him of his sword and green sash, put on a rough outer garment, handcuffs and fetters, each being chains about eighteen inches long, with triangular links, with rings at ends and are fastened on with bolts.)

Master of Infantry (having come up)—Why use me thus? Why treat me so? I am no enemy; I am a prince[60] of the house of Judah, and demand an audience with your sovereign.

Master of Cavalry (captain of Persian guards)—A prince of the house of Judah! You can only obtain an audience with his majesty in the garb of a slave and captive.[61] Do you submit to this?

Candidate (prompted)—I do.

[Candidate and Master of Infantry with Master of Cavalry and guards go to the center of the Council again, the candidate having sackcloth over his head.]

Master of Cavalry (eight raps on floor.)

Warder—Sovereign Master, there is an alarm.

Note 60.—"Having passed the barriers and entered the Persian dominions, he was taken captive, clothed in the habiliments of a slave, and put in chains; but not discouraged by this misfortune, he declared himself a prince of the house of Judah, and demanded an audience of the sovereign."—Sickels' Monitor, Part 4, page 12.

Note 61.—"He was told that he could only appear in the presence of the sovereign as a captive and slave; to which he consented, being impressed with a belief, that if by any means he could gain access to the king, he should succeed in the object of his journey."—Sickels' Monitor, Part 4, page 12.

Sovereign Master—Attend to the alarm.

Warder (drawing aside the curtains)—Who comes here?

Master of Cavalry—A detachment of his majesty's guards who have made prisoner of one who claims to be a prince of the house of Judah.

Warder—Who is he?

Master of Infantry—The first among his equals, a Mason by rank but a slave and captive by misfortune.

Warder—Where is he from?

Master of Infantry—Jerusalem.

Warder—What is his name?

Master of Infantry—Zerubbabel.

Warder—What does he desire?

Master of Infantry—An audience with your sovereign, if possible.

Warder—You will wait till the pleasure of the Sovereign Master is known. [Same dialogue between Warder and Sovereign Master.]

Sovereign Master (to warder)—Having ascertained that he is unarmed, you may let him enter.

Warder—Is he armed with any hostile weapon?

Master of Cavalry—He is not.

Warder—He has our Sovereign's permission to enter the council chamber. (The next veil is pulled aside and candidate enters.)

Sovereign Master—This is no enemy. This is Zerubbabel,[63] the friend and companion of my youth. Zerubbabel, having gained admittance to our presence, we demand of you that you make known to us the partic-

---

Note 68.—"Zerubbabel, having thus gained admission to the royal presence, was recognized by the king as the friend and companion of his youth, and was interrogated as to his motives in attempting to pass the barriers of his dominions."—Sickels' Monitor, Part 6, page 12.

INITIATION. 157

ular motive that induced you, without our permission and by force and arms, to invade the lines of our dominions?

Master of Infantry (for candidate)—Sovereign Master, the tears and entreaties[63] of my companions at Jerusalem who have so long and so often been impeded by their adversaries on the other side of the river, they having been compelled to cease work by force and power, have caused me to come up to crave your majesty's clemency, hoping you will restore me to your royal favor and grant me employment among the servants of your household.

Sovereign Master—I have often reflected with much pleasure on our early intimacy and friendship, and have heard with great satisfaction of your fame as a wise and accomplished Mason;[64] and having myself a profound veneration for that ancient and honorable institution, and having a sincere desire to become a member of the same, I will this moment grant your request on condition that you reveal to me the secrets of Freemasonry.

Master of Infantry (for candidate)—Sovereign Mas-

Note 63.—"Zerubbabel replied, that he was induced to seek the face of the king by the tears and complaints of his brethren and companions in Jerusalem, who were impeded, by their adversaries on the other side of the river, in the noble and glorious undertaking of rebuilding the house of the Lord, in which they had been permitted to engage by their late sovereign master, Cyrus, the king; that this great work having been made to cease by force and power, he had come to implore the sovereign that he might be restored to his confidence, and admitted amongst the servants of his household."—Sickels' Monitor, Part 4, page 13.

Note 64.—"The King answered, that he had often reflected, with peculiar pleasure, upon their former intimacy; that he had heard, with great satisfaction of his fame as a wise and accomplished ruler among the architects of his country; that having a profound veneration for an institution which was reputed to practice mysteries which were calculated to promote the glory of the nation and the happiness of the people, he would instantly restore him to favor, upon condition that he would reveal those mysteries which so eminently distinguished the architects of the Jews from those of all other nations."—Sickels' Monitor, Part 4, page 13.

ter, when our first most ancient Grand Master, Solomon, King of Israel, instituted the fraternity of Free and Accepted Masons, he taught us that Truth[65] was a divine attribute and the foundation of all virtue; to be good and true are the first lessons we are taught in Masonry. My obligations are sacred and inviolable, and if I can obtain your majesty's clemency only at the expense of my integrity, I humbly beg leave to decline your royal favor. I will cheerfully submit to an honorable exile or a glorious death.

Sovereign Master—Your virtue[66] and integrity are highly commendable and your fidelity to your trust is worthy of imitation. From this moment you are free. My guards will divest you of those chains and that badge of slavery and will clothe you with suitable habiliments to accompany me to a banquet.[67]

Sovereign Master (continuing)—Guards, strike off those chains, and may that garb of slavery never again disgrace the hands of a Mason, more particularly a prince of the house of Judah. (Order is obeyed.) Zerubbabel, we assign you a seat of rank and honor among

Note 65.—"Zerubbabel replied that their institution inculcated the doctrine that Truth is a divine attribute, and the foundation of every virtue; that to be good men and true was the first lesson they were taught; that his engagements were inviolable; that if he could obtain the royal favor only by the sacrifice of his integrity, he should humbly beg leave to renounce the protection of the sovereign, and cheerfully submit to an honorable exile or a glorious death."—Sickels' Monitor, Part 4, page 14.

Note 66.—"The King, struck with admiration at the firmness and discretion of Zerubbabel, declared that his virtue and integrity were truly commendable; that his fidelity to his engagements were worthy of imitation, and from that moment he was restored to his confidence."—Sickels' Monitor, Part 4, page 14.

Note 67.—"Darius, in the first year of his reign, gave a splendid and magnificent entertainment to the princes and nobility; and after they had retired, finding himself unable to sleep, he fell into discourse with his three favorite officers, to whom he proposed certain questions, telling them, at the same time, that he who should give him the most reasonable and satisfactory answer should be clothed in purple, drink from a golden cup, wear a silken tiara, and a golden chain about his neck."—Sickels' Monitor, Part 4, page 14.

the princes and nobles of the land. [They retire to a room where refreshments are served; the Sovereign Master and other officers with candidate passing through the lines, when the Sir Knights follow. After eating ten or fifteen minutes all but the officers and candidate, who are seated in the place of honor at or near head of table, retire from the room.]

Sovereign Master (at banquet hall)—It was the custom in ancient times at banquets like this among the princes and nobles of the land, for the king to propose certain questions[68] and he that could give the most satisfactory answer should be clothed in purple and fine linen, should wear a golden chain around his neck and drink out of a golden cup. There has a question occurred to me this evening. Which is the greatest, the strength of wine, of the king, or of women?[69]

Chancellor (rising)—Sovereign Master, I think wine is the strongest.

Master of Palace (rising)—Sovereign Master, I think the king is the strongest.

Master of Infantry (for candidate, as Zerubbabel)—Sovereign Master. I think women[70] are the strongest; but above all things, Truth beareth the victory.

Sovereign Master—Zerubbabel, you have made a very important addition[71] which deserves consideration. Sir

Note 68.—"He then proposed this question: Which is greatest, the strength of wine, of the king, or of women?"—Sickels' Monitor, Part 4, page 15.

Note 69.—"The discussion from 1 Esdras, iii. and iv., in which the respective powers of wine, women and the king are estimated, is introduced into the Red Cross with dramatic effect."—Morris' Dict., Art. Red Cross Knight.

Note 70.—"To this the first answered, Wine is the strongest; the second, that the King was strongest; and the third (who was Zerubbabel), that women were stronger, but above all things, Truth beareth the victory."—Sickels' Monitor, Part 4, page 15.

Note 71.—"The King, being forcibly struck with the addition Zerubbabel had made to his question, ordered that the princes and nobles should assemble on the following day, to hear the subject discussed."—Sickels' Monitor, Part 4, page 15.

Knights, you will now return to the council chamber, where you will be called upon to substantiate with arguments the opinions you have advanced. Let the banquet be broken up! [The trumpet sounds, the lines are formed as before and the Sovereign Master and officers, with candidate, passing through them, resume their stations.]

Sovereign Master—Sir Knight Chancellor, you will state your reasons[72] for your opinion that wine is the strongest.

"THE STRENGTH OF WINE.

"O ye princes and rulers, how exceeding strong is wine! it causeth all men to err that drink it; it maketh the mind of the king and the beggar to be all one; of the bondmen and the freemen; of the poor man and of the rich; it turneth also every thought into jollity and mirth, so that a man remembereth neither sorrow nor debt; it changeth and elevateth the spirits, and enliveneth the heavy hearts of the miserable. It maketh a man forget his brethren, and draw his sword against his best friends. O ye princes and rulers, is not wine the strongest, that forceth us to do these things?"— *Simons' Book of the Commandery, page 15.*

Sovereign Master—Sir Knight Master of the Palace, you will now state your reason for your opinion that the power of kings is the greatest.

"THE POWER OF THE KING.

"It is beyond dispute, O princes and rulers, that God has made man master of all things under the sun; to command them, to make use of them, and apply them

Note 72.—"On the following day the King assembled together the princes and nobility, to hear the questions debated. The first began as follows, upon the strength of wine."—Sickels' Monitor, Part 4, page 15.

to his service as he pleases; but whereas men have only dominion over other sublunary creatures, kings have an authority even over men themselves, and a right of ruling them by will and pleasure. Now he that is master of those who are masters of all things else hath no earthly thing above him."—*Simons' Book of the Commandery, page 16.*

Sovereign Master—Zerubbabel,[73] we will now hear the reasons for your opinion and the important addition you have made.

"THE POWER OF WOMEN AND TRUTH.

"O princes and rulers, the force of wi is not to be denied; neither is that of kings, that unites so many men in one common bond of allegiance; but the supremacy of *woman* is yet above all this; for *kings* are but the gifts of women, and they are also the mothers of those that cultivate our *vineyards*. Women have the power to make us abandon our very country and relations, and many times to forget the best friends we have in the world, and, forsaking all other comforts, to live and die with them. But when all is said, neither they, nor wine, nor kings, are comparable to the almighty force of TRUTH. As for all other things, they are mortal and transient, but Truth alone is unchangeable and everlasting; the benefits we receive from it are subject to no variations or vicissitudes of time and fortune. In her judgment is no unrighteousness, and she is the strength, wisdom, power and majesty of all ages. Blessed be the God of Truth."—*Simons' Book of the Commandery, page 16.*

Note 73.—"The incidents of Zerubbabel's life are also referred to in several other degrees, such as Knight of the Red Cross, Knight of the East and Prince of Jerusalem."—**Mackey's** Lexicon. Art. Zerubbabel.

All—Great is Truth,[74] and mighty above all things.

Sovereign Master—Zerubbabel, "ask what thou wilt and I will give it thee, because thou art found wisest among thy companions."—*Simons' Book of the Commandery, page 17.*

Master of Infantry (for candidate, as Zerubbabel)— "O king, remember thy vow, which thou hast vowed, to build Jerusalem in the day when thou shouldest come to thy kingdom, and to restore the holy vessels which were taken away out of Jerusalem. Thou hast also vowed to build up the Temple, which was burned when Judah was made desolate by the Chaldees. And now, O king, this is that I desire of thee, that thou make good the vow, the performance whereof, with thine own mouth, thou hast vowed to the King of heaven."— *Simons' Book of the Commandery, page 17.*

Sovereign Master—It shall be done. I will punctually fulfill my vow. Letters and passports[75] shall immediately be issued to my officers throughout the land, and they shall give you and those that accompany you a safe conveyance to Jerusalem, where you shall no longer be hindered or impeded in rebuilding your city and Temple until the same shall be completed.

Sovereign Master (hands him a green sash and continues)—This green sash which you were deprived of by my guards, I now with much pleasure restore to you,

---

Note 74.—"When Zerubbabel had finished speaking, the princes and rulers cried out: 'Great is Truth, and mighty above all things.'"—Sickels' Monitor, Part 4, page 17.

Note 75.—"Then Darius, the King, stood up and embraced him, and gave him passports and letters to his governors and officers, that they should safely convey both him, and those that should go with him, to Jerusalem; and that they should not be delayed or hindered from building the city and the Temple until they should be finished. He also restored all the holy vessels remaining in his possession, that had been taken from Jerusalem, when the children of Israel were carried away captive to Babylon, and reserved by Cyrus."—Sickels' Monitor, Part 4, page 18.

and I will make it the insignia[76] of a new order calculated to perpetuate the remembrance of the events which have caused the renewal of our friendship. Its color will remind you that Truth is a divine attribute and shall prevail and forever flourish in immortal green."[77]

Sovereign Master—I will now confer on you the highest honor in our power at this time to bestow, and will create you the first knight of an order instituted for the purpose of inculcating the almighty force and importance of Truth. You will now kneel. (Candidate kneels.)

Sovereign Master (continuing)—By virtue of the high power and authority in me vested as the successor of Darius, King of Persia, I receive and constitute you a Knight of the Red Cross. Arise, Sir Knight ———, and receive a hearty welcome among us.

Sovereign Master (hands him a sword and continues)—This sword which you were deprived of by my guards I now with much pleasure restore to you. In the hands of a true and courteous knight it is endowed with three most excellent qualities: Its hilt with faith, its blade with hope, and its point with charity, and it teaches us that when we draw our swords in a just and

Note 76.—"The green sash is restored, and adopted as the insignia of the order, designed to perpetuate the remembrance of the event which caused the renewal of long separated, but pure friendship. Its color is intended to remind us that Truth is a divine attribute, and shall prevail, and which must forever flourish in immortal green."—Sickels' Monitor, Part 4, page 18.

Note 77.—"The drapery of the throne is green; a green banner is suspended above the throne; on it are three triangles joined, with a red cross in the center of each; underneath are arranged the emblems of the order.

"The Knights wear a green sash, trimmed with red, from which is suspended a sword and trowel, crosswise.

"The symbolic color of the order is green.

"The motto of the order is: 'Magna est veritas, et prevalebit'—Great is Truth, and will prevail."—Sickels' Monitor, Part 4, page 5.

right cause, having faith in God, we may reasonably hope for victory, ever remembering to extend the point of charity to a fallen foe. Take it, return it to its scabbard and there let it remain until consumed by rust ere you draw it in the cause of injustice and oppression.

[Sovereign Master now gives and explains the Persian pass as on page 136, invests him with the Red Cross word, Veritas, as on page 137, then with the grand sign, grip and word, as on page 137.]

Sovereign Master—The grand sign alludes to the blowing of the trumpet upon the walls and watchtowers of the Council, but more particularly to that part of the penalty of your obligation: "When the last trump shall sound, I be forever excluded from the society of all true and courteous knights."

Sovereign Master (continuing)—The motto of our order is, *Magna est veritas, et prevalebit*, which signifies Truth is mighty and it will prevail.

CHAPTER XVI.

KNIGHTS OF THE RED CROSS, OR ELEVENTH DEGREE.

LECTURE, OR EXAMINATION.

Sovereign Master—Are you a Knight of the Red Cross?

Candidate—That is my profession.

Sovereign Master—By what will you be tried?

Candidate—By the test of Truth.

Sovereign Master—Why by the test of Truth?

Candidate—Because none but good men and true are entitled to the honors of our order.

Sovereign Master—Where were you constituted a knight of this order?

Candidate—In a just and lawfully constituted Council of Knights of the Red Cross.

Sovereign Master—What number composes such a Council?

Candidate—There is an indispensable number and a constitutional number.

Sovereign Master—What is the indispensable number?

Candidate—Three.

Sovereign Master—Under what circumstances may three Knights of the Red Cross form and operate a Council of this order?

Candidate—Three Knights of the Red Cross, being also Knights Templar and hailing from three different commanderies, may, under the sanction of a warrant from some Grand Commandery or from the Grand Encampment of the United States, form and operate a Council of Knights of the Red Cross for the dispatch of business.

Sovereign Master—What is the constitutional number?

Candidate—Seven, nine, eleven, or more.

Sovereign Master—When composed of eleven, of whom does it consist?

Candidate—The Sovereign Master, Chancellor, Master of the Palace, Prelate, Master of Cavalry, Master of Infantry, Master of Finance, Master of Dispatches, Standard Bearer, Sword Bearer, and Warder.

Sovereign Master—What were the circumstances attending your reception into this illustrious order?

Candidate—I was conducted to the door of the Council, where a regular demand was made by eight distinct knocks.

Sovereign Master—What was said to you from within?

Candidate—Who comes here?

Sovereign Master—Your answer?

Candidate—A companion Royal Arch Mason, who, having taken all the necessary preceding degrees, now solicits the honor of being received and constituted a Knight of the Illustrious Order of the Red Cross.

Sovereign Master—What were you then asked?

Candidate—If it was of my own free will and accord; if I was worthy and well qualified; if I had made suitable proficiency in the preceding degrees; all of which being answered in the affirmative, I was asked by what further right or benefit I expected to gain admission.

Sovereign Master—Your answer?

LECTURE.

Candidate—By the Royal Arch Word.

Sovereign Master—Have you the Royal Arch Word?

Candidate—I have, and with your assistance will give it. (Candidate, with Sovereign Master and a third person, give the Royal Arch Word, as explained page 146.)

Sovereign Master—What followed?

Candidate—I was directed to wait with patience until the Most Excellent Prelate was informed of my request and his answer returned.

Sovereign Master—What was his answer?

Candidate—Let him be admitted.

Sovereign Master—What were you then informed?

Candidate—That the Council there assembled represented the Grand Council convened at Jerusalem in the first year of Darius, King of Persia, to deliberate upon their unhappy situation during the reign of Artaxerxes and Ahasuerus and to devise some means whereby they might obtain the favor of their new sovereign and gain his consent to proceed in rebuilding their city and Temple.

Sovereign Master—What followed?

Candidate—The Most Excellent Prelate then informed me that if I was desirous of joining in their deliberations it was necessary that I should assume the name and character of Zerubbabel, a prince of the house of Judah, whose hands laid the foundation of the second Temple and whose hands, the Lord had promised, should finish it.

Sovereign Master—What followed?

Candidate—The Most Excellent Prelate then read a lesson from the fathers, stating the impediments with which they were troubled by their adversaries on the other side of the river and the grievous accusations which were brought against them before the king.

Sovereign Master—What followed?

Candidate—My conductor then addressed the most Excellent Prelate thus: Most Excellent Prelate, our Sovereign Lord, Darius, having ascended the throne of Persia, new hopes are entertained of his protection and support in the grand and glorious work of rebuilding our city and Temple; for the King, when but a private man, made a vow to God that should he ever ascend the throne of Persia he would order all the holy vessels now at Babylon back to Jerusalem; and now our most excellent and worthy companion Zerubbabel offers his valuable services in the hazardous enterprise of traversing the Persian dominions and seeking admission to the King, when the first favorable moment will be seized to remind him of his vow and request a fulfillment of the same; and from his known piety no doubts can be entertained of obtaining his consent, which will remove our enemies far hence and we be no longer hindered or impeded in our grand and glorious work.

Sovereign Master—What was the Most Excellent Prelate's reply?

Candidate—Zerubbabel, the Council with great joy accepts your noble and generous offer and will immediately invest you with the necessary passwords which will enable you to make yourself known to the friends of our cause wherever you may meet them and insure to you their friendship and protection; but before entering upon an undertaking of such vast importance it is necessary that you take upon yourself a solemn obligation to be faithful to the trust reposed in you. I arm you with this sword to enable you to defend yourself against your enemies.

Sovereign Master—Did you assume that obligation?

Candidate—I did, in due form.

Sovereign Master—What was that due form?

Candidate—Kneeling on my left knee, my right hand grasping the hilt of my sword, my left hand resting on the Holy Bible, square and compass and two cross swords, in which due form I took upon me the salemn oath and obligation of Knight of the Red Cross.

Sovereign Master—Repeat it. (Candidate repeats it. See page 152.)

Sovereign Master—What followed?

Candidate—The Most Excellent Prelate directed me to arise and invested me with a green sash as a mark of friendship and esteem and directed me to wear it as a constant memorial to stimulate me to the practice of every virtue, and that its color, green, was to remind me that the memory of him who falls in a just and righteous cause, shall forever flourish like the green bay tree.

Sovereign Master—What followed?

Candidate—The Most Excellent Prelate then directed my conductor to invest me with the Jewish pass.

Sovereign Master—Give me the Jewish pass. (Candidate, usually with Master of Infantry, gives Jewish pass as on page 135.

Sovereign Master—What followed?

Candidate—I then began my journey and was frequently hailed by guards, all of whom I was enabled to pass in safety by means of the pass I had received, until I arrived at a bridge represented as reaching into Persian territory. I attempted to pass this bridge which I found strongly guarded, the Persian pass was demanded and being unable to give it, I was attacked, overpowered and made a prisoner.

Sovereign Master—What followed?

Candidate—After remonstrating in vain against their violence, I told them that I was a prince of the house of Judah and demanded an audience with their Sovereign.

Sovereign Master—Their answer?

Candidate—"You can only obtain an audience with his majesty in the garb of a slave and captive."

Sovereign Master—Did you submit to this?

Candidate—I did, being firmly persuaded that could I by any means gain access to the presence of the Sovereign, I should be able to accomplish the object of my mission.

Sovereign Master—What followed?

Candidate—They deprived me of my outward apparel, sash and sword, and, having confined my hands and feet in chains, the links thereof of a triangular form, they put sackcloth and ashes on my head.

Sovereign Master—Why were the links of a triangular form?

Candidate—The Assyrians having learned that among the Jews the triangle was an emblem of Deity, caused their links to be made of a triangular form, thinking thereby to add to the misery of their captives.

Sovereign Master—What followed?

Candidate—I was conducted to the door of the council chamber, where the alarm being given by eight knocks, the Warder demanded, Who comes here?

Sovereign Master—What answer was returned?

Candidate—"A detachment of his majesty's guards, who have made prisoner of one who claims to be a prince of the house of Judah."

Sovereign Master—What was then said to you?

Candidate—I was asked, "Who are you?"

Sovereign Master—Your answer?

Candidate—"The first among my equals, a Mason by rank, but a slave and captive by misfortune."

Sovereign Master—What was then demanded of you?

Candidate—"Where are you from."

Sovereign Master—Your answer?

Candidate—"Jerusalem."

Sovereign Master—What were you then asked?

Candidate—My name.

Sovereign Master—Your answer?

Candidate—'Zerubbabel."

Sovereign Master—What were you then asked?

Candidiate—"What is your desire?"

Sovereign Master—Your answer?

Candidate—"An audience with your Sovereign, if possible."

Sovereign Master—What was then said to you?

Candidate—I was directed to wait with patience till the pleasure of the Sovereign Master was known.

Sovereign Master—What was the answer?

Candidate—That having ascertained that I was unarmed I should be admitted.

Sovereign Master—How were you received?

Candidate—I was conducted in front of the Sovereign Master, who received me with kindness and attention and patiently listened to my request.

Sovereign Master—What did the Sovereign Master then observe to the Council?

Candidate—"This is no enemy; this is Zerubbabel, the friend and companion of my youth!"

Sovereign Master—What followed?

Candidate—The Sovereign thus addressed me: "Zerubbabel, having gained admittance to our presence we demand of you that you make known to us the particular motive that induced you, without our permission and by force and arms, to invade the lines of our dominions."

Sovereign Master—Your answer?

Candidate—"Sovereign Master, the tears and entreaties of my companions at Jerusalem who have so long and so often been impeded by their adversaries on the other side of the river, they having been compelled to cease work by force and power, have caused me to come up to crave your majesty's clemency, hoping you will restore me to your royal favor and grant me employment among the servants of your household."

Sovereign Master—What was the Sovereign's reply?

Candidate—"Zerubbabel, I have often reflected with much pleasure upon our early intimacy and friendship and have heard with great satisfaction of your fame as a wise and accomplished Mason, and having myself a profound veneration for that ancient and honorable institution and having a sincere desire to become a member of same, I will this moment grant your request on condition that you reveal to me the secerts of Freemasonry."

Sovereign Master—Did you consent to that!

Candidate—I did not.

Sovereign Master—What was your reply?

Candidate—"Sovereign Master, when our first most ancient Grand Master, Solomon, King of Israel, instituted the fraternity of Free and Accepted Masons, he taught us that truth was a divine attribute and the foundation of all virtue; to be good and true are the first lessons we are taught in Masonry. My obligations are sacred and inviolable, and if I can obtain your Majesty's clemency only at the expense of my integrity, I humbly beg leave to decline your royal favor; I will cheerfully submit to an honorable exile or a glorious death."

Sovereign Master—What was the Sovereign's reply?

Candidate—"Zerubbabel, your virtue and integrity are highly commendable and your fidelity to your trust is worthy of imitation; from this moment you are free; my guards will divest you of those chains and that badge of slavery and will clothe you with suitable habiliments to accompany me to a banquet. Guards, strike off those chains, and may that garb of slavery never again disgrace the hands of a Mason, more particulary a prince of the house of Judah. Zerubbabel, we assign you a seat of rank and honor among the princes and nobles of the land."

Sovereign Master—What followed?

Candidate—The guards being drawn up in the courtyard, the Warder informed the Sovereign Master that the guards were in readiness, waiting his pleasure.

Sovereign Master—What followed?

Candidate—He then ordered the guards to attend him to the banquet hall.

Sovereign Master—What occurred there?

Candidate—After having participated in a liberal entertainment the Sovereign Master said: "It was the custom in ancient times at banquets like this among the princes and nobles of the land, for the king to propose certain questions and he that could give the most satisfactory answer should be clothed in purple and fine linen, should wear a golden chain around his neck and drink out of a golden cup. There has a question occurred to me this evening. Which is the greatest, the strength of wine, of the king or of women?"

Sovereign Master—What answers were returned?

Candidate—The Chancellor said wine was the strongest; the Master of the Palace said the king was the strongest; but I, being fully persuaded that the time had come in which I could remind the King of his vow and request the fulfillment of it, replied that women were stronger than either of the former, but above all things Truth beareth the victory.

Sovereign Master—What followed?

Candidate—The King being deeply struck with the addition I made to the question ordered us to be prepared with proper arguments to substantiate the opinions we had advanced, on the day following.

Sovereign Master—What followed?

Candidate—On the day following, the Council being convened, the Chancellor was called upon for his answer and thus replied: "O ye princes and rulers, how exceeding strong is wine!" etc. [See page 160.]

Sovereign Master—What followed?

Candidate—The Master of the Palace thus replied: "It is beyond dispute, O princes and rulers," etc. [See page 160.]

Sovereign Master—What followed?

Candidate—I then being called upon for my defense answered as follows: "O princes and rulers, the force of wine is not to be denied, neither is that of kings," etc. [See page 161.]

Sovereign Master—What followed?

Candidate—The King being deeply impressed with the force of the arguments I had used involuntarily exclaimed: "Great is Truth, and mighty above all things. Zerubbabel, ask what thou wilt and I will give it thee, because thou art found wisest among thy companions."

Sovereign Master—Your answer?

Candidate—"O king, remember thy vow, which thou hast vowed," etc. [See page 162.]

Sovereign Master—What followed?

Candidate—The Sovereign Master thus addressed me: "Zerubbabel, it shall be done. I will punctually fulfill my vow. Letters and passports shall immediately be issued to my officers throughout the land, and they shall give you and those that accompany you a safe conveyance to Jerusalem where you shall no longer be hindered or impeded in rebuilding your city and Temple until the same shall be completed."

Sovereign Master—What followed?

Candidate—The Sovereign Master then invested me with a green sash and thus addressed me: "This green sash which you were deprived of by my guards, I now with much pleasure restore to you, and I will make it the insignia of a new order calculated to perpetuate the remembrance of the events which have caused the renewal of our friendship. Its color will remind you that Truth is a divine attribute and shall prevail and forever flourish in immortal green. I will now confer on you the highest honor in our power at this time to bestow, and will create you the first knight of an order instituted for the purpose of inculcating the almighty force and importance of Truth."

Sovereign Master—What followed?

Candidate—The Sovereign Master then directed me to kneel and said: "By virtue of the high power and authority in me vested as the successor of Darius, King of Persia, I receive and constitute you a Knight of the Illustrious Order of the Red Cross."

Sovereign Master—What followed?

Candidate—The Sovereign Master then directed me to arise and presenting me with a sword, thus addressed me: "This sword which you were deprived of by my guards I now with much pleasure restore to you. In the hands of a true and courteous knight, it is endowed with three most excellent qualities; its hilt with faith, its blade with hope, and its point with charity, and it teaches us that when we draw our swords in a just and righteous cause, having faith in God we may reasonably hope for victory, ever remembering to extend the point of charity to a fallen foe. Take it, return it to its scabbard and there let it remain until consumed by rust ere you draw it in the cause of injustice and oppression."

Sovereign Master—What followed?

Candidate—The Sovereign Master then invested me with the Persian pass.

Sovereign Master—Give it. [Given same as on page 136, with the accompanying words, Tatnai and Shethar-bozani.]

Sovereign Master—Who were they?

Candidate—They were governors of Persian provinces and enemies of the Jews.

Sovereign Master—What followed?

Candidate—The Sovereign Master then invested me with the Red Cross word.

Sovereign Master—Give it. [The word Veritas, is given as explained, page 137.]

Sovereign Master—How do you translate the word?

Candidate—Truth.

Sovereign Master?—What followed.

Candidate—The Sovereign Master then invested me with the grand sign, grip and word of a Knight of the Red Cross.

Sovereign Master—Give them. [The grand sign, grip and word, Libertas, are given. See page 137-138.]

Sovereign Master—To what does the sign allude?

Candidate—To the blowing of the trumpet upon the walls and watch-towers of the Council, but more particularly to that part of the penalty of the obligation: "when the last trump shall sound, I be forever excluded from the society of all true and courteous knights."

Sovereign Master—What is the motto of our order?

Candidate—*Magna est veritas, et prevalebit.*

Sovereign Master—Translate it.

Candidate—Truth is mighty and it will prevail.

CHAPTER XVII.

KNIGHTS OF THE RED CROSS, OR ELEVENTH DEGREE.

CLOSING CEREMONIES.

Sovereign Master—Sir Knight Chancellor, are you a Knight of the Red Cross?

Chancellor—That is my profession.

Sovereign Master—By what will you be tried?

Chancellor—By the test of truth?

Sovereign Master—Why by the test of truth?

Chancellor—Because none but good men and true are entitled to the honors of our order.

Sovereign Master—Where were you constituted a knight of this order?

Chancellor—In a just and lawfully constituted Council of Knights of the Red Cross.

Sovereign Master—What number composes such a Council?

Chancellor—There is an indispensable number and a constitutional number.

Sovereign Master—What is the indispensable number?

Chancellor—Three.

Sovereign Master—Under what circumstances may three Knights of the Red Cross form and operate a Council of this order?

Chancellor—Three Knights of the Red Cross being also Knights Templar and hailing from three different

CLOSING CEREMONIES.

commanderies, may, under the sanction of a warrant from some Grand Council or from the Grand Encampment of the United States, form and operate a Council of Knights of the Red Cross, for the dispatch of business.

Sovereign Master—What is the constitutional number?

Chancellor—Seven, nine, eleven or more.

Sovereign Master—When composed of eleven, of whom does it consist?

Chancellor—The Sovereign Master, Chancellor, Master of the Palace, Prelate, Master of Cavalry, Master of Infantry, Master of Finance, Master of Dispatches, Standard Bearer, Sword Bearer and Warder.

[Sometimes the Sovereign Master asks the station and duties of each officer, exactly the same as in opening. See pages 138-143.]

Sovereign Master—Sir Knight Chancellor, it is my will and pleasure that this Council of Knights of the Red Cross be now closed; requiring all Sir Knights present to govern themselves according to the sublime principles of our order. Communicate this order to the Master of the Palace and he to the Sir Knights.

Chancellor—Sir Knight Master of the Palace, it is the will and pleasure of the Sovereign Master, that this Council of Knights of the Red Cross be now closed, requiring all Sir Knights present to govern themselves according to the sublime principles of our order. Communicate this order to the Sir Knights.

Master of Palace—It is the will and pleasure of the Sovereign Master that this Council of Knights of the Red Cross be now closed. Take notice and govern yourselves according to the sublime principles of the order. Look to the east. [The signs from first degree up are now given.]

Sovereign Master (eight raps).

Chancellor (eight raps).

Master of Palace (eight raps).

Sovereign Master—I now declare this Council of Knights of the Red Cross closed in form. Sir Knight Warder, inform the Sentinel. (Warder informs the Sentinel).

DIAGRAM OF A COMMANDERY OF KNIGHTS TEMPLAR. 181

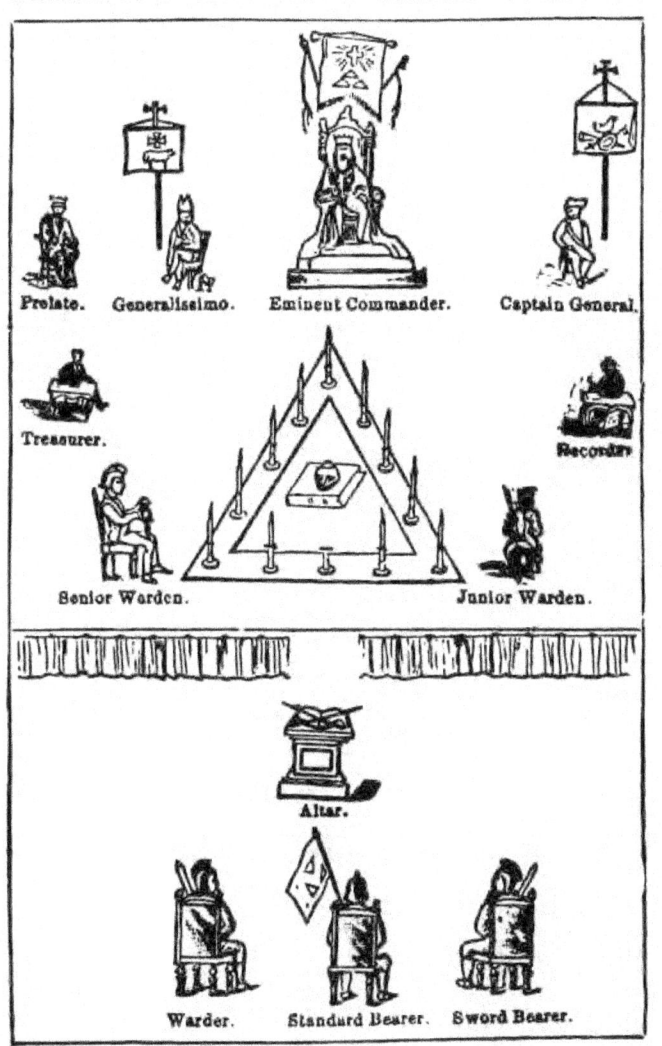

CHAPTER XVIII.

TWELFTH, OR KNIGHTS TEMPLAR[78] DEGREE.

OPENING CEREMONIES.

Eminent Commander[79]—Sir Knight Captain General, it is my order that this Commandery of Knights Templar be now prepared for my reception. Sir Knight Generalissimo[80], accompany me to my apartment. (Eminent Commander and Generalissimo retire.)

Captain General (at post of Eminent Commander)—Attention, Sir Knights Clothe and equip yourself as Knights Templar.[81] (Order is obeyed.)

Captain General—Sir Knight Senior Warden, you

Note 78.—"The connection between the Knights Templar and the Freemasons has been repeatedly asserted by the enemies of both institutions, and as often admitted by their friends. Lawrie on this subject holds the following language: 'We know that the Knights Templar not only possessed the mysteries, but performed the ceremonies and inculcated the duties of Freemasons.'"—Mackey's Lexicon, Art. Knight Templar.

Note 79.—"An assembly of Knights Templar is called a Commandery, and has the following officers:

"1. The Commander, whose title is 'Eminent;' his station is on the throne in the east, dressed in the full uniform of the order. His jewel is the Passion Cross, with rays of light at the crossings."—Sickels' Monitor, Part 4, page 26.

Note 80.—"His station is on the right of the Eminent Commander, and his jewel is a square surmounted by a paschal lamb."—Mackey's Lexicon, Art. Generalissimo.

Note 81.—"An attempt has been made with indifferent success to connect the history of this institution with Freemasonry. Some of the Masonic historians of the last century boldly affirm that the Knights Templar were Masons and connect them with the Druses, long inhabitants of Mount Lebanon. There is nothing in Masonic tradition to justify such belief; on the contrary the three essential qualifications of ancient Masonry are averse to the idea of a Christianised system."—Morris' Dict., Art. Templar Knight.

OPENING CEREMONIES.   183

will see that this Commandery of Knights Templar is in order for the reception of the Eminent Commander.

Senior Warden—Sir Knight Warder, satisfy yourself that all present are Knights Templar.

Warder (looking around)—All present are Knights Templar.

Senior Warden—When a commandery of Knights Templar is about to be opened, what is the first duty?

Warder—To see that the Sentinel is at his post and the asylum duly guarded.

[The following movements are explained, pages 126 to 134.]

Senior Warden—Attention, Sir Knights! Fall in!
Senior Warden—Front!
Senior Warden—Right—Dress!
Senior Warden—Front!
Senior Warden—From the right count twos!
Senior Warden—Form divisions! Right—face!
Senior Warden—Officers—posts!
Senior Warden—Form lines for reception of Eminent Commander!
Junior Warden—Second Division. By file left—march!
Junior Warden—By file left—march!
Junior Warden—Halt!
Junior Warden—Front!
Junior Warden—Left—dress!
Junior Warden—Front! [Junior Warden takes his place at head of Second Division.]
Senior Warden (before Second Division was in line) —First Division. Front!
Senior Warden—Right—Dress!
Senior Warden—Front! [The lines are now formed

184 KNIGHTS TEMPLAR DEGREE.

as in diagram, page 128.]

Senior Warden—Sir Knight Captain General, the lines are duly formed.

Captain General—Sir Knight Junior Warden, repair with the Standard Bearer and Sword Bearer to the apartment of the Eminent Commander and inform him that the lines are formed and await his pleasure.

Junior Warden—Sir Knights Standard Bearer and Sword Bearer, repair with me to the apartment of the Eminent Commander.

Junior Warden—Sir Knights Standard Bearer and Sword Bearer. Left—face! [Exactly the same movements take place as are described on pages 125-129.]

Junior Warden (at the apartment of Eminent Commander)—Eminent Commander, the lines are formed and await your pleasure.

Eminent Commander—Sir Knight Generalissimo,[82] accompany me to the asylum. [See page 125.]

Captain General (as the trumpet sounds)—Attention, Sir Knights! Form cross! (Each throws his right foot forward about eighteen inches, throwing the weight of the body forward and extending the right arm forward and upward crosses swords with opposite Knight, swords crossing about four inches from the points. [See page 131.] The officers, with escort, pass through the lines under the crossed swords, from the west to the east, when they take their stations and the Junior Warden, called Master of Infantry on page 129, with Standard Bearer and Sword Bearer, march around to their post again.)

Eminent Commander (from his post)—Sir Knights,

Note 82.—"Generalissimo.—The second officer in a Commandery of Knights Templar, and one of its representatives in the Grand Commandery."—Mackey's Lexicon, Art. Generalissimo.

OPENING CEREMONIES.

carry—swords!

Eminent Commander—Sir Knight Generalissimo,[83] it is my order that the lines be formed for inspection and review.

Generalissimo—Sir Knight Captain General, it is the order of the Eminent Commander that the lines be formed for inspection and review.

[The lines are formed for inspection and review as explained on pages 126-128.]

Captain General—Sir Knight Generalissimo, the order of the Eminent Commander has been obeyed.

Generalissimo—Eminent Commander, the lines are formed for inspection and review.

Eminent Commander—Sir Knight Generalissimo, accompany me in the inspection and review.

Captain General (as officers approach)—Present—swords! (All present swords, and as the officers appear in front of a Sir Knight he twirls the sword with his thumb and forefinger so as to show both sides of the blade. They inspect the First Division in passing through to the west, and the Second Division in returning.)

Eminent Commander (having returned to his post) —Carry—swords!

Eminent Commander—Sir Knight Generalissimo, advance and communicate the Pilgrim Warrior's pass!

Generalissimo—Maher-shalal-hash-baz.[84] (Given as follows:)

Note 83.—"His duty is to receive and communicate all orders, signs and petitions; to assist the Eminent Commander, and, in his absence to preside over the Commandery."—**Mackey's Lexicon, Art. Generalissimo.**

Note 84.—"Maher-shalal-hash-baz.—This Hebrew term signifying 'hastenbooty, speedspoil,' is introduced into the order of Knights Templar. The term is found in Isaiah 8: 1-4, but the propriety of its introduction into Masonry is not easily shown."—**Morris' Dict., Art. Maher-shalal-hash-baz.**

KNIGHTS TEMPLAR DEGREE.

Pilgrim Warrior's Pass.

PILGRIM WARRIOR'S PASS.

This is given in the same manner as the Persian pass, page 136.

Four sword cuts are given, the fourth being toward the neck, either cut No. 1 or 2, when the Pilgrim Warrior's pass, *Maher-shalal-hash-baz*,[85] is given "under an arch of steel." See cut.

Eminent Commander—Receive it from your right. (Generalissimo turns to knight on his right and in like manner demands the Pilgrim Warrior's pass, receives it in the same way, when the knight demands it of the one next him, and so on down the First Division till it reaches the Junior Warden, when he steps one pace forward, faces the east, and says:)

Junior Warden—Eminent Commander, the Pilgrim Warrior's pass has come down to me through the lines.

Eminent Commander—Advance to the east and give me the same.

Eminent Commander (having received the word in the same manner as before)—The word has come down to me through the lines correct.

Eminent Commander—Sir Knight Junior Warden, about—face; to your post—march!

Note 85.—"**Maher-shalal-hash-baz.**—Four Hebrew words which the prophet Isaiah was ordered to write upon a tablet and which were afterwards to be the name of his son. They signify 'make haste to the prey, fall upon the spoil' and were prognostic of the sudden attack of the Assyrians. They may be said, in their Masonic use, to be symbolic of the readiness for action which should distinguish a warrior."—**Mackey's** Lexicon, Art. Maher-shalal-hash-baz.

OPENING CEREMONIES.

[The word having been passed through both divisions the Eminent Commander says:]

Eminent Commander—Sir Knight Generalissimo, advance and communicate the Pilgrim Penitent's pass.

Generalissimo—Golgotha.[86] (Given same as Persian pass, page 136, and same as Pilgrim Warrior's pass.)

Eminent Commander (after Pilgrim Penitent's pass has been given)—Sir Knight Generalissimo, it is my order that the triangle be now formed preparatory to our devotions.

Generalissimo—Sir Knight Captain General, it is the order of the Eminent Commander that the triangle be now formed preparatory to our devotions.

Captain General—Second Division. Right—face! By file left—march! (These orders are executed.)

Captain General—By file left—march! (They march a pace further than the length of the division.)

Captain General—By the left flank into line—march! (They turn to the left and, marching up, fill the spaces in the line of the First Division, thus forming one line.)

Captain General—Right—dress!

Captain General—Front!

Captain General From the right count threes! (They count—one, two three; one, two, three, etc., and as in counting "twos," each one who says "three" is in the Third Division, etc.)

Captain General—Form division! Right—face! (All face to the right, and each No. "one" stands fast, while the "twos" take one oblique step to the right and

---

Note 86.—"Golgotha.—This word, which is the Hebrew name of the place where the Saviour was crucified, is introduced with much propriety into the order of Knights Templar. It is a Choldee term signifying, the place of a skull. A fabulous tradition affirms that Adam was buried there, and that the place thus received its name. The skull affixed to the ordinary emblem of the crucifix alludes to this tradition."—Morris' Dict., Art. Golgotha.

the "threes" two oblique steps to the right, when they stand three abreast.)

Captain General—Officers—posts! (Officers take stations as follows: Senior Warden, to right of First Division, faced to the right; Sword Bearer to right of Second Division, faced to the right; Standard Bearer in center of Second Division, faced to the right; Warder to the left of the Second Division, faced to the right; the Junior Warden on the right of the Third Division, faced to the right.)

Captain General—Close—intervals—march! (The first file of three stands fast while the other files close up to about one foot apart.)

Captain General—Form triangle!

[The different officers now give orders as follows:]

Senior Warden—First Division. Countermarch by file left!

Sword Bearer—Second Division. By file left!

Junior Warden—Third Division. Mark time!

Captain General—March! (At the word march the different movements previously ordered begin. Marking time consists in moving the feet without marching.)

Senior Warden (when head of First Division has reached the place where base of triangle is to rest)—First Division. Halt!

Senior Warden—Right face!

Senior Warden—Left dress!

Senior Warden—Front!

[The Second Division, led by Sword Bearer, marches its length to the left, then files to the left, and when opposite the Senior Warden files left again, halting when the read of the division reaches the left of the First Division and is lined at right angles with it.]

Sword Bearer—Second Division. Halt!
Sword Bearer—Front!
Sword Bearer—Right dress!
Sword Bearer—Front!

[The Third Division continues to mark time until the Second Division has filed to the north and passed its length north.]

Junior Warden—Third Division. By file left—March! [On passing its length the division again files to the left or north precisely as the Second Division did, but it halts as soon as it has passed its length to the north, its right resting on the left of the Second Division.]

Junior Warden—Third Division. Halt!
Junior Warden—Front!
Junior Warden—Right dress!
Junior Warden—Front! [The three divisions now form three sides of a square along the north, south and west.]

Captain General—First Division, left; Third Division, right—wheel—march! [These divisions wheel as ordered until within about three paces of each other.]

Captain General—Halt! [The two Wardens align their respective divisions by the usual orders.]

Captain General—Sir Knight Generalissimo, the triangle is formed.

Generalissimo—Eminent Commander, the triangle is formed for devotions.

Eminent Commander—Sir Knights Generalissimo, Captain General and Prelate,[47] repair with me to the triangle for the performance of our devotions.

Note 87.—"The Lodge de la Parfaite Intelligence, at Liege (France) contained in December, 1770, the Prince Bishop, and the greatest part of his chapter, and all the office bearers were dignitaries of the church."—Robison's Proofs of a Conspiracy, page 65.

Eminent Commander—Attention, Sir Knights. Return swords! To your devotions! (They kneel on the right knee, deposit their helmets on the floor before them, and then interlace their fingers by crossing their arms and giving right hand to knight on the left and left hand to knight on the right. The Prelate leads and usually the "Lord's Prayer" is used, when all unite with him.)

OPENING PRAYER, KNIGHTS TEMPLAR DEGREE.

"Our Father which art in heaven, hallowed be thy name. Thy kingdom come. Thy will be done in earth as it is in heaven. Give us this day our daily bread. And forgive us our debts, as we forgive our debtors. And lead us not into temptation, but deliver us from evil. For thine is the kingdom, and the power, and the glory, forever. Amen."—*Simons' Book of the Commandery, page 27.*

Eminent Commander—Sir Knight Generalissimo, give me the immaculate word. (Generalissimo and Eminent Commander give the grip and immaculate word as follows:)

Knights Templar Grip.

KNIGHTS TEMPLAR GRIP AND WORD.

Fingers of right hands and left hands interlaced and, of course, arms crossed, as shown in cut.

IMMACULATE WORD. *Immanuel.*[aa] (Spoken as arms are crossed.

Note 88.—"Immanuel.—This term, signifying 'God with us' is introduced in the order of Knights Templar."—Morris' Dict., Art. Immanuel.

OPENING CEREMONIES. 191

[When at devotions the grip and "word" are given while still kneeling, and though arms are crossed, the fingers of each are interlaced with one knight on his right and the other on his left.]

Eminent Commander—Receive it from your right. (Generalissimo demands the word, receives it same as described, and the knight next him does the same of the knight on his right.)

Eminent Commander—Recover helmets. Arise, Sir Knights. Attention to giving the signs. (Led by the Eminent Commander the due guards and signs from Entered Apprentice up are now given, and the Knights Templar, as follows:)

DUE GUARD OF A KNIGHT TEMPLAR.

Thumb of right hand under the chin, as shown in cut, fingers closed in hand.

This alludes to the penalty of the obligation. Head placed on the highest spire in Christendom.

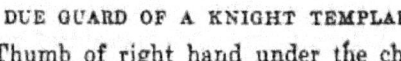
Due-Guard K. T.

Eminent Commander—Attention, Sir Knights! About—face! To your posts—march! (All march to their posts, when the regular opening "lecture" is in order.)

Eminent Commander—Sir Knight Generalissimo, are you a Knight Templar?[89]

Generalissimo—That is my title.

Note 89.—"Rite known as the Order of Modern Templars or Knights Templar, comprising three degrees, practiced in the United States of America and Great Britain. As the successor of the secular Templars of the Jesuit system of Strict Observance, this rite was arranged in France in 1804."—**Rebold's History of Freemasonry, page 229.**

Eminent Commander—Where were you created a Knight Templar?

Generalissimo—In a just and lawful Commandery of Knights Templar.

Eminent Commander—What number composes such a Commandery?

Generalissimo—There is an indispensable number and a constitutional number.

Eminent Commander—What is the indispensable number?

Generalissimo—Three.

Eminent Commander—Under what circumstances may three Knights Templar open and form a Commandery?

Generalissimo—Three Knights Templar, hailing from three different Commanderies, may, under the sanction of a warrant from some Grand Commandery or from the Grand Encampment of the United States, form and operate a Commandery of Knights Templar for the dispatch of business.

Eminent Commander—What is the constitutional number?

Generalissimo—Nine,[90] eleven, or more.

Eminent Commander—When composed of eleven, of whom does it consist?

Generalissimo—The Eminent Commander, Generalissimo, Captain General, Prelate, Senior Warden, Junior Worden, Treasurer, Recorder, Standard Bearer, Sword Bearer, and Warder.

Note 90.—"To protect the pious pilgrims thus exposed to plunder and death, nine noble knights, who had previously distinguished themselves at the siege of Jerusalem, united in a brotherhood, and bound themselves by a solemn compact to aid one another in clearing the highways of infidels and robbers and in protecting the pilgrim through the passes and defiles of the mountains to the Holy City. These Knights called themselves the Poor Fellow Soldiers of Jesus Christ."—Mackey's Lexicon, Art. Knight Templar.

OPENING CEREMONIES.

Eminent Commander—What is the Warder's station in the Commandery?

Generalissimo—On the left of the Standard Bearer in the west and on the left of the Second Division.

Eminent Commander—What are your duties there, Sir Knight Warder?

Warder—To announce the approach and departure of the Eminent Commander, to post the Sentinel and to see that the asylum is duly guarded.

Eminent Commander—What is the Sword Bearer's station in the Commandery?

Warder—On the right of the Standard Bearer in the west and on the right of the Second Division.

Eminent Commander—What are your duties, Sir Knight Sword Bearer?

Sword Bearer—To assist in the protection of the banners of the order, and to watch all signals from the Eminent Commander and see that they are promptly obeyed.

Eminent Commander—What is the Standard Bearer's station in the Commandery?

Sword Bearer—In the west and in the center of the Second Division.

Eminent Commander—What are your duties, Sir Knight Standard Bearer?

Standard Bearer—To display, protect and support the banners" of the order.

Eminent Commander—Why is your station in the west?

Standard Bearer—That the brilliant rays of the ris-

Note 91.—"Their banner was half black, half white, called Beauseant, that 'a to say in the Gallic tongue Bienseant, (well becoming,) because they are fair and favorable to the friends of Christ, but black and terrible to his enemies." *Mackey's Lexicon, Art. Knight Templar.*

ing sun shedding their lustre on the banners of the order, may encourage and animate all true and courteous knights and confound and dismay their enemies.

Eminent Commander—What is the Recorder's station in the Commandery?

Standard Bearer—On the left, in front of the Captain General.

Eminent Commander—What are your duties, Sir Knight Recorder?

Recorder—Faithfully to record the proceedings of the Commandery, collect the revenue and pay the same over to the Treasurer.

Eminent Commander—What is the Treasurer's station in the Commandery?

Recorder—On the right, in front of the Generalissimo.

Eminent Commander—What are your duties, Sir Knight Treasurer?

Treasurer—To receive in charge all the funds and property of the Commandery, pay all orders drawn on the treasury and render a just and faithful account of the same when required.

Eminent Commander—What is the Junior Warden's station in the Commandery?

Treasurer—On the northwest angle of the triangle, on the right of the Third Division and on the left when formed in single line.

Eminent Commander—What are your duties, Sir Knight Junior Warden?

Junior Warden—To attend on poor and weary pilgrims, traveling from afar; to accompany them on their journey, to answer all questions for them and recommend them to the hospitality of the Eminent Commander.

OPENING CEREMONIES. 195

Eminent Commander—What is the Senior Warden's station in the Commandery?

Junior Warden—At the southwest angle of the triangle, on the right of the First Division and on the right of the whole when formed in single line.

Eminent Commander—What are your duties Sir Knight Senior Warden?

Senior Warden—To attend on Pilgrim Warriors to comfort and support Pilgrim Penitents and after due trial introduce them into the asylum.

Eminent Commander—What is the Prelate's station in the Commandery?

Senior Warden—On the right of the Generalissimo.

Eminent Commander—What are your duties, Sir Knight Prelate?"

Prelate—To minister at the altar and offer up prayers and oblations to Deity."

Eminent Commander—What is the Captain General's station in the Commandery?

Prelate—On the left of the Eminent Commander.

Eminent Commander—What are your duties Sir Knight Captain General?

Captain General—To see that the proper officers make all due preparations for the various meetings of

---

NOTE 92.—"TRIANGLE, TRIPLE.—This is another of the numerous forms in which the triangle is arranged, and like all the others it is used as a symbol of Deity, though perhaps it is here made to assume a still more sacred character from its triple form. As such it has been adopted as the most appropriate jewel of the Illustrious Prelate in a Commandery of Knights Templars."—*Mackey's Lexicon, Art. Triangle, Triple.*

NOTE 93.—"In this prayer [prayer prescribed in the charter of York] we perceive no mention made of a Trinity, the Deity invoked being none other than the Great Architect of the Universe, that Great First Cause recognized by the Noachidean doctrine, and the belief in the eternal existence of which can readily be concurred in by men of every confession."—*Rebold's History of Freemasonry, page 848.*

the Commandery, and that the asylum is in suitable array for the introduction of candidates and the dispatch of business, and to receive and communicate all orders and signals issued by the Eminent Commander to the officers of the lines.

Eminent Commander—What is the Generalissimo's station in the Commandery?

Captain General—On the right of the Eminent Commander.

Eminent Commander—What are your duties, Sir Knight Generalissimo?

Generalissimo—To receive and communicate all orders, signals and petitions; to assist the Eminent Commander in his various duties and in his absence to preside in the Commandery.

Eminent Commander—What is the Eminent Commander's station in the Commandery?

Generalissimo—In the east.

Eminent Commander—What are his duties?

Generalissimo—To distribute alms to poor and needy pilgrims traveling from afar, feed the hungry, clothe the naked, bind up the wounds of the afflicted; inculcate the principles of charity" and hospitality, and govern the Commandery with justice and moderation

Eminent Commander—Sir Knight Generalissimo, it is my order that a Commandery of Knights Templar be now opened for the dispatch of such business as may regularly come before it, requiring all Sir Knights present to govern themselves according to the sublime principles of our order. Communicate this order to

---

NOTE 94.—"The peculiar characteristics of this magnanimous order are charity and hospitality; therefore those who assume the responsibilities of Knights Templar, are bound by solemn vows to give alms to the poor and weary; to succor the needy, feed the hungry, clothe the naked, and bind up the wounds of the afflicted."—*Sickels' Monitor, Part 4, page 83.*

Sir Knight Captain General and he to the Sir Knights.

Generalissimo—S.r Knight Captain General, it is the order of the Eminent Commander that a Commandery of Knights Templar be now opened for the dispatch of such business as may regularly come before it; requiring all Sir Knights present to govern themselves according to the sublime principles of our order. Communicate this order to the Sir Knights.

Captain General—Sir Knights, it is the order of the Eminent Commander that a Commandery of Knights Templar be now opened for the dispatch of such business as may regularly come before it; take notice and govern yourselves according to the sublime principles of our order. [The signs are now given from E. A. Deg. up. See pages 35 to 40, 65, 66, 96, 97 and 138. Before declaring the Commandery opened the Eminent Commander frequently delivers the following:]

OPENING CHARGE KNIGHTS TEMPLAR DEGREE.

"James, a servant of God and of the Lord Jesus Christ, to the twelve tribes which are scattered abroad, greeting. My brethren, count it all joy when ye fall into divers temptations; knowing this, that the trying of your faith worketh patience. But let patience have her perfect work, that ye may be perfect and entire, wanting nothing. If any of you lack wisdom, let him ask of God, that giveth to all men liberally and upbraideth not; and it shall be given him. But let him ask in faith nothing wavering. For he that wavereth is like a wave of the sea, driven with the wind and tossed. For let not that man think that he shall receive anything of the Lord. A double-minded man is unstable in all his ways. Let the brother of low degree rejoice in that he is exalted. If any man among you seem to be religious, and bridleth not his tongue, but deceiveth his own heart; this man's religion is vain. Pure religion and undefiled before God and the Father is this: To visit the fatherless and widows in their affliction, and to keep himself unspotted from the world.—James 1: 1-10; 26, 27." —*Simons' Book of the Commandery, page 28.*

Eminent Commander (twelve raps, 000-000-000-000.)
Generalissimo (twelve raps.)
Captain General (twelve raps.)
Eminent Commander—I now declare —— Commandery, —— ——, open in form. Sir Knight Warder, inform the Sentinel.

[As all the business of the Commandery, except initiation in the two previous degrees, even to balloting for candidates must be transacted in this degree and only by Knights Templar, reading the minutes of the previous communication, reading and referring petitions, reports of committees, balloting on candidates, and other business here follows, unless it is a "special communication for work," *i. e.*, initiation.]

CHAPTER XIX.

Twelfth, or Knights Templar" Degree.

INITIATION.

Eminent Commander—Sir Knight Warder, ascertain if there are any candidates in waiting for this order of knighthood.

Warder—Eminent Commander, there is in the anteroom ———, a Knight of the Red Cross, who having taken all the necessary preceding degrees, now solicits the honor" of being dubbed and created a knight of this most valiant and magnanimous order of Knights Templar.

Eminent Commander—Sir Knight Junior Warden, repair to the ante-room and conduct ———, a Knight of the Red Cross, to the "Chamber of Reflection,"" where you will place before him three questions, to which you will require his answer in writing. After

---

Note 95.—"The first assembly of this congress [A Masonic congress at Wilhelmsbad, Germany, convoked by Duke Ferdinand of Brunswick, General Grand Master of all the 'Strict Observance Lodges'] took place on the 16th July, 1782. All the grand officers of all the provinces of the Templar system, and delegates from all their lodges were present, as also many delegates of other rites then extant in Germany and France. After thirty sittings, none of the questions upon the origin, doctrines, etc., had been resolved in a satisfactory manner; when finally, upon the proposition of the French delegates of the Templar system from the province of Burgundy, the views of the congress were thus expressed: 'Modern Freemasons are not only *not* the true successors of the Knights Templar, but, as worthy recipients of the three symbolic degrees, they can not be.'"—*Rebold's History of Freemasonry, page* 222.

Note 96.—"Section 62, Article IV. Constitution of Grand Encampment, U. S. A.—No subordinate Commandery shall confer the orders of knighthood for a less sum than twenty dollars."—*Myers' Templar Manual, page* 159.

Note 97.—"Chamber of Reflection.—In the French and Scotch rites, a small room adjoining the lodge, in which, preparatory to initiation, the candidate is enclosed for the purpose of indulging in those serious meditations which its sombre appearance and the gloomy emblems with which it is furnished are calculated to produce. It is also used in the degree of Knights Templar for a similar purpose."—*Mackey's Lexicon, Art., Chamber of Reflection.*

he has reflected upon them in silence and solitude;
when he has testified to the purity of his intentions by
performing the required ablutions, you will return with
his answer. (Junior Warden conducts him, hood-
winked, into a small room where the walls, furniture
and everything is painted black and the only light is
one small taper. Seating him in a chair at a table
where the taper burns, he says:)

Junior Warden—Companion, you are now seated in
the Chamber of Reflection; before you is the Holy Bible,
that rule and guide of our faith and practice; you will
also find certain questions," which you will carefully
read, and answer in writing, signing your name to them,
after which, in testimony of the purity of your intentions, you will perform your ablutions, for which you
will find water and a napkin before you. I am now
about to leave you alone and will signify my departure
by an alarm at the door. On hearing it you will remove the bandage from your eyes and proceed as I have
directed, and when you have concluded, you will signify
it by giving a like alarm from within. (Junior Warden goes out and gives three raps on the door. Candidate removes the hoodwink and discovers on the table
before him, a Bible bowl of water and a skull and cross
bones, which often disconcerts him. Before him is a paper on which he finds the following questions:)

Table in the Chamber of Reflection.

First—Should you ever be called

NOTE 98.—"RECEPTION.—The novitiate for the honors of this magnanimous order is required to answer several interrogatories, touching his faith in the Christian religion, and his strict conformity to the rules and regulations of the order."—*Sickels' Monitor, Part 4, page 29.*

upon to draw your sword, will you wield it in defense of the Christian religion? [After this he writes, Yes.]

Second—Does your conscience upbraid you for any known or overt act unrepented of? [He writes No, after this.]

Third—Do you solemnly promise to conform to all the ceremonies, rules and regulations of this Commandery as all valiant and magnanimous Sir Knights have done, who have traveled this way before you? [To this he writes Yes, and signs his name to the whole or to each question separately. He then washes and wipes his hands and gives three raps on the door.]

Junior Warden (entering)—Have you answered the questions?

Candidate—I have. (Hands him the paper with written questions and answers.)

Junior Warden—You will wait with patience till the pleasure of the Eminent Commander is made known.

Junior Warden (twelve stamps on the floor with his foot, outside the door.)

Warder—Eminent Commander there is an alarm.

Eminent Commander—Ascertain the cause.

Warder—Who comes here?

Junior Warden————, a Knight of the Red Cross, now in the Chamber of Reflection,[99] who having received all the necessary preceding degrees now wishes the honor[100] of being dubbed and created a knight of

---

NOTE 99.—"CHAMBER OF REFLECTION.—This is simply the Masonic preparation room, adapted to the peculiar purposes of the orders of knighthood."—*Morris' Dict., Art. Chamber of Reflection.*

NOTE 100.—"The prescribed fees for the orders of knighthood can not be remitted by a Commandery, directly or indirectly."—*Myers' Templar Manual, page 175.*

this most valiant and magnanimous order of Knights Templar.

Warder—Has he answered the necessary questions?

Junior Warden—He has, in writing, and in testimony of his sincerity has performed the required ablution.

Warder—Present them. (Junior Warden hands him the questions and answers.)

Warder—Let him wait the pleasure of the Eminent Commander.

[The same dialogue occurs between the Warder and the Eminent Commander.]

Eminent Commander—Present them (the questions and answers.)

Eminent Commander—Thus far his proceedings have been satisfactory, but as a further trial of his patience and perseverance I shall enjoin upon him seven years of pilgrimage[101] which he will perform under the direction of the Junior Warden, dressed in pilgrim's weeds.

Warder (to Junior Warden)—The Eminent Commander decides that the questions are answered satisfactorily, but as a further trial of his patience and perseverance, enjoins upon him seven years of pilgrimage, which he will perform under your direction, in pilgrim's weeds.

Junior Warden (returns to Chamber of Reflection) —Companion, the Eminent Commander decides that the questions are answered satisfactorily, but as a fur-

---

NOTE 101.—"PILGRIM'S SHELL.—The shell was an ancient symbol of the Syrian goddess Astarte, who was the same as the Venus Pelagia, or Venus rising from the sea, of the Western mythology. The escalop or scollop shell (the *pecten* of Linæus) is found in great abundance on the shores of the Mediterranean and was worn in the time of the Crusades by pilgrims to the Holy Land as a memorial of the pious pilgrimage they were then performing or had already accomplished. Hence the scollop shell, staff and sandals form a part of the costume of a candidate in the ceremonies of the Templar's degree."—*Mackey's Lexicon, Art. Pilgrim's Shell.*

ther trial of your patience and perseverance, enjoins upon you seven years of pilgrimage, in pilgrim's weeds.

[Clothes him in pilgrim's weeds, a staff in right hand and scrip, containing bread and water, in left, sandals and a slouch hat, etc., as shown in cut.]

Junior Warden—Follow me! (They come to First Guard.)

First Guard—Who comes here?

Junior Warden—A weary pilgrim traveling from afar, to join with those who oft have gone before, and offer his devotions at the holy shrine.

Pilgrim penitent.

"EXHORTATION BY THE FIRST GUARD.

"———, I greet thee.

"Silver and gold have I none; but such as I have, give I unto thee.

["Here is some good bread and pure water, just such as pilgrims need; help yourself." The guard, feeling in his scrip, says: "Your bread is almost gone, I will put in some; your water is almost spent, I will replenish it."]

"Hearken to a lesson to cheer thee on thy way and assure thee of success.

"Let the brother of low degree rejoice in that he is exalted. Come unto Me, all ye that are weary and heavy laden, and I will give you rest.

"Christ also suffered for us, leaving us an example that we should follow his steps. For ye were as sheep going astray; but are now returned Shepherd and Bishop of your souls.

"Let, therefore, brotherly love continue.

"Farewell, ———. God speed thee."—*Simons' Book of the Commandery, page 29.*

Second Guard (to Junior Warden, who, followed by candidate, has passed on)—Who comes here?

Junior Warden—A weary pilgrim traveling from afar to join with those who oft have gone before, and offer his devotions at the holy shrine.

"EXHORTATION BY THE SECOND GUARD.

"———, I greet thee.

["Here is some good bread and pure water, just such as pilgrims need; help yourself." The guard feeling in his scrip, says; "Your bread is almost gone, I will put in some; your water is almost spent, I will replenish it."]

"Hearken to a lesson to cheer thee on thy way and assure thee of success.

"To do good and communicate, forget not: for with such sacrifices God is well pleased.

"Be not forgetful to entertain strangers: for thereby some have entertained angels unawares.

"Remember them that are in bonds, as being bound with them; and them which suffer adversity, as being yourselves also in the body.

"Be not weary in well doing; for in due time ye shall reap, if ye faint not.

"Farewell, ———. God speed thee."—*Simons' Book of the Commandery, page 30.*

Third Guard (to Junior Warden and candidate)—Who comes here?

Junior Warden—A weary pilgrim[102] traveling from

NOTE 102.—"The loss of a leg or arm by a petitioner disqualifies him from receiving the orders of knighthood."—*Myers' Templar Manual, page 134.*

afar, to join with those who oft have gone before and offer his devotions at the holy shrine.

"EXHORTATION BY THE THIRD GUARD.

"———, I greet thee.

["Here is some good bread and pure water, just such as pilgrims need; help yourself." The guard feeling in his scrip, says: "Your bread is almost gone, I will put in some; your water is almost spent, I will replenish it."]

"Hearken to a lesson to cheer thee on thy way and assure thee of success.

"Charity covereth a multitude of sins. If a brother or sister be naked, and destitute of daily food; and one of you say unto them, Depart in peace, be ye warmed and be ye filled; notwithstanding ye give them not those things which are needful for the body; what doth it profit?

"Now, may He who is able send you forth into the world, 'thoroughly furnished unto all good works,' keep you from falling into vice and error, improve, strengthen, establish and perfect you.

"Be thou faithful unto death, and I will give thee a crown of life.

"Farewell, ———. God speed thee."—*Simons' Book of the Commandery, page 31.*

[The Scripture readings termed "Exhortation by First Guard," "Second Guard" and "Third Guard", are entirely different in different jurisdictions. The following is from *Myers' Templar Manual:*]

"EXHORTATIONS.
"FIRST.

"———, I greet thee.

"Silver and gold have I none, but such as I have give I unto thee.

"Hearken to a lesson to cheer thee on thy way, and assure thee of success.

"And Abraham rose up early in the morning, and took *bread* and a *bottle of water* and gave it unto Hagar (putting it on her shoulder) and the child, and sent her away, and she departed and wandered in the wilderness, and the water was spent in the bottle, and she cast the child under one of the shrubs; and the angel of God called to Hagar out of heaven, saying, Arise, lift up the lad and hold him in thine hand, for I will make him a great nation; and God opened her eyes, and she saw a well of water. By faith Abraham sojourned in the land of promise as in a strange country, dwelling in tabernacles; for he looked for a city which had foundations, whose builder and maker is God. Be ye therefore followers of God as dear children, rejoicing in the Lord always; and again I say, rejoice.

"Farewell ———. God speed thee on thy way."

"SECOND.

"———, I greet thee.

"If a brother or sister be naked and destitute of daily food, and one of you say, Depart in peace, be ye warmed and filled, and ye give them not of those things which are needful for the body, what doth it profit? To do good and communicate forget not, for with such sacrifices God is well pleased. Beware, lest any man spoil you through philosophy and vain deceit; after the traditions of men; after the rudiments of the world and not after Christ; for in him dwelleth all the fullness of the Godhead bodily.

"Farewell ———. God speed thee on thy way."

"THIRD.

"———, I greet thee.

"He that receiveth you receiveth Me, and he that receiveth Me receiveth Him that sent Me. Come unto Me all ye that labor and are heavy laden, and I will give you rest. Take My yoke upon you and learn of Me, for I am meek and lowly in heart, and ye shall find rest unto your souls, for My yoke is easy and my burden is light. Whosoever shall give to drink unto one of these little ones a cup of cold water only, in the name of a disciple, verily I say unto you he shall in no wise lose his reward.

"Farewell ———. God speed thee on thy way."

Junior Warden (with candidate at asylum door; twelve raps.)

Warder—Eminent Commander, there is an alarm.

Eminent Commander—Ascertain the cause.

Warder—Who comes here?

Junior Warden—A poor and weary pilgrim, traveling from afar, who having performed three long years of pilgrimage, now desires, if it so pleases the Eminent Commander, to dedicate the four remaining years to deeds of more exalted usefulness, and if found worthy, his strong desire is to be admitted among those valiant knights whose well-earned fame has spread both far and wide for deeds of charity and pure beneficence.

Warder—What security can he offer that he is no impostor?

Junior Warden—The commendation of your Junior Warden, who recommends to the Eminent Commander a remission of the four remaining years.

Warder—Let him wait with patience and perseverence till the pleasure of the Eminent Commander is made known.

[The same dialogue occurs between Warder and Eminent Commander.]

Eminent Commander—What security can he offer that he is no impostor?

Warder—The commendation of a valiant and magnanimous Sir Knight, our Junior Warden, who recommends to the Eminent Commander a remission of the our remaining years.

Eminent Commander—This being the case, Sir Knight Prelate, you will conduct the weary pilgrim to the holy altar, where after he has taken upon himself the solemn vow of the order, invest him with sword and buckler, so that as a pilgrim warrior he may perform four years' warfare as a trial of his constancy and courage.

Senior Warden—Attention, Sir Knights! Form avenue! [This is the same as forming CROSS; the knights being formed in two rows on each side of altar, from east to west facing inward, with swords crossed a few inches from the point. See page 131. The avenue being formed the Prelate with candidate advance through the lines to the altar.]

Prelate (to candidate)—Thou hast craved permission to pass through our solemn ceremonies and enter the asylum of our Commandery, but before you can be permitted to do so, you must take upon yourself the solemn vows of our order. If it is still your wish to proceed you will kneel at our sacred altar in due form. [He kneels on two cross swords, placing his hands on cross swords which lie on the Bible, the cross swords of the knights forming an arch of steel overhead.]

KNIGHTS TEMPLAR OBLIGATION.

I, ———, of my own free will and accord and in the

INITIATION. 209

presence of the Sovereign Architect of the Universe and this Commandery of Knights Templar, do hereby and hereon most solemnly and sincerely promise and vow that I will ever keep and conceal the secrets[103] of this order of knighthood, and never reveal the same except it be to a true and lawful Sir Knight of the order, or within the body of a regular and duly constituted Commandery of the same, until after due trial strict examination, or lawful information I find him o them justly entitled to receive the same.

I furthermore promise and vow that I will support and maintain the constitution, rules and edicts of the Grand Encampment[104] of the United States, the statutes and regulations of the Grand Commandery of the the State of ———, the by-laws, rules and regulations of ——— Commandery,[105] ———, or those of any other Grand or Subordinate Commandery of Knights from whose jurisdiction I may hereafter hail, so far as the same shall come to my knowledge.

I furthermore promise and vow that I will answer

NOTE 103.—"I am particularly struck by a position of Abbe Barruel, 'That *Irreligion and unqualified Liberty and Equality, are the genuine and original Secret of Freemasonry, and the ultimatum of a regular progress through all its degrees!*' He supports this remarkable position with great ingenuity and many pertinent facts."—*Robison's Proofs of a Conspiracy*, page 893.

NOTE 104.—"It was by members of this 'association [Order of Knights of the Temple] that Knight Templarism, as known in America—comprising the three degrees, viz: Knight of the Red Cross, Knight Templar and Knight of Malta—was introduced into the United States in 1808, and which degrees now compose the highest grades of the American Masonic system. Delegates from seven Encampments of Knights Templar and one Council of Red Cross—none of which were located south or west of New York—organized in New York city, on the 20th of June, 1816, a General Grand Encampment for the United States. At this assembly Hon. De Witt Clinton of New York, was elected General Grand Master, and Thomas Smith Webb, Esq., of Boston, his Deputy."—*Rebold's History of Freemasonry*, page 226.

NOTE 105.—"Each Commandery has penal jurisdiction over all knights, non-affiliated as well as affiliated, for violation of moral or Templar law within its territorial jurisdiction."—*Myers' Templar Manual*, page 174.

KNIGHTS TEMPLAR DEGREE.

and obey all summons from a regular Commandery of Knights Templar or from a Sir Knight of the order, if within the distance of forty miles, natural infirmities and unavoidable accidents alone excusing me.

I furthermore promise and vow that I will help, aid and assist with my counsel, my prayers and my sword all poor and destitute Sir Knights of the order, their widows and orphans, they applying to me as such, and I finding them worthy and can do so without material injury to myself or family.

I furthermore promise and vow that I will go the distance of forty miles barefooted and on frozen ground to save the life or relieve the distress of a worthy Sir Knight, should his necessities require and my circumstances permit.

I furthermore promise and vow not to be present at the opening of a Commandery of Knights Templar except there be present at least nine regular knights, myself included, or the representatives of three different Commanderies working under legal warrants.

I furthermore promise and vow not to be present at the conferring of the order upon any one except he shall have regularly received all the necessary preceding degrees, to the best of my knowledge and belief.

I furthermore promise and vow that I will wield my sword in the defense of innocent maidens,[106] destitute

---

NOTE 106.—"The book *Des Erreurs et de la Verite*, must therefore be considered as a classical book of these opinions. We know that it originated in the Loge des Chev. Bienfaisants at Lyons. We know that this lodge stood, as it were, at the head of French Freemasonry and that the fictitious order of Masonic Knights Templar was formed in this Lodge and was considered as the model of all the rest of this mimic chivalry. They proceeded so far in this mummery, as even to have the clerical tonsure. The Duke of Orleans, his son, the Elector of Bavaria and some other German princes did not scruple at this mummery in their own persons. In all the Lodges of Reception, the Brother Orator never failed to declaim on the topics of superstition, blind to the exhibition he was then making, or indifferent to the vile hypocrisy of it. We have in the lists of orators and office-bearers many names of persons who have had an opportunity at last of proclaiming their sentiments in public. Lequinio, author of the most profligate b... ever disgraced a press, the *Prejuges vaincus per la Raison*, was Warden ... Lodge *Compacte Sociale*."—*Robison's Proofs of a Conspiracy*, page 44.

widows, helpless orphans and the Christian[107] religion.

All this I most solemnly and sincerely promise and vow, with a firm and steadfast resolution to keep and perform the same, binding myself under no less penalty[108] than that of having my head smote off and placed on the highest spire in Christendom, should I ever willfully or knowingly violate any part of this solemn obligation of a Knight Templar, so help me God and keep me steadfast to keep and perform the same.

Prelate—Arise!

Prelate—Pilgrim, by thy sandals, scrip and staff I judge thee to be a child of Humility. Charity and hospitality are the grand characteristics of this valiant and magnanimous order. In the character of a knight you are bound to give alms to poor and weary pilgrims, traveling from afar; to succor the needy, clothe the naked, feed the hungry, and bind up the wounds of the afflicted. We here wage war against the enemies of innocent maidens, destitute widows, helpless orphans and the Christian religion. If thou art desirous of enlisting in this noble and glorious warfare, lay aside thy

---

NOTE 107.—"The Mason Lodges in France [where Templarism was born] were the hot-beds, where the seeds were sown and tenderly reared, of all the pernicious doctrines which soon after choked every moral or religious cultivation, and have made the society worse than a waste—have made it a noisome marsh of human corruption, filled with every rank and poisonous weed."—*Robison's Proofs of a Conspiracy*, page 30.

NOTE 108.—"It were ... a Commandery to sustain a charge and then refuse to inflict any punishment. —*Myers' Templars' Manual, page 88.*

Pilgrim warrior.

staff and take up the sword, fighting thy way manfully and with valor running thy course. [He takes the sword and buckler.] And may the Almighty who is a strong tower of defense to all those who put their trust and confidence in him, be now and forever thy strength and thy salvation.

Prelate (continuing)—Pilgrim, having now taken up the sword we expect that you will make a public declaration of the cause in which you wield it. Do as I do and repeat after me, "I will wield my sword (flourishes sword over his head) in the defense of innocent maidens, (sword flourish) destitute widows, (flourish) helpless orphans (flourish) and the Christian religion (another flourish).

Prelate (continuing)—Pilgrim, placing confidence in this thy profession, Sir Knight our Senior Warden will invest you with the Pilgrim Warrior's pass and under his direction, as a trial of your courage and constancy, we assign to you four years' warfare, and may success and victory attend you. Senior Warden instructs the candidate in giving the Pilgrim Warrior's pass on page 186.]

Senior Warden—Pilgrim, follow me, do as I do and repeat after me: I will wield my sword, etc. [same as before, swinging their swords in same manner, when they pass to the First Guard.]

First Guard—Who comes here?

Senior Warden—A pilgrim warrior, traveling from afar, seeking the accomplishment of valorous deeds to ennoble his name.

INITIATION.

First Guard—Whither bound?
Senior Warden—To the asylum.[109]
First Guard—How do you expect to gain admission?
Senior Warden—By the Pilgrim Warrior's pass.
First Guard—Advance and give it: (Given same as on page 186.)
Second Guard—Who comes here?
Senior Warden—A pilgrim warrior traveling from afar, seeking the accomplishment of valorous deeds to ennoble his name.
Second Guard—Whither bound?
Senior Warden—To the asylum.
Second Guard—How do you expect to gain admission?
Senior Warden—By the Pilgrim Warrior's pass.
Second Guard—Advance and give it. (He gives it and passes on.)
Third Guard—Who comes here?
Senior Warden—A pilgrim warrior, etc.
Third Guard—Whither bound?
Senior Warden—To the asylum.
Third Guard—How do you expect to gain admission?
Senior Warden—By the Pilgrim Warrior's pass.
Third Guard—Advance and give it. (He gives it and passes on.)
Senior Warden (at asylum door, twelve raps.)
Warder—Eminent Commander, there is an alarm.
Eminent Commander—Ascertain the cause.
Warder—Who comes here?
Senior Warden—A pilgrim warrior, who having per-

NOTE 109.—"The inner portion of a Commandery of Knights Templar is termed the asylum. It is the apartment in which the final ceremonies of an initiation are performed. The idea of an asylum is evidently borrowed from that of cities of refuge under the Mosaic Law."—*Morris' Dic. art. Asylum.*

formed three long years of warfare now solicits the remission of the remaining year, and craves the honors and awards that await the valiant Templar.

Warder—What security can he offer that he is no impostor?

Senior Warden—The commendations of your Senior Warden, who recommends to the Eminent Commander a remission of the remaining year.

Warder—By what further right or benefit does he expect to gain admission?

Senior Warden—By the Pilgrim Warrior's pass.

Warder—Has he that pass?

Senior Warden—He has.

Warder—Advance and communicate it. (He gives it.)

Warder—You will wait with courage and constancy until the pleasure of the Eminent Commander i made known. [Same dialogue between Warder and Eminent Commander follows.]

Eminent Commander—Let him enter the asylum.

Warder (to Senior Warden)—Let him enter the asylum. (Senior Warden and candidate approach in front of Eminent Commander.)

Eminent Commander—Pilgrim, having now gained admission within our asylum, what profession have you to make in testimony of your fitness to be received a knight among our number?

Senior Warden (for candidate)—I now declare in all truth and soberness that I hold no enmity or ill-will against a soul on earth that I would not cheerfully reconcile, should I find in turn a corresponding disposition.

Eminent Commander—Pilgrim, the sentiments you utter are worthy of the cause in which you are engaged,

INITIATION.   215

but we require still stronger proofs of your faithfulness. The proofs that we demand are that you participate with us in five libations."¹⁰ The elements of these libations are four of them wine and water; the fifth pure wine; this being accomplished we will receive and rank you a knight among our number. Have you any repugnance to participate in these libations?

Senior Warden—We are willing to conform to all the established usages and customs of the order.

Eminent Commander—Advance to the base of the triangle and do as I do and repeat after me.

First Libation—To the memory of our ancient Grand Master, Solomon, King of Israel. (Both take a wineglass of wine and water from the table, drink it and then give the drinking sign, by drawing glass across throat.)

Second Libation—To the memory of our ancient Grand Master, Hiram, King of Tyre. (Both drink and give sign.)

Third Libation—To the memory of our ancient operative Grand Master, Hiram Abif, the widow's son, who lost his life in the defense of his integrity. (Both drink again and give sign.)

Eminent Commander—Pilgrim, these libations in honor of the illustrious Grand Masters of Ancient Craft Masonry are taken in acknowledgement of our connection with, and veneration for, that ancient and honorable institution; but the order to which you

---

NOTE 110.—"LIBATION.—The libation was a very ancient ceremony, and among the Greeks and Romans, constituted an essential part of every sacrifice. The material of the libation differed according to the different deities in honor of whom they were made, but wine was the most usual. Libations are still used in some of the higher degrees of Masonry."—*Mackey's Lexicon, Art. Libation.*

now seek to unite, is founded upon the Christian''' religion and the practice of the Christian virtues;''² you will therefore attend to a lesson from the holy evangelist. (Prelate reads.)

FIRST "LESSON FROM THE HOLY EVANGELIST.

"Then one of the twelve, called Judas Iscariot, went unto the chief priests and said unto them, What will ye give me, and I will deliver him unto you? And they covenanted with him for thirty pieces of silver. And from that time he sought opportunity to betray him. Now the first day of the feast of unleavened bread, the disciples came to Jesus, saying unto him, Where wilt thou that we prepare for thee to eat the passover? And he said, Go into the city to such a man and say unto him, The Master saith, My time is at hand; I will keep the passover at thy house with my disciples. And the disciples did as Jesus had appointed them; and they made ready the passover. Now when the even was come, he sat down with the twelve. And as they did eat, he said, Verily I say unto you, that one of you shall betray me. And they were exceeding sorrowful, and began every one of them to say unto him, Lord, is it I? And he answered and said, He that dippeth his hand with me in the dish, the same shall betray me. The Son of man goeth, as it is written of him; but wo unto that man by whom the Son of man is

---

NOTE 111.—"The rule of St. Bernard, which had been adopted for their government, prescribed for them a dress, consisting of a white mantle, 'that those' as the rule expressed it, 'who have cast behind them a dark life, may know that they are to commend themselves to their Creator by a pure and white life.' To this Pope Eugenius, some years afterward, added a r l cross as a symbol of martyrdom."—*Mackey's Lexicon., Art. Knight Templar.*

NOTE 112.—"In 1128, they received a rule or system of regulations from the Pope, which had been drawn expressly for them by St. Bernard."—*Mackey's Lexicon, Art. Knight Templar.*

betrayed! It had been good for that man if he had not been born. Then Judas, which betrayed him, answered and said, Master, is it I? He said unto him, Thou hast said.—Matt. 26: 14-25."—*Simons' Book of the Commandery, page 32.*

Eminent Commander—Pilgrim, the twelve tapers you here observe burning around this triangle correspond in number to the apostles of our Saviour while on earth, one of whom fell by transgression and betrayed his Lord and Master; and, as a constant admonition for you to pursue the paths of truth, virtue and brotherly love and a perpetual memorial of the apostasy of Judas Iscariot,"[1] you are required by the rules of our order to extinguish one of these tapers; and let it teach you this important lesson, that he who would violate his vow or betray his trust is worthy of no better fate than that which Judas suffered. [Candidate extinguishes one taper, when the Generalissimo and Captain General uncover the human skull resting on the Bible in the center of the table on a coffin.]

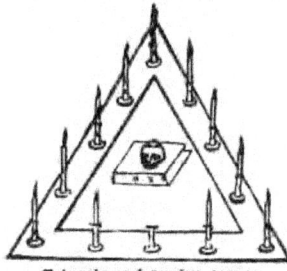
Triangle and twelve tapers.

Eminent Commander—Pilgrim, you here behold an emblem of mortality upheld by Divinity. a human skull resting on the Holy Scriptures, which teaches us that amidst all the trials and vicissitudes of life that we are destined to endure while traveling through this vale of tears, a firm reliance on Divine Providence can

---

NOTE 118.—"The defection of Judas Iscariot is marked as the infamous model of treachery, through all ages.—*Morris' Dict., Art. Jesus Christ.*

alone insure us that comfort and consolation in the gloomy hour of dissolution which the world can neither give nor take away. You will again attend to a lesson from the holy evangelist. (Prelate reads.)

SECOND "LESSON FROM THE HOLY EVANGELIST.

"Then cometh Jesus with them unto a place called Gethsemane, and saith unto the disciples Sit ye here, while I go and pray yonder. And he took with him Peter and the two sons of Zebedee, and began to be sorrowful and very heavy. Then saith he unto them, My soul is exceeding sorrowful, even unto death; tarry ye here, and watch with me. And he went a little farther, and fell on his face, and prayed, saying, O my Father, if it be possible, let this cup pass from me; nevertheless, not as I will, but as thou wilt. And he cometh unto the disciples, and findeth them asleep, and saith unto Peter, What! could ye not watch with me one hour! Watch and pray, that ye enter not into temptation; the spirit indeed is willing, but the flesh is weak. He went away again the second time, and prayed, saying, O my Father, if this cup may not pass away from me, except I drink it, thy will be done. And he came and found them asleep again for their eyes were heavy. And he left them, and went away again, and prayed the third time, saying the same words. Then cometh he unto his disciples, and saith unto them, Sleep on now, and take your rest; behold the hour is at hand, and the Son of man is betrayed into the hands of sinners. Rise, let us be going; behold, he is at hand that doth betray me. And while he yet spake, lo! Judas, one of the twelve, came, and with him a great multitude, with swords and staves, from the chief priests and elders of the people. Now he that betrayed him, gave them a sign, saying, Whomsoever I shall kiss, that same is he: hold him fast. And forthwith he came to Jesus, and said, Hail, Master; and kissed him.—Matt. 26: 36-50."—*Simons Book of the Commandery, page 33.*

Eminent Commander (taking skull in his hands)— How striking is this emblem of mortality, once animated like us, but now has ceased to act and think. Its vital energies are extinct, and all the powers of life have ceased their operations. To such an end pilgrim and Sir Knight, are we all hastening. Then let us improve the short space allotted to us that when our weak and frail bodies like this memento shall be reduced to sepulchral dust and ashes, our disembodied spirits may soar aloft to that blessed region where dwells light and life eternal. You will again attend to a lesson. (Prelate reads.)

THIRD "LESSON FROM THE HOLY EVANGELIST.

"When Pilate saw that he could prevail nothing, but that rather a tumult was made, he took water, and washed his hands before the multitude, saying, I am innocent of the blood of this just person; see ye to it. Then answered all the people, and said, His blood be on us and on our children. Then released he Barabbas unto them; and when he had scourged Jesus, he delivered him to be crucified. Then the soldiers of the governor took Jesus into the common hall, and gathered unto him the whole band of soldiers. And they stripped him, and put on him a scarlet robe. And when they had platted a crown of thorns they put it upon his head, and a reed in his right hand; and they bowed the knee before him, and mocked him, saying, Hail, king of the Jews! And they spit upon him, and took the reed and smote him on the head. And after that they had mocked him, they took the robe off from him, and put his own raiment on him, and led him away to crucify him. And as they came out, they found a man of Cyrene, Simon by name: him they compelled to bear his cross. And when they were come unto a place called Golgotha, that is to say. A place of a skull, they gave him vinegar to drink, mingled with gall; and when he had tasted thereof, he would not drink. And they crucified him and parted his garments, casting lots; that it might be fulfilled which was spoken by the prophet; They parted my garments among them, and upon my vesture did they cast lots. And sitting down, they watched him there; and set up over his head his accusation, written, THIS IS JESUS THE KING OF THE JEWS.—Matt. 27: 24-37."—*Simons' Book of the Commandery, page 35.*

Eminent Commander—Pilgrim, we will now participate in the fourth libation, to the memory of Simon of Cyrene, who was compelled to bear the cross. (Both drink and give the drinking sign.)

Eminent Commander—Pilgrim, before you can be permitted to participate in the fifth libation, I shall enjoin upon you one years' penance, as a trial of your faith and humility, which you will perform under the direction of our Senior and Junior Wardens, with this emblem of humility a human skull, in one hand, and this emblem of faith, a lighted taper, in the other; take them and travel to the sepulchre of our Saviour. (Accompanied by the Wardens he marches around awhile, and is finally conducted to the door of a small, dark

INITIATION. 231

room, when Senior Warden gives twelve stamps on floor.)

Guard—Who comes here?

Senior Warden—A pilgrim penitent, who craves permission here awhile to rest and offer up his devotions.

Guard—How does he expect to gain admission?

Senior Warden—By the benefit of the Pilgrim Penitent's pass.

Guard—Has he that pass?

Senior Warden—He has it not; I have it for him.

Guard—Advance and communicate it. (It is given, same as Pilgrim Warrior's pass on page 186, and under the swords the word GOLGOTHA, is whispered.)

Guard—You have my permission to enter the Sepulchre. [Candidate kneels as directed in the entrance and the Senior Warden reads.]

FOURTH "LESSON FROM THE HOLY EVANGELIST.

"Although it is appointed unto all men once to die, yet the Scriptures inform us that the Saviour of the world arose from the dead, and ascended into heaven; there forever he is seated on the throne of majesty on high; and they also assure us, that all who have received him for their righteousness, and put their trust in him, shall rise to life everlasting.

"In the end of the Sabbath, as it began to dawn, toward the first day of the week, came Mary Magdalene and the other Mary, to see the sepulchre. And behold there was a great earthquake; for the angel of the Lord descended from heaven, and came and rolled back the stone from the door, and sat upon it. His countenance was like lightning, and his raiment white as snow: and for fear of him the keepers did shake, and become as dead men. And the angel answered and said unto the women, Fear not ye: for I know that ye seek Jesus, which was crucified. He is not here: for he is risen, as he said. Come, see the place where the Lord lay: and go quickly, and tell his disciples that he is risen from the dead; and behold he goeth before you into Galilee; there shall ye see him: lo! I have told you. And they departed quickly from the sepulchre, with fear and great joy, and did run to bring his disciples word.

And as they went to tell his disciples, behold Jesus met them, saying, All hail. And they came and held him by the feet, and worshiped him.

"And he led them out as far as to Bethany; and he lifted up his hands and blessed them. And it came to pass, while he blessed them, he was parted from them and carried up into heaven. And they worshiped him and returned to Jerusalem with great joy."—*Simons' Book of the Commandery, page 36.*

[Candidate is now bid to arise, is conducted near the table, and the room being darkened, he beholds at some distance a brilliantly lighted transparency, representing the resurrection and ascension of Christ, when the knights sing the following:]

ODE.

"Music—*Old Hundred.*

"The rising God forsakes the tomb!
Up to his Father's court he flies;
Cherubic legions guard him home,
And shout him welcome to the skies.

"Break off your tears, ye saints, and tell
How high our Great Deliv'rer reigns;
Sing how he spoil'd the hosts of hell,
And led the monster, Death, in chains.

"Say live forever, wondrous King,
Born to redeem, and strong to save;
Then ask the tyrant, 'Where's thy sting?
And where's thy vict'ry, boasting grave?'"

—*Simons' Book of the Commandery, page 39.*

Prelate—Pilgrim, the scene before you represents the conclusion of the hallowed sacrifice offered by the Redeemer of the world to propitiate the anger of an offended Deity. This sacred volume informs us that our Saviour after having suffered the pains of death descended into the place of departed spirits; that on the third day he burst the bands of death, triumphed over the grave, and in due time ascended with transcendent majesty to heaven, where he now sits on the right hand of our Heavenly Father, a Mediator and Intercessor for all those who put their faith in him. I will now invest you with an emblem of that faith. (Suspends a black cross from his neck.) It is also an emblem of our order, which you will wear as a constant memorial for you to imitate the virtues of that immaculate Jesus[114] who died that you may live.

Pilgrim, the scenes through which you are now passing are calculated to deeply impress the mind, and I hope will have a happy and lasting effect upon your faith, life and conduct.

You were first, as a trial of your patience and perseverance, enjoined to perform seven years' pilgrimage. It represented to you the great pilgrimage of life through which we are all passing. We are all weary pilgrims, anxiously looking forward toward that asylum where we shall rest from our labors and be at peace forever.

You were next, as a trial of your courage and constancy, enjoined to perform four years' warfare. It represented to you the constant warfare with the lying

---

NOTE 114.—"JESUS CHRIST.—The birth, life, death, resurrection and ascension of this exalted personage constitute the sublime lessons of the Knights Templar order, which is emphatically the Christian branch of Masonry. The passage from the Gospels that describe his Passion are read during the ceremonies."—*Morris Dict., Art. Jesus Christ.*

vanities and deceits of this wicked world, in which it is necessary for us always to be engaged.

You are now, as a trial of your faith and humility, performing a penance. Of this our Lord and Saviour has left us a bright example; for although he was the eternal Son of God, he humbled himself to be born of a woman, to endure the pains and afflictions incident to human nature, and finally to suffer a cruel and ignominious death upon the cross.

It is also a trial of that faith which will conduct you safely over the dark gulf of everlasting death and land your enfranchised spirit in the peaceful abode of the blessed.

Pilgrim, keep ever in your memory this awful truth: You know not how soon you may be called to render an account to that Supreme Judge from whom not even the most minute act of your life is hidden. For although you now stand erect in all the pride of beauty and streng h of manhood, in a few short hours you may become a pale and lifeless corpse. This moment even, while I yet speak, the angel of death may receive the fatal mandate to strike you from the roll of existence, and the friends who now surround you be called upon to perform the last sad duty of laying you in the ground a banquet for worms, and this fair body become as the miserable relic you now hold in your hand. [He ho ds a skull in one hand, a taper in the other.]

Man that is born of a woman is of few days and full of sorrow, he cometh up as a flower and is cut down, He fleeth also as a shadow and continueth not. In the midst of life we are in death; of whom may we seek for succor, but of thee, O God, who for our sins art most justly displeased.

INITIATION. 225

I heard a voice from heaven saying unto me write, "from henceforth blessed are the dead who die in the Lord, even so saith the Spirit, for they rest from their labors." Be ye also ready, and rest assured that a firm faith in the truths therein revealed will afford you comfort and consolation in the gloomy hour of dissolution, and insure to you eternal and immortal happiness in the world to come. Amen and amen. [The room is lighted up again and the Wardens conduct him to the asylum curtain, or door, when Senior Warden stamps on floor twelve times.]

Warder—Eminent Commander, there is an alarm.

Eminent Commander—Ascertain the cause.

Warder—Who comes here? Who dares approach our sacred asylum and disturb our meditations?

Senior Warden—A pilgrim penitent, who, having performed his allotted year of penance, now seeks to participate in the fifth libation and thereby seal his faith.

Warder—What security does he offer that he is no impostor?

Senior Warden—The commendations of two valiant and magnanimous knights, our Senior and Junior Wardens.

Warder—By what further right or benefit does he expect to gain admission within our asylum.[115]

Senior Warden—By the benefit of the Pilgrim Penitent's pass.

Warder—Has he that?

Senior Warden—He has it not, but I have it for him.

Note 115.—"Asylum.—During the session of a Commandery of Knights Templar, a part of the room is called the asylum; the word has hence been adopted, by the figure synecdoche, to signify the place of meeting of a Commandery."—**Mackey's Lexicon**, Art., Asylum.

Warder—Advance and give it.

Senior Warden—GOLGOTHA. (Given same as explained page 221.)

Warder—You will wait with faith and humility until the pleasure of the Eminent Commander is made known.

Warder (at his post)—Eminent Commander, the alarm is caused by a pilgrim penitent, who, having performed his allotted year of penitence, now seeks to participate in the fifth libation and thereby seal his faith.

Eminent Commander—What security does he offer that he is no impostor?

Warder—The commendations of two valiant and magnanimous knights, our Senior and Junior Wardens.

Eminent Commander—By what further right or benefit does he expect to gain admission within our asylum?

Warder—By the benefit of the Pilgrim Penitent's pass.

Eminent Commander—Has he that?

Warder—He has it not, but his conductor has it for him.

Eminent Commander—Advance and give it.

Warder—GOLGOTHA. (Given same as before.)

Eminent Commander—Let him enter. (Warder communicates the answer and they enter.)

Eminent Commander—Who have you there in charge, Sir Knights?

Senior Warden—A pilgrim penitent, who, having performed his alloted year of penance, now seeks to participate in the fifth libation and thereby seal his faith.

Eminent Commander—Pilgrim, your *year* of penance is indeed ended, but your *term* of penance is not ended,

INITIATION. 227

neither can it end until this mortal shall have put on immortality; for all men have erred, and error needs repentance. In granting your request we can only offer you coarse diet, rough habit and severe duties. If on these conditions you are still desirous of enlisting under our banners, you will advance and kneel at the base of the triangle. (He kneels as indicated.)

Eminent Commander (continuing)—Pilgrim, the fifth libation is taken in the most solemn and impressive manner. We cannot too often be reminded that we are born to die, and the fifth libation is an emblem of that bitter cup of death of which we must all, sooner or later, partake, and from which the Saviour of the world was not exempt.

It is taken in the most solemn manner, in pure wine and from this cup. (Shows him a human skull into which he pours the wine.) To show you that we practice no imposition, I now give you this pledge. (Drinks, and after drinking turns the skull bottom up to show it is empty, when he pours in more wine and hands skull to candidate. In some Commanderies the Eminent Commander here adds: "Have you any repugnance to participate in the fifth libation?" when Senior Warden answers for candidate: "I am willing to conform to the requirements of the order.")

FIFTH LIBATION.

Eminent Commander (continuing)—Repeat after me. This pure wine I now take in testimony of my belief in the mortality of the body and the immortality of the soul; and as the sins of the whole world were once visited upon the head of our Saviour, so may all the sins of the person whose skull this once was, in

KNIGHTS TEMPLAR DEGREE.

addition to my own, be heaped upon my head, and may this libation appear in judgment against me, both here and hereafter, should I ever knowingly or willfully violate this my most solemn vow of a Knight Templar; so help me God and keep me steadfast. You will partake of the wine. (Candidate drinks the wine from the skull.)

Enforcing Fifth Libation.

Eminent Commander—Attention,, Sir Knights! (Knights form around candidate.) Handle swords!

Eminent Commander—Draw swords!

Eminent Commander—Charge! (See cut.)

Eminent Commander—Pilgrim, you here behold the swords of your companions presented to your unprotected breast, ever ready to avenge any wilful violation of the vows you have just taken.

Eminent Commander—Form cross! (Swords are crossed over candidate's head.)

Eminent Commander (continuing)—But while you remain faithful to these vows I give you the mystic assurance of this glittering arch of steel that these with thousands of others will leap from their scabbards in the defense of your cause.

Eminent Commander—Attention, Sir Knights! Return swords!

Eminent Commander—To your posts—march!

Eminent Commander—Pilgrim, this is called the sealed libation, and an agreement so made, or obligation entered into, is considered by Knight Templars as more sacred and binding than any others. You will again attend to a lesson. (Prelate reads.)

FIFTH "LESSON FROM THE HOLY EVANGELIST.

"And in those days Peter stood up in the midst of the disciples, and said, (the number of the names together were about an hundred and twenty,) Men and brethren, this Scripture must needs have been fulfilled which the Holy Ghost by the mouth of David spake before concerning Judas, which was guide to them that took Jesus. For he was numbered with us, and had obtained part of this ministry. Now, this man purchased a field with the reward of iniquity; and falling headlong, he burst asunder in the midst, and all his bowels gushed out. And it was known unto all the dwellers at Jerusalem; insomuch as that field is called, in their proper tongue, Aceldama, that is to say, The field of blood. For it is written in the book of Psalms, Let his habitation be desolate, and let no man dwell therein; and his bishopric let another take. Wherefore, of these men which have companied with us, all the time that the Lord Jesus went in and out among us, beginning from the baptism of John unto that same day that he was taken up from us, must one be ordained to be a witness with us of his resurrection. And they appointed two, Joseph, called Barsabas, who was surnamed Justus, and Matthias. And they prayed, and said, Thou, Lord. which knowest the hearts of all men, show whether of these two thou hast chosen, that he may take part of this ministry and apostleship, from which Judas by transgression fell, that he might go to his own place. And they gave forth their lots; and the lot fell upon Matthias; and he was numbered with the eleven apostles.—Acts 1:15-26."—*Simons' Book of the Commandery, page 39.*

Generalissimo—Eminent Commander, I see by the extinguished taper on our triangle there is a vacancy in our asylum; I move it be filled by some one who has passed through our solemn ceremonies.

Eminent Commander—We will fill it by lot. Let the lot be cast. (They cast lots and candidate is chosen.)

Eminent Commander—Pilgrim, the lot has fallen upon you.[116] In token of your acceptance of this high honor, you will re-light the extinguished taper, (candidate lights it; three raps, all rise), and may the Lord lift upon you the light of his reconciled countenance and keep you from falling.

Eminent Commander (continuing)—You will now kneel. By virtue of the high power and authority in me vested, as the representative[117] of Hugh de Payens and Geoffery de St. Omer, I do now dub and create you,

---

Note 116.—"The vacancy produced by the apostasy and death of Judas Iscariot being now filled, a hearty welcome is extended to the bosom of a society whose principles are designed to defend and protect the true and faithful among them."—**Sickels' Moniter, Part 4, page 40.**

Note 117.—"The Preceptor then said: 'In the name of God, and of Mary our dear Lady, and in the name of St. Peter of Rome, and of our father the Pope, and in the name of all the brethren of the Temple we receive you to all the good works of the order."—**Mackey's Lexicon, Art. Knight Templar.**

INITIATION.   231

———, a knight[118] of this most valiant[119] and magnanimous order of Knights Templar.[120]

Eminent Commander (continuing)—Arise, Sir Knight! and with this hand (reaches out his hand) receive a hearty welcome into the bosom of a society ever ready to assist, protect and defend you. I now

Note 118.—"The Pilgrim Penitent, having performed his term of penance, is entitled to receive the rewards that await the valiant Templar." —Sickels' Monitor, Part 4, page 39.

Note 119.—"The history of this valiant and magnanimous order is full of interest. Originally established to protect and defend those who came on pilgrimages to the holy shrines, they assumed the name of 'Poor Fellow Soldiers of Christ.' Taking vows of poverty and celibacy, the device upon the great seal of the order was two knights riding upon one horse. Their costume was a white mantle, teaching them to commend themselves to God by a spotless life; to this a red cross was afterward added as an emblem of martyrdom. Their banner, styled "Beauseant," was composed of alternate stripes of black and white, implying that while they were fair and engaging to their friends, they were dark and terrible to their enemies.

"The prosperity of this order was unprecedented. The most eminent warriors and noblemen of Europe entered its ranks. The Knights of the Temple became the bulwark of the Holy Land against the Saracens. France, England and other countries formed associations (Priories) of Templar Knights, each with its own Grand Master and other officers. Such great wealth was accumulated in the treasuries of the order that in the year 1185 its annual income represented a sum equal to thirty millions of dollars. But wealth and prosperity naturally led to licentiousness, neglect of Templar law and in the end destruction. In the year 1307, the Grand Master of the order, Jaques de Molay, was arrested at Paris with sixty of his knights and imprisoned upon charges of idolatry and other crimes. Shortly afterward all the Knights Templar in France were put in prison at Paris. May 12, 1310, fifty-four of them were burnt alive. March 18, 1314, the Grand Master, with three of his most eminent officers, suffered in like manner. The great possessions of the order were now confiscated and the society suppressed, both by the Pope and the leading monarchs of Europe."—Morris' Dict., Art. Templar Knight.

Note 120.—"Since the beginning of the present century, the principal rites created have been the Ancient and Accepted Scottish Rite, the Rite of Misraim and the Rite of Memphis. Regarding some two or three others, however, as worthy of notice, we will mention them:

"1. The order of Modern Templars, constituted the 4th of November, 1804, by virtue of an old constitution, found in the possession of a brother, and according to which the founders afterward pretended to be the legitimate successors of the Knights of the Temple."—Rebold's History of Freemasonry, page 226.

with much pleasure present you with the sword.[121] In the hands of a valiant and magnanimous knight it is endowed with the most excellent qualities; its hilt with justice impartial; its blade with fortitude undaunted and its point with mercy, and it teaches us this important lesson: That we should be well assured of the justice of the cause in which we draw our swords. Being thus assured, we should persevere with the most undaunted fortitude, until we have subdued our enemies, then consider them as such no longer, but extend to them the most noble attribute of Deity, mercy. Take it and wield it valiantly in the cause of knighthood.

Eminent Commander—I will now invest you with the due-guard of a Knight Templar. (Gives it as on page 191.) And this is the grand hailing sign:

KNIGHT TEMPLAR GRAND HAILING SIGN.

Right foot crossed[122] over the left as shown in cut. Arms and hands extended and head inclined to the right. Then say, "*In hoc signo vinces,*" the motto of the order. It is pretended that Christ hung on the cross in this manner.

K. T. Grand Hailing Sign.

Note 121.—"The sword, in the hands of a valiant and magnanimous knight, is endowed with the sublime qualities of Justice, Fortitude and Mercy."—Sickels' Monitor, Part 4, page 40.

Note 122.—"Cross Legged.—It was an invariable custom in the Middle Ages, in laying out the body of a Knight Templar after death, to cross one leg over the other; and in all the monuments of these knights now remaining in the various churches of Europe, there will always be found an image of the person buried sculptured on the stone, lying on a bier in this cross-legged position. Templars of the present day will readily connect this posture with an appropriate portion of the degree as now conferred. When in the 6th century a portion of the Knights Templar of Scotland united themselves with a Masonic lodge at Stirling they were commonly known by the name of the 'Cross-legged Masons.' It was I presume given in allusion to this funeral posture of the Templars, and a 'Cross-legged Mason' would, therefore, be synonymous with a Masonic Knight Templar"—Mackey's Lexicon, Art. Cross-Legged.

INITIATION.   233

KNIGHTS TEMPLAR GRIP.

Knights Templar Grip.

A. interlaces the fingers of his right hand with left hand of B. and his left hand with right hand of B., arms of each being crossed as shown in cut; then say "IMMANUEL," which is the immaculate word.

Eminent Commander (handing him a baldric or K. T. sash)—Wear this baldric, the ensign of our order; (hands him a metal star) and this star the emblem of the reward which the great Captain of our Salvation has promised to those who conquer in his name. Wear his emblem of himself, he being the bright morning star whose rising brought health and salvation to mankind and light to them who sat in darkness and the shadow of death. Bear this ever in mind and continue his faithful soldier until death.

[Sometimes a long history of the degree now follows, called a lecture, and it may be in narrative form as in some previous degrees, or in catechetical or dialogue form.]

CHAPTER XX.

Twelfth, or Knights Templar Degree.
LECTURE, OR EXAMINATION.

Eminent Commander—Are you a Knight Templar?[123]

Candidate—That is my title.

Eminent Commander—Where were you created a Knights Templar?

Candidate—In a just and lawful Commandery of Knights Templar.

Eminent Commander—What number compose such a Commandery?

Candidate—There is an indispensable number and a constitutional number.

Eminent Commander—What is the indispensable number?

Candidate—Three.

Eminent Commander—Under what circumstances may three Knights Templar open and form a Commandery?

Candidate—Three Knights Templar, hailing from three different Commanderies, may, under the sanction

---

Note 123.—"We have every reason for believing that the knights who visited Palestine organized their chivalric system upon the model of the Masonic institutions which existed there, and into which we may also presume, that most of them were admitted. Upon this subject we have something more than mere conjecture to direct us, for we are informed by Adler, who wrote an account of the Association of Druses on Mount Libanus, that the Knights Templar were actually members of the Syriac fraternities."—Mackey's Lexicon, Art. Knighthood, Orders of.

of a warrant from some Grand Commandery or from the Grand Encampment of the United States, form and operate a Commandery of Knights Templar for the dispatch of business.

Eminent Commander—What is the constitutional number?

Candidate—Nine, eleven, or more.

Eminent Commander—When composed of eleven, of whom does it consist?

Candidate—The Eminent Commander, Generalissimo, Captain General, Prelate, Senior Warden, Junior Warden, Treasurer, Recorder, Standard Bearer, Sword Bearer and Warder.

[The catechism in reference to position of each officer in the Commandery and his duties, as on pages 193 to 196, is next in order, but is often omitted in the "lecture."]

Eminent Commander—What were the preparatory circumstances attending your reception into this most valiant and magnanimous order?

Candidate—I was conducted to the Chamber of Reflection, where I was left in silence and solitude to reflect upon three questions which were left me in writing.

Eminent Commander—What were your answers?

Candidate—They were satisfactory to the Eminent Commander, but as a trial of my patience and perseverance he enjoined upon me the performance of seven years of pilgrimage clothed in pilgrim's weeds.

Eminent Commander—What followed?

Candidate—I was then invested with sandals, staff and scrip and commenced my tour of pilgrimage, but soon was accosted by a guard who demanded of me: "Who comes here?"

Eminent Commander—Your answer?

Candidate—A weary pilgrim, traveling from afar to join with those who oft have gone before and offer his devotions at the holy shrine."

Eminent Commander—What said the guard?

Candidate—"Pilgrim, I greet thee. Silver and gold have I none; but such as I have, give I unto thee."

Eminent Commander—What followed?

Candidate—After having participated in the refreshments the guard said: "Pilgrim, hearken now to a lesson to cheer thee on thy way and assure thee of success."

Eminent Commander—What followed?

Candidate—He then read the following lesson: "Let the brother of low degree rejoice in that he is exalted. Come unto Me, all ye that are weary and heavy laden, and I will give you rest.

"Christ also suffered for us, leaving us an example that we should follow his steps. For ye were as sheep going astray; but are now returned unto the Shepherd and Bishop of your souls.

"Let, therefore, brotherly love continue."

Eminent Commander—What followed?

Candidate—He then took me by the hand and said, "Farewell, brother. God speed thee."

Eminent Commander—What followed?

Candidate—I still pursued my pilgrimage, but was often accosted by guards from whom I received the same friendly treatment as from the first.

Eminent Commander—Where did your pilgrimage end?

Candidate—At the door of the asylum, where, after giving the alarm by twelve knocks, the Warder appeared and demanded, "Who comes here?"

Eminent Commander—Your answer?

Candidate—"A poor and weary pilgrim, traveling from afar, who, having performed three long years of pilgrimage, now desires, if it so please the Eminent Commander, to dedicate the four remaining years to deeds of more exalted usefulness, and if found worthy his strong desire is to be admitted among those valiant knights whose well earned fame has spread both far and wide for deeds of charity and pure beneficence."

Eminent Commander—What were you then asked?

Candidate—"What security can you offer that you are no impostor?"

Eminent Commander—Your answer?

Candidate—"The commendation of your Junior Warden, who recommends to the Eminent Commander a remission of the four remaining years."

Eminent Commander—What followed?

Candidate—The Eminent Commander then addressed the Most Excellent Prelate: "This being the case, Sir Knight Prelate, you will conduct this weary pilgrim to the holy altar, where, after he has taken upon himself the solemn vow of the order, invest him with sword and buckler so that as a pilgrim warrior he may perform four years' warfare as a trial of his constancy and courage."

Eminent Commander—What followed?

Candidate—An avenue was formed and I was conducted to the holy altar by the Most Excellent Prelate, where in due form I took upon me the vow of a Knight Templar.

Eminent Commander—What was that due form?

Candidate—Kneeling on both knees upon cross

swords, my body erect, my hands resting upon the Holy Bible, square, compass, and cross swords lying thereon, in which due form I took upon me the solemn vow of a Knight Templar.

Eminent Commander—Repeat it.

Candidate—"I, ———, of my own free will," etc. [See page 208.]

Eminent Commander—What followed?

Candidate—The Most Excellent Prelate directed me to arise and thus addressed me: "Pilgrim, by thy sandals, scrip and staff I judge thee to be a child of humility. Charity and hospitality are the grand characteristics of this valiant and magnanimous order. In the character of a knight you are bound to give alms to poor and weary pilgrims traveling from afar, to succor the needy, clothe the naked, feed the hungry and bind up the wounds of the afflicted.

"We here wage war against the enemies of innocent maidens, destitute widows, helpless orphans and the Christian religion; if thou art desirous of enlisting in this noble and glorious warfare, lay aside thy staff and take up the sword, fighting thy way manfully and with valor running thy course, and may the Almighty, who is a strong tower of defense to all those who put their trust and confidence in him, be now and forever thy strength and thy salvation."

Eminent Commander—What followed?

Candidate—Having laid aside my staff and taken up the sword, the Most Excellent Prelate continued: "Pilgrim, having now taken up the sword, we expect that you will make a public declaration of the cause in which you wield it."

Eminent Commander—Your answer?

Candidate—"I will wield my sword in defense of innocent maidens, destitute widows, helpless orphans and the Christian religion."

Eminent Commander—What was the Prelate's reply?

Candidate—"With confidence in this thy profession, Sir Knight our Senior Warden will invest you with the Pilgrim Warrior's pass, and under his direction, as a trial of your courage and constancy, we assign to you four years' warfare; and may success and victory attend you."

Eminent Commander—What followed?

Candidate—I then commenced my tour of warfare and made professions of the cause in which I would wield my sword.

Eminent Commander—Where did your tour of warfare end?

Candidate—At the door of the asylum, where, on giving the alarm by twelve knocks, the Warder appeared and demanded, "Who comes here?"

Eminent Commander—Your answer?

Candidate—"A pilgrim warrior, who, having performed three long years of warfare, now solicits the remission of the remaining year and craves the honors and awards that await the valiant Templar."

Eminent Commander—What was then demanded of you?

Candidate—"What security can you offer that you are no impostor?"

Eminent Commander—Your answer?

Candidate—"The commendations of your Senior Warden, who recommends to the Eminent Commander a remission of the remaining year."

Eminent Commander—What was then demanded?

Candidate—"By what further right or benefit do you expect to gain admission?"

Eminent Commander—Your answer?

Candidate—"By the Pilgrim Warrior's pass."

Eminent Commander—Give it. (It is given as on page 186.)

Eminent Commander—What was then said to you?

Candidate—I was directed to wait with courage and constancy until the pleasure of the Eminent Commander was made known.

Eminent Commander—What answer was returned?

Candidate—"Let him enter the asylum."

Eminent Commander—What did the Eminent Commander then observe?

Candidate—"Pilgrim, having now gained admission within our asylum, what profession have you to make in testimony of your fitness to be received a knight among our number?"

Eminent Commander—Your answer?

Candidate—"I now declare in all truth and soberness that I hold no enmity or ill-will against a soul on earth that I would not cheerfully reconcile, should I find in him a corresponding disposition."

Eminent Commander—What was the Eminent Commander's reply?

Candidate "Pilgrim, the sentiments you utter are worthy of the cause in which you are engaged, but we require still stronger proofs of your faithfulness. The proofs that we demand are that you participate with us in five libations. The elements of these libations are four of them wine and water, the fifth, pure wine. This being accomplished we will receive and rank you a knight among our number."

Eminent Commander—What was the first libation?

Candidate—To the memory of our ancient Grand Master, Solomon, King of Israel.

Eminent Commander—What was the second libation.

Candidate—To the memory of our ancient Grand Master, Hiram, King of Tyre.

Eminent Commander—What was the third libation?

Candidate—To the memory of our ancient operative grand Master, Hiram Abif, the widow's son, who lost his life in defense of his integrity.

Eminent Commander—What followed?

Candidate—The Eminent Commander then addressed me: "Pilgrim, these libations in honor of the Illustrious Grand Masters of Ancient Craft Masonry are taken in acknowledgment of our connection with, and veneration for, that ancient and honorable institution; but the order to which you now seek to unite is founded upon the Christian religion and the practice of the Christian virtues; you will therefore attend to a lesson from the Holy Evangelist."

Eminent Commander—What followed?

Candidate—The Most Excellent Prelate then read a lesson relative to the apostasy of Judas Iscariot. (See page 216.)

Eminent Commander—What followed?

Candidate—The Eminent Commander then addressed me: "Pilgrim, the twelve tapers you here observe burning around this triangle correspond in number to the apostles of our Saviour while on earth, one of whom fell by transgression and betrayed his Lord and Master; and, as a constant admonition for you to pursue the paths of truth, virtue and brotherly love, and as a perpetual memorial of the apostasy of Judas Iscariot, you are required by the rules of our order to extinguish one of these tapers, and let it teach you this important lesson, that he who would violate his vow or betray his trust is worthy of no better fate than that which Judas suffered."

Eminent Commander—What followed?

Candidate—The relics were uncovered and the Eminent Commander thus addressed me: "Pilgrim, you here behold an emblem of mortality (skull and cross bones) resting on the Holy Scriptures, which teaches us that amidst all the trials and vicissitudes of life that we are destined to endure while traveling through this vale of tears, a firm reliance on Divine Providence can alone assure us that comfort and consolation in the gloomy hour of dissolution, which the world can neither give nor take away."

Eminent Commander—What followed?

Candidate—The Most Excellent Prelate then read a lesson to me with respect to the bitter cup. [See page 218.]

Eminent Commander—What followed?

Candidate—The Eminent Commander took the skull in his hand and pronounced the following soliloquy: "How striking is this emblem of mortality, once animated, like us, but now has ceased to act and think. Its vital energies are extinct, and all the powers of life have ceased their operations. To such an end, pilgrim and Sir Knight, we are all hastening. Then let us improve the short space of time allotted us, that, when our weak and frail bodies, like this memento, shall be reduced to sepulchral dust and ashes, our disembodied spirits may soar aloft to that blessed region where dwell light and life eternal."

Eminent Commander—What followed?

Candidate—The Most Excellent Prelate then read a lesson relative to the crucifixion. [See page 219.]

Eminent Commander—What was the fourth libation?

Candidate—To the memory of Simon of Cyrene, who was compelled to bear the cross.

Eminent Commander—What followed?

Candidate—The Eminent Commander then addressed me: "Pilgrim, before you can be permitted to participate in the fifth libation I shall enjoin upon you one year's penance, as a trial of your faith and humility, which you will perform under the direction of our Senior and Junior Wardens, with this emblem of humility, a human skull, in one hand, and this emblem of faith, a lighted taper, in the other. Take them and travel to the sepulchre of our Saviour."

Eminent Commander—What followed?

Candidate—I then commenced my tour of penance and passed in a humble posture through the sepulchre where the fourth lesson was read by the Senior Warden relative to the resurrection. [See page 221.]

Eminent Commander—Where did your tour of penance end?

Candidate—It has not ended, neither can it end until this mortal shall put on immortality; for all men have erred, and error needs repentance.

Eminent Commander—Were you then permitted to participate in the fifth libation?

Candidate—I was.

Eminent Commander—Where?

Candidate—Within the asylum.

Eminent Commander—How gained you admittance?

Candidate—After having passed my year of penance I returned to the door of the asylum, where, on giving the alarm, the Warder appeared and demanded, "Who comes here?"

Eminent Commander—Your answer?

Candidate—"A pilgrim penitent, who, having performed his alloted year of penance, now seeks to participate in the fifth libation and thereby seal his faith."

Eminent Commander—What was then demanded of you?

Candidate—"What security does he offer that he is no impostor?"

Eminent Commander—Your answer?

Candidate—"The commendations of two valiant and magnanimous knights, our Senior and Junior Wardens."

Eminent Commander—What was then demanded of you?

Candidate—By what further right or benefit I expected to gain admittance within the asylum.

Eminent Commander—Your answer?

Candidate—"By the benefit of the Pilgrim Penitent's pass."

Eminent Commander—Did you give it?

Candidate—I gave it not; my conductor gave it for me.

Eminent Commander—Give it.

Candidate—"GOLGOTHA." (Given as explained, page 221.)

Eminent Commander—What was then said to you?

Candidate—"You will wait with faith and humility until the pleasure of the Eminent Commander is made known."

Eminent Commander—What was the answer of the Eminent Commander?

Candidate—That I should be admitted.

Eminent Commander—What did the Eminent Commander then demand?

Candidate—"Whom have you there in charge, Sir Knights?"

Eminent Commander—What answer was returned?

Candidate—"A pilgrim penitent, who, having performed his allotted year of penance, now seeks to participate in the fifth libation, and thereby seal his faith."

Eminent Commander—What did the Eminent Commander then observe?

Candidate—"Pilgrim, your *year* of penance is indeed ended, but your *term* of penance is not ended, neither can it end until this mortal shall have put on immortality, for all men have erred and error needs repentance. In granting your request we can only offer you coarse diet, rough habit and severe duties. If on these conditions you are still desirous of enlisting under our banners, you will advance and kneel at the base of the triangle."

Eminent Commander—What did the Eminent Commander then observe?

Candidate—"Pilgrim, the fifth libation is taken in the most solemn and impressive manner. We can not too often be reminded that we are born to die, and the fifth libation is an emblem of that bitter cup of death of which we must all sooner or later partake, and from which the Saviour of the world was not exempt. It is taken in the most solemn manner, in pure wine, and from this cup. [As indicated by the sentence in parentheses on page 227, in some Commanderies candidate is asked a question about his willingness to take the fifth libation.]

Eminent Commander—What followed?

Candidate—I then took the cup (a skull) in my hand and repeated after the Eminent Commander the following vow: "This pure wine I now take in testimony of my belief in the mortality of the body and the immortality of the soul; and as the sins of the whole world were once visited upon the head of our Saviour, so may all the sins of the person whose skull this once was, in addition to my own, be heaped upon my head, and may this libation appear in judgment against me, both here and hereafter, should I ever knowingly or wilfully violate this my most solemn vow as a Knight Templar; so help me God and keep me steadfast."

Eminent Commander—What was this vow called?

Candidate—The sealed libation.

Eminent Commander Why so?

Candidate—Because an agreement so made or obligation entered into is considered by Knights Templar as more sacred and binding than any other.

Eminent Commander—What followed?

Candidate—The Most Excellent Prelate then read the fifth lesson, relative to the election of Matthias. [See page 229.]

Eminent Commander—What followed?

Candidate—The Generalissimo thus addressed the Eminent Commander: "Eminent Commander, I see by the extinguished taper on our triangle there is a vacancy in our asylum; I move it be filled by some one who has passed through our solemn ceremonies."

Eminent Commander—What followed?

Candidate--The Eminent Commander then ordered the lots to be cast, which being done I was elected and the Eminent Commander thus addressed me: "Pilgrim, the lot has fallen upon you. In token of your acceptance of this high honor, you will re-light the extinguished taper, and may the Lord lift upon you the light of his reconciled countenance and keep you from falling."

Eminent Commander—What followed?

Candidate—The Eminent Commander then directed me to kneel, and said: "By virtue of the high power and authority in me vested, as the representative of Hugh de Payens and Geoffrey de St. Omer, I do now dub and create you ———, a knight of this most valiant and magnanimous order of Knights Templar."

Eminent Commander—What followed?

Candidate—The Eminent Commander then presented me with a sword and thus addressed me: "I now with much pleasure present you with the sword. In the hands of a valiant and magnanimous knight it is endowed with three most excellent qualities; its hilt with justice impartial; its blade with fortitude undaunted and its point with mercy,' and it teaches us this important lesson: That we should be well assured of the justice of the cause in which we draw our swords. Being thus assured, we should persevere with the most undaunted fortitude, until we have subdued our enemies, then consider them as such no longer, but extend to them that most noble attribute of Deity, mercy."

Eminent Commander—What followed?

Candidate—The Eminent Commander then communicated to me the due guard, pilgrim penitent's pass, **grand hailing sign, grip and word of a Knight Tem-**

plar.

Eminent Commander—Give the due guard. (Candidate gives it as follows:)

DUE GUARD OF A KNIGHT TEMPLAR.

Thumb of right hand under the chin, as shown in cut, fingers closed.

Eminent Commander—To what does it allude?

Candidate—To the penalty of my vow; to have my head smote off and placed on the highest spire in Christendom. [See page 211.]

Eminent Commander—Give the Pilgrim Penitent's pass. (Candidate does so as follows:)

PILGRIM PENITENT'S PASS.

Golgotha; given under an arch of steel. The same as the Persian pass, page 136. See cut.

Eminent Commander—Give the grand hailing sign.

LECTURE. 249

KNIGHTS TEMPLAR GRAND HAILING SIGN.

K. T. Grand Hailing Sign.

Right foot thrown over the left, arms extended, head inclined to the right. See cut.

Eminent Commander — To what does this sign allude?

Candidate—To the manner in which the Saviour expired upon the cross and expiated the sins of the world.

Eminent Commander—Give the grip and word.

KNIGHTS TEMPLAR GRIP AND WORD.

Knights Templar Grip.

One interlaces fingers of right hand with another's left hand and fingers of left hand with another's right hand, arms of each crossed, thus forming a cross.

WORD (given with grip), *Immanuel.*

Eminent Commander—What does the grip teach us?

Candidate—That as our fingers are thus strongly interlaced, so should the hearts of Knights Templar be firmly interlaced in friendship and brotherly love.

Eminent Commander—What is the motto of our order?

Candidate—*In hoc signo vinces.*

Eminent Commander—Translate it.

Candidate—By this sign we conquer.

CHAPTER XXI.

Twelfth, or Knights Templar Degree.

CLOSING CEREMONIES.

[Sometimes the ceremonies of closing include drill and sword practice as well as all the other exercises given in chapter XVIII., changed a trifle occasionally to suit the closing instead of opening ceremonies, and sometimes they are much more abbreviated than as here given.]

Eminent Commander (one rap)—Sir Knight Captain General, you will see that the asylum is made secure and inform the Sentinel that I am about to close this Commandery of Knights Templar and direct him to guard accordingly.

Captain General—Eminent Commander, the Sentinel is at his post and the asylum is duly guarded.

Eminent Commander (one rap)—Sir Knight Generalissimo, are you a Templar Knight?

Generalissimo—That is my title.

Eminent Commander—Where were you created a Knight Templar?

Generalissimo—In a just and lawful Commandery of Knights Templar.

Eminent Commander—What number composes such a Commandery?

Generalissimo—There is an indispensable number and a constitutional number.

CLOSING CEREMONIES.

Eminent Commander—What is the indispensable number?

Generalissimo—Three.

Eminent Commander—Under what circumstances may three Knights Templar open and form a Commandery?

Generalissimo—Three Knights Templar, hailing from three different Commanderies, may, under the sanction of a warrant from some Grand Commandery or from the Grand Encampment of the United States, form and operate a Commandery of Knights Templar for the dispatch of business.

Eminent Commander—What is the constitutional number?

Generalissimo—Nine, eleven or more.

Eminent Commander—When composed of eleven, of whom does it consist?

Generalissimo—The Eminent Commander, Generalissimo, Captain General, Prelate, Senior Warden, Junior Warden, Treasurer, Recorder, Standard Bearer, Sword Bearer and Warder.

Eminent Commander—What is the Warder's station in the Commandery?

Generalissimo—On the left of the Standard Bearer in the west and on the left of the Second Division.

Eminent Commander—What are your duties, Sir Knight Warder?

Warder—To announce the approach and departure of the Eminent Commander, to post the Sentinel and to see that the asylum is duly guarded.

Eminent Commander—What is the Sword Bearer's station in the Commandery?

Warder—On the right of the Standard Bearer in the west and on the right of the Second Division.

Eminent Commander—What are your duties, Sir Knight Sword Bearer?

Sword Bearer—To assist in the protection of the banners of the order; to watch all signals from the Eminent Commander and see that they are promptly obeyed.

Eminent Commander—What is the Standard Bearer's station in the Commandery?

Sword Bearer—In the west and in the center of the Second Division.

Eminent Commander—What are your duties, Sir Knight Standard Bearer?

Standard Bearer—To display, protect and support the banners of the order.

Eminent Commander—Why is your station in the west?

Standard Bearer—That the brilliant rays of the rising sun, shedding their luster on the banners of the order, may encourage and animate all true and courteous knights and confound and dismay their enemies.

Eminent Commander—What is the Recorder's station in the Commandery?

Standard Bearer—On the left, in front of the Captain General.

Eminent Commander—What are your duties, Sir Knight Recorder?

Recorder—Faithfully to record the proceedings of the Commandery, collect the revenue and pay the same over to the Treasurer.

Eminent Commander—What is the Treasurer's station in the Commandery?

Recorder—On the right, in front of the Generalissimo.

Eminent Commander—What are your duties, Sir Knight Treasurer?

Treasurer—To receive in charge all the funds and property of the Commandery, pay all orders drawn on the treasury and render a just and faithful account of the same when required.

Eminent Commander—What is the Junior Warden's station in the Commandery?

Treasurer—On the northwest angle of the triangle, on the right of the Third Division and on the left when formed in single line.

Eminent Commander—What are your duties, Sir Knight Junior Warden?

Junior Warden—To attend on poor and weary pilgrims, traveling from afar; to accompany them on their journey, to answer all questions for them and recommend them to the hospitality of the Eminent Commander.

Eminent Commander—What is the Senior Warden's station in the Commandery?

Junior Warden—At the southwest angle of the triangle, on the right of the First Division and on the right of the whole when formed in single line.

Eminent Commander—What are your duties, Sir Knight Senior Warden?

Senior Warden—To attend on pilgrim warriors, to comfort and support pilgrim penitents, and after due trial introduce them into the asylum.

Eminent Commander—What is the Prelate's station in the Commandery?

Senior Warden—On the right of the generalissimo.

Eminent Commander—What are your duties, Sir Knight Prelate?

Prelate—To minister at the altar and offer up prayers and oblations to Deity.

Eminent Commander—What is the Captain General's station in the Commandery?

Prelate—On the left of the Eminent Commander.

Eminent Commander—What are your duties, Sir Knight Captain General?

Captain General—To see that the proper officers make all due preparations for the various meetings of the Commandery, and that the asylum is in suitable array for the introduction of candidates and the dispatch of business, and to receive and communicate all orders and signals issued by the Eminent Commander to the officers of the lines.

Eminent Commander—What is the Generalissimo's station in the Commandery?

Captain General—On the right of the Eminent Commander.

Eminent Commander—What are your duties, Sir Knight Generalissimo?

Generalissimo—To receive and communicate all orders, signals and petitions; to assist the Eminent Commander in his various duties, and in his absence to preside in the Commandery.

Eminent Commander—What is the Eminent Commander's station in the Commandery?

Generalissimo—In the east.

Eminent Commander—What are his duties?

Generalissimo—To distribute alms to poor and needy pilgrims traveling from afar, feed the hungry, clothe the naked, bind up the wounds of the afflicted, inculcate the principles of charity and hospitality, and govern the Commandery with justice and moderation.

CLOSING CEREMONIES. 255

Eminent Commander (three raps, all rise)—Sir Knight Generalissimo, it is my order that this Commandery of Knights Templar be now closed; requiring all Sir Knights present to govern themselves according to the sublime principles of our order. Communicate this order to the Sir Knight Captain General, and he to the Sir Knights.

Generalissimo—Sir Knight Captain General, it is the order of the Eminent Commander that this Commandery of Knights Templar be now closed; requiring all Sir Knights present to govern themselves according to the sublime principles of our order. Communicate this order to the Sir Knights.

Captain General—Sir Knights, it is the order of the Eminent Commander that this Commandery of Knights Templar be now closed; requiring all Sir Knights present to govern themselves according to the sublime principles of our order. [The signs are now given from Entered Apprentice up.]

Eminent Commander (twelve raps, 000-000-000-000.)

Generalissimo (twelve raps.)

Captain General (twelve raps.)

Eminent Commander—I now declare this Commandery closed in form. Sir Knight Warder, inform the Sentinel.

CHAPTER XXII.

THIRTEENTH, OR KNIGHTS OF MALTA DEGREE.

OPENING CEREMONIES.

Eminent Commander—Sir Knight Warder, satisfy yourself that all present are Knights of Malta.[124]

Warder (having looked around)—All present are Knights of Malta.

Eminent Commander—The officers will take their respective places and stations.

Eminent Commander—Sir Knight Generalissimo, are you a Knight of Malta?

Generalissimo—I have been honored with that trust.

Eminent Commander—How many compose a Council[125] of the order of Malta?

Note 124.—"The Knights of St. John of Jerusalem, or Hospitalers of St. John, afterward called Knights of Rhodes and finally Knights of Malta, were founded about the commencement of the Crusades, as a military and religious order. In 1048, some pious merchants from Amalfi, in the kingdom of Naples, built a church and monastery at Jerusalem, which they dedicated to St. John the Almoner. The monks were hence called Brothers of St. John, or Hospitalers, and it was their duty to assist those sick and needy pilgrims whom a spirit of piety had led to the Holy Land. They assumed the black habit of the hermits of St. Augustine, distinguished only by a white cross of eight points on the left breast. They rapidly increased in numbers and in wealth, and at the beginning of the twelfth century were organized as a military order by Raymond du Puy, who added to their original vows of chastity, obedience and poverty, the obligation of defending the church against infidels. Raymond then divided them into three classes: Knights, who alone bore arms; Chaplains, who were regular ecclesiastics; and Servitors, who attended to the sick."—**Mackey's Lexicon**, Art. **Knight of Malta**.

Note 125.—"The Assembly is called a Council. The officers are, 1. Commander; 2. Generalissimo; 3. Captain General, 4. Prelate; 5. Senior Warden; 6. Junior Warden; 7. Treasurer; 8. Recorder; 9. First Guard, 10. Second Guard; 11. Standard Bearer; 12. Warder; 13. Sentinel."—**Sickels' Monitor, Part 4, page 42.**

Generalissimo—Seven or more.

Eminent Commander—When composed of twelve of whom do they consist?

Generalissimo—Eminent Commander, Generalissimo, Captain General, Prelate, Senior Warden, Junior Warden, Treasurer, Recorder, First and Second Guards, Standard Bearer and Warder.

Eminent Commander—The Warder's station?

Generalissimo—On the left of the Standard Bearer in the west.

Eminent Commander[126]—Sir Knight Warder, your duties?

Warder—To see that the council chamber is securely guarded, and attend to the reception of candidates.

Eminent Commander—The Standard Bearer's station?

Warder—In the west.

Eminent Commander—Sir Knight Standard Bearer, your duties?

Standard Bearer—To display and protect the banners of our order.

Eminent Commander—The First Guard's station?

Standard Bearer—On the right, in front of the Captain General, in the south.

Eminent Commander—Sir Knight First Guard, your duties?

First Guard—To challenge all strangers attempting to pass my station, and report them to the Captain General.

Eminent Commander—The Second Guard's station?

NOTE 126.—"The chief of the order was called 'Grand Master of the Holy Hospital of St. John of Jerusalem, and Guardian of the Army of Jesus Christ.' He was elected for life, and resided at the city of Valette. He was addressed by foreign powers with the title of Altezza Eminentissima, and enjoyed an annual revenue of about one million of guilders."—*Mackey's Lexicon, Art. Knight of Malta.*

First Guard—On the right, in front of the Generalissimo in the west.

Eminent Commander—Sir Knight Second Guard, your duties?

Second Guard—To challenge all strangers attempting to pass my station, and report them to the Generalissimo.

Eminent Commander—The Recorder's station?

Second Guard—On the left, in front of the Eminent Commander.

Eminent Commander—Sir Knight Recorder, your duties?

Recorder—Faithfully to record the proceedings of the Council; collect the revenue and pay it to the Treasurer.

Eminent Commander—The Treasurer's station?

Recorder—On the right, in front of the Eminent Commander.

Eminent Commander—Sir Knight Treasurer, your duties?

Treasurer—To receive in charge the funds and property of the Council, pay all orders drawn on the Treasurer and render a just and regular account of the same when required.

Eminent Commander—The Junior Warden's station?

Treasurer—On the right of the Second Division and on the left of the whole when formed in line.

Eminent Commander—Sir Knight Junior Warden, your duties?

Junior Warden—To take charge of the candidate, accompany him on his journey, answer questions for him and present his petition to the Generalissimo.

Eminent Commander—The Senior Warden's station?

OPENING CEREMONIES.

Junior Warden—On the right of the First Division and on the right of the whole when formed in line.

Eminent Commander—Sir Knight Senior Warden, your duties?

Senior Warden—To command the Sir Knights and form as the Eminent Commander shall direct.

Eminent Commander—The Prelate's station?

Senior Warden—On the right of the Eminent Commander.

Eminent Commander—Sir Knight Prelate, your duties?

Prelate—To minister at the altar and offer up prayers and oblations to Deity.

Eminent Commander—The Captain General's station?

Prelate—In the south.

Eminent Commander—Sir Knight Captain General, your duties?

Captain General—To examine all strangers reported to me by the First Guard and see that none pass my station except such as are duly qualified.

Eminent Commander—The Generalissimo's station?

Captain General—On the left of the Standard Bearer, in the west.

Eminent Commander—Sir Knight Generalissimo, your duties?

Generalissimo—To receive all candidates for the order, and after strict examination, if found worthy, recommend them to the Eminent Commander.

Eminent Commander—The Eminent Commander's station?

Generalissimo—In the east.

Eminent Commander—His duties?

Generalissimo—To preside over and govern his Coun-

KNIGHT OF MALTA DEGREE.

cil with impartiality, firmness and discretion; to confer the order upon all candidates who shall be found worthy and legally entitled to receive it, and to inculcate the duties of morality, benevolence and truth.

Eminent Commander—Sir Knight Generalissimo, it is my order that a Council of the Order of Malta[1] be now opened for the dispatch of such business as may regularly come before it, requiring all Sir Knights present to govern themselves according to the sublime principles of our order. Communicate this order to Sir Knight Captain General, and he to the Sir Knights.

Generalissimo—Sir Knight Captain General, it is the order of the Eminent Commander that a Council of the Order of Malta be now opened for the dispatch of such business as may regularly come before it, requiring all Sir Knights present to govern themselves according to the sublime principles of our order. Communicate this order to the Sir Knights.

Captain General—Attention, Sir Knights! (all rise) it is the order of the Eminent Commander that a Council of the Order of Malta be now opened for the dispatch of such business as may regularly come before it, requiring all Sir Knights to govern themselves according to the sublime principles of our order.

[The due guards and signs from Entered Apprentice up are now given. See Chapter XXV.]

NOTE 127.—"The Knights, or Hospitalers of St. John, afterward known as Knights of Rhodes, and finally called Knights of Malta, was a military religious order, established about the commencement of the Crusades.

"As early as 1048, some merchants from Amalfi, in Naples, being struck with the misery to which the pilgrims were exposed on their road to the Holy Land, obtained permission of the Caliph of Egypt to erect a church and build a monastery near the site of the Holy Sepulchre at Jerusalem, which they dedicated to St. John the Baptist. They entertained all pilgrims that came for devotion, and cured the diseased among them. They became eminent for their devotion, charity and hospitality. St. John the Baptist, being their patron, they were called Brethren Hospitalers of St. John the Baptist of Jerusalem, to distinguish them from the Knights of the Holy Sepulchre. They took the black habit of the Hermits of St. Augustine, and on the left breast wore a cross of eight points. In war they wore crimson, with a white cross, but in their monasteries, and on the day of their profession, the black garment only."—*Sickels' Monitor, Part 4, page 41.*

KNIGHT OF MALTA SIGN.

Both hands held out as if warming them; then quickly seize left hand near knuckle joint of little finger with thumb and forefinger of right hand, raising them in this position as high as the chin when they are jerked apart and hands and arms extended downward at an angle of forty-five degrees, fingers extended, palms down. This is supposed to represent Paul on the island of Melita, discovering a scorpion on his hand and jerking it off into the fire where he was warming.

Eminent Commander (ten raps.)
Generalissimo (ten raps.)
Captain General (ten raps.)

PRAYER AT OPENING.

"Our Father which art in heaven, hallowed be thy name. Thy kingdom come. Thy will be done on earth, as it is in heaven. Give us this day our daily bread. And forgive us our debts as we forgive our debtors. And lead us not into temptation, but deliver us from evil. For thine is the kingdom and the power, and the glory, forever. Amen."—*Simons' Book of the Commandery, page 42.*

Eminent Commander—I now declare a Council of the Order of Malta opened in form. Sir Knight Warder, inform the Sentinel. (This is done the same as in previous degrees, ten raps being given as the alarm.)

CHAPTER XXIII.

THIRTEENTH, OR KNIGHT OF MALTA DEGREE

INITIATION.

Eminent Commander—Sir Knight Junior Warden, take charge of the candidate. (Junior Warden goes to preparation room and coming to the door with candidate gives ten raps; three threes and one.)

Eminent Commander—Sir Knight Warder, attend to that demand.

Warder (ten raps; then opening door)—Who comes here?

Junior Warden—Sir Knight ———, who has been created and dubbed a knight of the valiant and magnanimous order of the Temple, now solicits the further honor of being created a knight of the order of Malta.[128]

Warder—What security can he offer that he is no impostor?

Junior Warden—The commendation of a true and courteous Sir Knight, the Junior Warden.

Warder—By what further right or benefit does he expect to obtain admission?

Junior Warden—By the benefit of the Pilgrim Penitent's pass.

Warder—Has he that pass?

Junior Warden—He has.

NOTE 128.—"As a Masonic grade, the degree of Knight of Malta, is in this country communicated in a Commandery of Knights Templar, as an appendant order thereto."—*Mackey's Lexicon, Art., Knight of Malta.*

Warder—Advance and give it.

Junior Warden—GOLGOTHA. (Given same as on page 248.)

Warder—The pass is right. You will wait until the Eminent Commander is informed of your request and his answer returned.

Warder (from his post)—Eminent Commander, there is without Sir Knight ———, who has been created and dubbed a knight of the valiant and magnanimous order of the Temple and now solicits the further honor of being created a knight of the order of Malta.

Eminent Commander—What security can he offer that he is no impostor?

Warder—The commendation of a true and courteous knight, our Junior Warden.

Eminent Commander—By what further right or benefit does he expect to obtain admission?

Warder—By the benefit of the Pilgrim Penitent's pass.

Eminent Commander—Has he that pass?

Warder—He has.

Eminent Commander—Advance and give it. (Given as on page 248.)

Eminent Commander—You have my permission to enter. (They enter and pass close by the east to the south and come to the First Guard.)

First Guard—Who comes here?

Junior Warden—A friend.

First Guard—Friend, stand!

First Guard—Sir Knight Captain General, a stranger wishes to pass.

Captain General—Who passes here?

Junior Warden—A Knight of the Temple.

KNIGHT OF MALTA DEGREE.

Captain General—Sir Knight, advance and give the pass. (Candidate gives Pilgrim Penitent's pass as explained page 248.)

Captain General—The word is right; pass on. (They pass to the west, to station of Second Guard.)

Second Guard—Who comes here?

Junior Warden—A friend, desirous of an interview with your Generalissimo.

Second Guard—Friend, stand, until the Generalissimo is informed of your request.

Second Guard—Sir Knight Generalissimo, a stranger desires an interview.

Generalissimo—Who passes here?

Junior Warden—Sir Knight ———, who has been created and dubbed a knight of the valiant and magnanimous order of the Temple, and is now desirous of the further honor of being created a knight of the order of Malta, for which purpose he solicits your high commendation with the Eminent Commander.

Generalissimo—Sir Knight, advance and give the pass. (Candidate gives Pilgrim Penitent's pass as before.)

Generalissimo—The word is right, but before granting your request I must require some evidence that you have made the requisite proficiency in the preceding degrees and orders to entitle you to the honor you ask. You will face the east and exhibit to me the signs of each degree as you advance. (Generalissimo takes his station on the right and Junior Warden on the left of the candidate and all advance together by the regular *steps* of the degrees giving signs and due guards of each as they advance.)

Generalissimo—The evidence is satisfactory.

Generalissimo—Eminent Commander, I have the

honor to present to you Sir Knight ———, who has been created and dubbed a knight of the valiant and magnanimous order of the Temple and now offers himself a candidate for the order of Malta. He has exhibited to me the requisite evidence of his proficiency in the preceding degrees and orders. I am also in possession of satisfactory assurances that he has taken upon himself the sealed obligation and therefore recommend him to you as fully entitled to the honor he solicits. [Generalissimo returns to his station leaving candidate in charge of Junior Warden.]

Eminent Commander—Sir Knight ———, I am happy to learn that you have been able to satisfy my Generalissimo in respect to your proficiency in the preceding degrees and that you are legally entitled to the further honor of being created a Knight of Malta; before proceeding to confer which, however, let us in accordance with a time honored Masonic usage unite with our Excellent Prelate in an address to the Throne of Mercy.

Eminent Commander—Attention, Sir Knights! (all rise) to your devotions! (Knights crm in a hollow square around the altar, candidate, with Junior Warden and Prelate inside, all kneel on right knee helmets on left shoulder held by left hand, when led by the Prelate all repeat the Lord's Prayer.)

Eminent Commander—Arise, Sir Knights! (They put on their helmets and rise.)

Eminent Commander—The Order of Malta[129] is appendant to the Order of the Temple and in this country is conferred either in the asylum[130] of a Command-

---

NOTE 129.—"The Grand Encampment of the United States, in 1856, abolished the order of Knights of Malta as being unnecessary and embarrassing; but in 1862 restored it to the anomalous place it had previously occupied in the system of Encampment Masonry."—*Morris' Dict., Art. Maltese Knight.*

NOTE 130.—"This order must be conferred in an asylum of a legal Commandery of Knights Templar, or in a Council of the Order of Malta, regularly convened for the purpose, distinct from, and *after*, the Templar's Order."—*Sickels' Monitor, Part 4, page 48.*

KNIGHT OF MALTA DEGREE.

ery or a Council regularly convened for that purpose. Your sealed obligation supercedes the necessity of my laying you under a particular one in reference to this order. I must, however, require that you make the solemn declaration which I am authorized to propose to you. [With uncovered head, sword drawn and held by the blade in left hand, his right hand on his bowels the candidate repeats after the Eminent Commander the following:]

OBLIGATION, KNIGHT OF MALTA.

I, ———, solemnly pledge my honor as a knight, having reference to my sealed obligation, that I will not assist or be present at conferring this order while under the jurisdiction of the United States of America, upon any person who shall not have regularly received the several degrees of Entered Apprentice, Fellow Craft, Master Mason, Past Master, Most Excellent Master, Royal Arch, Knights of the Red Cross and Knights Templar, to the best of my knowledge and belief, and then only within the asylum of a legal Commandery of Knights Templar or a Council of the Order of Malta regularly constituted.

Eminent Commander (continuing)—This order like all the degrees of Masonry through which you have passed has its sign, grip and word. The first sign is given in this way: (Gives it same as on page 261.) It is called MELITA, the ancient name of the island of Malta'" and alludes to the shipwreck of St. Paul.

The Scriptures inform us that when that distinguished

NOTE 181.—"MALTA.—The name of this island is associated with the order of knights who under the successive titles of Knights Templar, Knights of St. John, Knights of Rhodes and finally Knights of Malta, filled the Christian world for 700 years with the prowess of their arms. In the order of Maltese Knights, the visit of Paul to this island is alluded to."—*Morris' Dict., Art. Malta.*

INITIATION.

Apostle was on his passage to Rome, to be tried before AUGUSTUS CÆSAR he was cast away on the island of Melita and that the natives entertained him and his fellow sufferers with great kindness. "They kindled a fire, and received us every one, because of the present rain and because of the cold. And when Paul had gathered a bundle of sticks and laid them on the fire, there came a viper out of the heat, and fastened on his hand. And when the barbarians saw the venomous beast hang on his hand, they said among themselves, No doubt this man is a murderer, whom, though he hath escaped the seas, yet vengeance suffereth not to live. And he shook off the beast into the fire and felt no harm. Howbeit they looked when he should have swollen, or fallen down dead suddenly; but after they had looked a great while, and saw no harm come to him, [they changed their minds, and said that he was a god.] —Acts 28: 1-6."—*Simons' Book of the Commandery, page 43.*

[Sometimes the foregoing Scripture quotation is read by the Prelate.]

Eminent Commander (continuing)—The grand sign and grip of the order are given in this way:

GRAND SIGN AND GRIP, KNIGHT OF MALTA.

Knight of Malta grand sign and grip.

Eminent Commander (to candidate)—Thomas, reach hither thy finger and feel the print of the nails. (They join right hands, each forcing the forefinger into the palm of the other's hand.)

Eminent Commander—Reach hither thy hand and thrust it into my side. (Each extends his left hand and arm thrusting it into the other's left side, right hands still joined.)

Eminent Commander—MY LORD.

Candidate (prompted)—AND MY GOD.

Eminent Commander—They allude to the unbelief of Thomas. We learn from the Scriptures that after the Saviour had arisen from the dead he appeared to his disciples when they were assembled together on the evening of the first day of the week.

MONITORIAL.

"But Thomas, one of the twelve, called Didymus, was not with them when Jesus came. The other disciples, therefore, said unto him, We have seen the Lord. But he said unto them, Except I shall see in his hands the prints of the nails, and put my finger into the print of the nails, and thrust my hand into his side, I will not believe. And after eight days, again his disciples were within, and Thomas with them. Then came Jesus, the doors being shut, and stood in the midst, and said, Peace be unto you. Then saith he to Thomas, Reach hither thy finger, and behold my hands; and reach hither thy hand and thrust it into my side; and be not faithless, but believing. And Thomas answered and said unto him, My Lord and my God.—St. John 20: 24-28."—*Simons' Book of the Commandery, page 44.*

Eminent Commander (continuing)—The name of this grip is IMMANUEL. It teaches us that there is an unbelief which transcends a rational scepticism; that we should possess a power of faith to receive divine truth even though unaccompanied by physical evidence and thus entitle us to the commendation of our Divine Teacher; "Blessed are they that have not seen and yet have believed."

The principal words of this degree are, *Rex Regum, Dominus Dominorum*. It signifies "King of kings and Lord of lords."

INITIATION.

The initials of the motto of the order, I. N. R. I.[132] you will see encircled upon our banner. They are the initials of the Latin words, *Jesus Nazarenus Rex Judaorum,* signifying Jesus of Nazareth the King of the Jews, [In Latin I and J are interchangeable.] The word formed by these initials, INRI, is the grand word of a Knight of Malta.

The cross upon the banner is the cross of Calvary on which the Saviour was crucified. It is used in these ceremonies in preference to the military cross of the order, on account of the relation the motto of the order bears to it and the solemn and interesting associations which when viewed together they are calculated to awaken in the mind. The Sir Knights will now be seated. [Candidate is also seated in front of the Eminent Commander.]

HISTORY,[133] OR LECTURE.

Eminent Commander (to candidate)—I will now recount briefly a few of the circumstances which led to the institution of this order:

NOTE 132.—"I. N. R. I.—The initials of the Latin sentence which was placed upon the cross: *Jesus Nazarenus Rex Judaorum.* The Rosicrucians used them as the initials of one of their hermetric secrets: *Igne Natura Renovatur Integra*—'By fire, nature is perfectly renewed.' They also adopted them to express the names of their three elementary principles, salt, sulphur, and mercury, by making them the initials of the sentence, *Igne Nitrum Roris Invenitur.* These speculations may afford some interest to the Rose Croix Mason and the Knight Templar."—*Mackey's Lexicon, Art. I. N. R. I.*

NOTE 133.—"After long and bloody contests with the Turks and Saracens, they were finally driven from Palestine in the year 1191. Upon this they attacked and conquered Cyprus, which, however, they lost after eighteen years occupation; they then established themselves at the Island of Rhodes, under the Grand Mastership of Fulk de Villaret, and assumed the title of Knights of Rhodes. On the 15th of December, 1442, after a tranquil occupation of this island for more than two hundred years, they were finally ejected from all their possessions by the Sultan Soliman the Second. After this disaster they successively retired to Castro, Messina and Rome, until the Emperor Charles V., in 1530, bestowed upon them the island of Malta, upon the condition of their defending it from the depredations of the Turks, and the corsairs of Barbary, and of restoring it to Naples, should they ever succeed in recovering Rhodes. They now took the name of Knights of Malta."—*Mackey's Lexicon, Art. Knight of Malta.*

KNIGHT OF MALTA DEGREE.

After the suppression of the order of Knights Templar by the Council of Vienne in 1312, a considerable portion of their assets were conferred upon the Knights of St. John, with which order they were, by a general decree in the papacy of Clement V., annexed and incorporated.

This decree was not generally submitted to. The Templars and the Knights of St. John were formerly rival orders, between whom there had long existed a spirit of jealousy, which on various occasions led to the deadliest animosity. The recollection of these events had kindled a fire in the bosoms of a portion of the Templars which the most dreadful misfortunes could not extinguish.

Those Templars who could not reconcile themselves to the union of the two orders continued to maintain a distinct organization.

The Grand Master Molay in anticipation of his own fate, had appointed[134] by charter of transmission John Mark Larmienus of Jerusalem as successor. Under this charter the Grand Chapter of France has from that time to the present continued to practice the ancient rites of the order.

Dennys, Prince of Portugal, adverse to the destruction of an order, a branch of which he had taken under his protection, adroitly avoided the fate which threatened it by the nominal fiction of converting its title into that of the Order of Christ, th supremacy of which he declared thenceforth to be vested in the crown.

NOTE 134.—"The traditions of the order, preserved by the French knights, affirm that De Molay, in anticipation of martyrdom, appointed John Mark Larmienus his successor, and that an unbroken line of Grand Masters has been maintained in that country to the present day. This, however, is flatly contradicted by the English and Scotch historians of the order."—*Morris' Dict., Art. Templar Knight.*

Under this title the Templars in Portugal have continued to flourish undisturbed to the present day.

The papal persecution had reached every state in Europe and scattered the members of the order throughout Christendom. Some became errant while others connected themselves with the Teutonic and other orders of knighthood and others again formed independent Chapters, and by avoiding the political questions of the day were enabled quietly to hold their meetings.

The Templars connected themselves with the Knights of St. John under the following circumstances: After the Christians had been driven out of Palestine in 1291, those Templars who had been engaged in the holy wars, repaired to Cyprus and settled in Limasol. There they remained until 1306, when the Grand Master Molay and his principal officers were treacherously summoned to France by Clement V., the unworthy instrument of Philip the Fair. On their arrival they were immediately thrown into prison. The Templars remained at Limasol justly apprehensive of the result of the unjust and cruel proceedings which had been instituted against the Grand Master and his companions, and foreseeing the probable destruction of the order established themselves in 1310 at the island of Rhodes then under the Grand Master of the Knights of St. John. This was the first direct approach to that union of the two orders which was subsequently firmly decreed by Clement, and henceforth the orders so united were known as the Knights of Rhodes until 1512, when the island fell into the hands of the Turks.

After the capitulation at Rhodes the order successively retreated to Candia, Venice, Viterbo, Villa Franca and Syracuse, when in 1530 the Emperor Charles V.

granted them the island of Malta as a permanent residence. At this time they took the name of Knights of Malta, or the Order of St. John of Jerusalem.

At that period it was the only one of the military orders of Palestine that continued to be recognized by the sovereign powers of Europe. About this period its ramifications extended throughout all Christendom and it maintained General Priories on the Continent and England. These, added to its immense possessions and wealth, were to its members great and desirable personal advantages and enabled the order to exercise a more extensive and powerful influence in all public affairs than was at that time enjoyed by any other class or association of men.

With a view to protect themselves from imposition and that the members of the deceased order of knighthood and the recent members of their own order, should not improperly avail themselves of the privileges and credit which their valor and perseverance had won for them, they instituted the order of Knights of Malta.

The order continued in possession of the island of Malta until 1798, when it was betrayed by some French Knights into the hands of Bonaparte, after which the station of the order was established at Catania in Sicily, where it remained until 1826, when the Pope permitted the Chapter and the government to remove to France.

Eminent Commander (continuing)—And now Sir Knight, in behalf of my companions, I again bid you a hearty welcome to all the rights and privileges, even to the disinerested friendship and unbounded hospitality which have ever and we trust will long continue to distinguish, adorn and characterize these noble orders.

With the age and the occasion which gave them birth their adventurous and warlike spirit have passed away, but their moral and beneficent character still remains bright in all its primitive beauty and loveliness, to excite as in the days of their greatest glory that spirit of refined and moral chivalry which should prompt us to press onward in the cause of truth and justice, stimulate us to exertion in behalf of the destitute and oppressed, to wield the sword if need be when "pure and undefiled religion" calls us in her defense and in a brother's cause to do *all* that may become man.

They also teach the triumph of immortality; that although death hath its sting, its infliction is but for a moment; that this frail organization, though here subject to the many "ills that flesh is heir to," possesses an ethereal principle that shall soar to the realms of endless bliss and beyond the power of change, to live forever.

CHARGE TO CANDIDATE, KNIGHT OF MALTA DEGREE.

"SIR KNIGHT:—Having passed through the several degrees and honorary distinctions of our ancient and honorable institution—in your admission to the tesselated Masonic ground floor—your ascent into the middle chamber—your entrance to the unfinished *sanctum sanctorum*—your regularly passing the several gates of the Temple—induction to the oriental chair—witnessing the completion and dedication of that superb model of excellence, the Temple, which h s immortalized the names of our ancient Grand Masters, and the justly celebrated craftsmen; having wrought in the ruins of the first Temple, and from its sacred Royal Arch brought to light incalculable treasures and advantages to the craft; having duly studied into the way and manner of their concealment; also having been engaged in the hazardous enterprise of traversing an enemy's dominions, and there convincing a foreign prince that truth is great and will prevail; therefore, you are now admitted to a participation in those labors which are to effect the erection of a temple more glorious than the first, even that beauteous temple of holiness and innocence, whose pillars are Charity, Mercy and Justice, the foundation of which is in the breast of every one who has tasted that the Lord is gracious: to whom you come as unto a living stone, disallowed indeed of men, but chosen of God and precious.

"And now, Sir Knight, we bid you welcome to all these rights and privileges, even to that disinterested friendship and unbounded hospitality which ever has, and we hope and trust ever will continue to adorn, distinguish and characterize this noble order.

"It will henceforth become your duty, and should be your desire, to assist, protect and befriend the weary, way-worn traveler, who finds the heights of fortune inaccessible and the thorny paths of life broken, adverse and forlorn; to succor, defend and protect the innocent, the distressed and the helpless, ever standing forth as a champion to espouse the cause of the Christian religion.

"You are to inculcate, enforce and practice virtue; and amidst all the temptations which surround you, never be drawn aside from the path of duty, or forgetful of those due guards and pass words which are necessary to be had in perpetual remembrance; and while one hand is wielding the sword for your companion in danger, let the other grasp the mystic Trowel and widely diffuse the genuine cement of Brotherly Love and Friendship.

"Should calumny assail the character of a brother Sir Knight, recollect that you are to step forth and vindicate his good name, and assist him on all necessary occasions. Should assailants ever attempt your honor, interest or happiness, remember, also, at the same time, you have the counsel and support of your brethren, whose mystic swords, combining the virtues of Faith, Hope and Chari y, with Justice, Fortitude and Mercy will leap from their scabbards in defense of your just rights, and insure you a glorious triumph over all your enemies.

"On this occasion permit me, Sir Knight, to remind you of our mutual engagements, our reciprocal ties; whatever may be your situation or rank in life you will find those, in similar stations, who have dignified themselves and b en useful to mankind. You are therefore called upon to discharge all your duties with fidelity and patience, whether in the field, in the senate, on the bench, at the bar, or at the holy altar. Whether you are placed upon the highest pinnacle of worldly grandeur, or glide more securely in the humble vale of obscurity, unnoticed, save by a few, it matters not, for a few rolling suns will close the scene, when naught but holiness will serve as a sure password to gain admission into that REST prepared from the foundation of the world.

"If you see a brother bending under the cross of adversity and disappointment, look not idly on, neither pass by on the other side, but fly to his relief. If he be deceived, tell him the truth; if he be calumniated, vindicate his cause; for, although in some instances he may have erred, still recollect that indiscretion in him should never destroy humanity in you.

"Finally, Sir Knights, as *Memento mori* is deeply engraved on all sublunary enjoyments, let us ever be found in the habiliments of righteousness, traversing the straight path of rectitude, virtue, and true holiness, so that having discharged our duty here below, performed the pilgrimage of life, burst the bands of mortality, passed over the Jordan of death, and safely landed on the broad shore of eternity, there, in the presence of myriads of attending angels, we may be greeted as brethren, and received into the extended arms of the blessed Immanuel, and forever made to participate in his heavenly kingdom."—*Sickels' Monitor, Part 4, page 44.*

CHAPTER XXIV.

THIRTEENTH, OR KNIGHT OF MALTA DEGREE.

LECTURE, OR EXAMINATION.

Eminent Commander—Sir Knight ———, are you a Knight of Malta?

Candidate—I have been honored with that trust.

Eminent Commander—Where did you receive that honor?

Candidate—In a regular and duly constituted Council of the Order of Malta.

Eminent Commander—At what time?

Candidate—After I had been dubbed and created a knight of the valiant and magnanimous order of the Temple.

Eminent Commander—Have you a sign belonging to this order?

Candidate—I have.

Eminent Commander—Show it. (Candidate gives the sign as on page 261.)

Eminent Commander—What is that called?

Candidate—The sign of a Knight of Malta.

Eminent Commander—To what does it alluds?

Candidate—To the shipwreck of St. Paul.

Eminent Commander—Explain that circumstance.

Candidate—Sacred history informs us that when that distinguished Apostle was on his passage to Rome to be tried by Augustus Cæsar, he was cast away on the island of Melita and that the natives entertained him and his fellow-sufferers with great kindness. They kindled a fire and received every one of them because of the rain and cold.

Eminent Commander—What followed?

Candidate—"And when Paul had gathered a bundle of sticks, and laid them on the fire, there came a viper out of the heat, and fastened on his hand. And when the barbarians saw the venomous beast hang on his hand, they said among themselves, No doubt this man is a murderer, whom, though he hath escaped the seas, yet vengeance suffereth not to live. And he shook off the beast into the fire, and felt no harm. Howbeit they looked when he should have swollen, or fallen down dead suddenly; but after they had looked a great while, and saw no harm come to him, [they changed their minds, and said that he was a god.]—*Simon's Book of the Commandery, page 43.*

Eminent Commander—Have you another sign and grip?

Candidate—I have.

Eminent Commander—Communicate them to your next Sir Knight. (Candidate with the Sir Knight next to him give grand sign and grip as on page 267.)

Eminent Commander—What are they called?

Candidate—The grand sign and grip of the order.

Eminent Commander—To what do they allude?

Candidate—To the unbelief of Thomas.

Eminent Commander—How are they explained?

Candidate—After our Saviour had arisen from the dead he appeared unto his disciples when they were assembled together on the evening of the first day of the week.

Eminent Commander—What followed?

Candidate—"But Thomas, one of the twelve, called

Didymus, was not with them when Jesus came. The other disciples, therefore, said unto him, We have seen the Lord. But he said unto them, Except I shall see in his hands the prints of the nails, and put my finger into the print of the nails, and thrust my hand into his side, I will not believe. And after eight days, again his disciples were within, and Thomas with them. Then came Jesus, the doors being shut, and stood in the midst, and said, Peace be unto you. Then saith he to Thomas, Reach hither thy finger, and behold my hands; and reach hither thy hand, and thrust it into my side; and be not faithless, but believing. And Thomas answered, and said unto him, My Lord and my God.—St. John 20: 24–28."—*Simons' Book of the Commandery, page 44.*

Eminent Commander—What is the name of that grip?

Candidate—Immanuel.

Eminent Commander—What does it teach?

Candidate—That there is an unbelief that transcends a rational scepticism; that we should possess a power of faith to receive Divine truth, though unaccompanied by physical evidence and thus entitle us to that commendation of our Divine Teacher. "Blessed are they that have not seen and yet have believed."

Eminent Commander—What are the principal words of this order?

Candidate—*Rex regum, Dominus dominorum.*

Eminent Commander—Translate them.

Candidate—King of kings and Lord of lords.

Eminent Commander—What is the motto of the order?

Candidate—*Jesus Nazarenus, Rex Judaeorum.*

Eminent Commander—Translate it.

Candidate—Jesus of Nazareth, King of the Jews.

CHAPTER XXV.

THIRTEENTH, OR KNIGHTS OF MALTA DEGREE.

CLOSING CEREMONIES.

Eminent Commander—Sir Knight Generalissimo, are you a Knight of Malta?

Generalissimo—I have been honored with that trust.

Eminent Commander—How many compose a Council of the order of Malta?

Generalissimo—Seven or more.

Eminent Commander—When composed of twelve of whom do they consist?

Generalissimo—Eminent Commander, Generalissimo, Captain General, Prelate, Senior Warden, Junior Warden, Treasurer, Recorder, First and Second Guards, Standard Bearer and Warder. [Same questions as in opening, chapter XXII., here follow.]

Eminent Commander—Sir Knight Generalissimo, it is my order that this Council of the Order of Malta be now closed. Communicate this order to Sir Knight Captain General, and he to the Sir Knights.

Generalissimo—Sir Knight Captain General, it is the order of the Eminent Commander that this Council of the Order of Malta be now closed. Communicate this order to the Sir Knights.

Captain General—Attention, Sir Knights! (all rise.) It is the order of the Eminent Commander that this Council of the Order of Malta be now closed.

[The due guards and signs from Entered Apprentice up, are now given in concert.]

Eminent Commander (ten raps.)
Generalissimo (ten raps.)
Captain General (ten raps.)

"EXHORTATION AT CLOSING.

"Finally, my brethren, be strong in the Lord, and in the power of his might. Put on the whole armor of God, that ye may be able to stand against the wiles of the devil. For we wrestle not against flesh and blood, but against principalities, against powers, against the rulers of the darkness of this world, against spiritual wickedness in high places. Wherefore, take unto you the whole armor of God, that ye may be able to withstand in the evil day, and having done all, to stand. Stand, therefore, having your loins girt about with truth, and having on the breastplate of righteousness; and your feet shod with the preparation of the Gospel of peace; above all, taking the shield of faith, wherewith ye shall be able to quench all the fiery darts of the wicked. And take the helmet of salvation and the sword of the Spirit, which is the Word of God."— *Sickels' Monitor, Part 4, page 49.*

Eminent Commander—I now declare this Council of the Order of Malta closed in form. Sir Knight Warder inform the Sentinel. [This is done the same as in opening.]

ANALYSIS COMMANDERY DEGREES.

ANALYSIS OF COMMANDERY DEGREES

Ceremonies of the Council and Commandery Degrees May Be Known from the Ritual.—Knight Templars Break the Lord's Day.—Triennial Conclaves Attract Loose Women.—The Order Promotes Lewdness Among Members and a Disregard of Other of God's Commands.—Templarism Tends to Destroy Marriage.—Knight Templarism Counterfeits the Teachings of Christ.—Ignores Regeneration by Repentance and Faith.—Newspapers on the Conclave.—From the Chicago Inter Ocean, Times and the Religious Press.

The thoughtful reader will continually compare the notes which are found in this volume with the Ritual published above it. It is frequently said by lodge men that one who is not a member of an Order cannot have any knowledge as to what the secret work really is, but everyone who reads the exposition of the lodge ceremonies here given and the extracts from Masonic "Books of the Chapter or of the Commandery, Lexicons and Texts on Masonic Jurisprudence" will at once perceive how each fits into the other. It would not be at all difficult for one to trace the whole course of initiation from Entered Apprentice to Knights of Malta, by the monitorial work to which reference has been made. The practical conclusion to be derived from this fact is that one may know the ceremonies of the Council and Commandery as fully without ever uniting with the Masonic Order, as he can if he pays his money and submits to the degradation of initiation. This fact has become so well known to intelligent lodge men, that those of them who are fairly truthful have ceased to affirm that non-masons cannot know Masonry. I speak personally with lodge men every few months assuming the truth of revelations as

COUNCIL AND COMMANDERY FOUND IN RITUAL. 283

made in this and other books, and I find that these gentlemen admit the truth of the Ritual as herein revealed, and undertake to justify the Order, if at all, on the basis of the facts as stated.

If the reader, in conversation with Masters or Knights should find them denying the subtantial truth of the revelation herein contained, he may rest assured that they are either not members of the Order at all, or are lying to him. Of course there are clandestine Masonic bodies. These may, and possibly do, modify the ceremonies, oaths and penalties in conferring the degrees. Then, too, there are regular Masonic bodies which for the sake of securing members who will not submit to the humiliation of regular initiations, omit portions of the Ritual. Then there are the Masons made at sight, that is men who, because of their standing, are admitted as lodge men without any ceremonies at all. But all Royal, Select and Superexcellent Masters and Knights of the Red Cross, Knights Templar and Knights of Malta, who have been in real Masonic bodies, regularly admitted to these degrees, have passed through the ceremonies, have taken the obligations and are subject to the penalties herein set forth.

PUBLIC ASSEMBLIES OF KNIGHTS TEMPLAR

All who have studied the lodge question understand that in addition to the secret work of the Order, there are also public occasions, which in one way and another reveal the character and tendencies of the institution. The most prominent of the open gatherings of the Knights Templar are what they call their "Conclaves." Every three years, in some large city, there have been held, for many years, these gatherings. Respecting them, two or three things might be said. First: They usually involve a nation wide contempt and profanation of the Sabbath. Great trains having hundreds of these Knights, so-called, are made up, Friday, Saturday or Sabbath, and for hundreds of miles go thundering over the broken law of God. If it be said that many professed Christians also ride on such trains, we must sorrowfully admit the truth of the statement; but it is not true that Christians as individuals, or organizations, make up great trains to convey large numbers of persons for hundreds or thousands of miles on the Sabbath Day; and, while we must admit that the treatment which professed Christians give to the Sabbath Day is very far from what it should be, we can affirm without doubt or hesitation that the Church is innocent of this wholesale Sabbath desecration, which the lodges of our country are now practising.

The second characteristic of these conclaves of Knights Templar is the terrible amount of drunkenness which is associated with them. It is credibly reported that on several occasions the Knights Templar from the Pacific Coast, when starting for a conclave, have brought with them wine, not by the barrel or case, but by the carload, and at times the camping grounds of the Knights has been so cluttered with wine bottles during the night's drinking, that they have been carried away by the wagon load in the morning.

The vices of Sabbath breaking and drunkenness are intimately associated. Drunkenness leads to Sabbath breaking and Sabbath breaking conducts to drunkenness. The saloon system in our country from ocean to ocean wars against the Sabbath Day. In every great city the saloons not only sell liquor during the days and hours which they are permitted to sell, but they also sell at night and on the Sabbath Day, when by law they are supposed to be closed. The reason for mentioning this characteristic of the Knights Templar is the fact that they profess to be Christians; making this profession, their national contribution to this universal demoralizing trade calls for sterner condemnation.

The third characteristic of these great lodge assemblies is the fact that houses of ill-repute are so largely patronized by these Knights, who have sworn to draw their swords in defense of innocent maidens, destitute widows, suffering orphans and the Christian religion. No doubt there are differences in different conclaves, but the testimony of those who have been conversant with a number of these conclaves held in our own country, is that the disreputable houses of the city are fairly crowded with these men, many of whom do not even take the trouble to remove their uniforms.

Deacon Philo Carpenter of Chicago said many years ago that the conductors of the Burlington line said to him that the meeting of the Grand Lodge of Illinois was attended by women of loose character from all parts of the State, as regularly as by the representatives of the lodges themselves. To the thoughtful student the explanation of this dark and loathsome fact is not far to seek. The Bible speaks continually of idolatry as adultery. The rightful relation of the human soul to God is continually referred to in the Bible as marriage. God calls himself the husband of the believer, and believers who turn away to false gods are said to have broken their covenant with Jehovah. It is one of the world wide facts in connection with religions that false religions assail the home as directly as they do the Church. Among the Mormons and Mohammedans, in China and Japan, there is nothing that corresponds to Christian marriage. The reason is that the religions of these countries are not Christian. Not being Christian, how can there be Christian institutions?

A gentleman who had withdrawn from the Masonic Order said that he did so because he found himself becoming, in his thoughts, disloyal to his wife. He said that he was horrified at the thoughts and feelings which were arising in his heart; that he talked the subject over plainly with his wife, and that they both agreed that it was association with the Masonic lodge which was separating them. He abandoned the Order and his home remained pure and happy. He did not understand the reason, but all who know that false religions naturally tend to disrupt homes can understand what he simply felt.

FRIENDS DO HIS COMMANDMENTS

This principle our Lord lays down as fundamental in His kingdom. His friends are those who do His commandments. Masons who have understood that Christ is excluded from the first seven degrees of Masonry, have sometimes been quite pleased to find that in the Commandery His name occurs; that long passages of Scripture which deal with His life, death and resurrection, are read, and that prayers are offered to God through Him. They apparently forget that the only way into this place where, as they suppose, Christ is honored, is through the long lodge road where He is ignored; but they should understand, even from the Ritual of the Council and Commandery, that Knights Templar Masonry is no more Christian than that of Blue Lodge or Chapter. "Ye are my friends if ye do whatsoever I command you." "Not every one that saith unto me, Lord, Lord, shall enter into the kingdom of heaven, but he that doeth the will of my Father which is in heaven." One can scarcely understand the stupidity which would lead one to suppose that a man or an organization could be acceptable to Christ because it pronounces His name, if it does not at the same time obey His commands. Is it not rather adding insult to injury to be mouthing the name and reading about the life of Jesus Christ while living in disobedience of His Commands and disregard of His example? It would be laughable, if it were not tragic, to see men marching along the streets smoking cigars and rushing into liquor shops, using profane language, etc., and at the same time wearing the cross of Jesus on their gloves, on their hats or caps, on swords, and other articles of clothing. How all hell must ring with laughter when such men kneel, clasp hands and together repeat the Lord's prayer, and then rise to go on with their profane and wicked living!

One of my choicest friends, a man who was a Knight Templar, a Knight of Pythias and an Odd Fellow, and I think connected with one or two other lodges, told me that when he was in the lodges he was committing every sin he knew about excepting murder; yet he was an acceptable member of the organizations, and was a district deputy grand master for one of them. He said that after he was converted, when he was on his knees in the chapter, the men on each side of him were the same sort of persons that he had been. Prior to that time he said that he had never thought that it was wrong for such men as he had been, and they were, to kneel down and repeat prayers, but having himself become a Christian, he said it seemed unspeakably horrible for him to be kneeling there between two men of immoral and wicked lives, repeating together the Lord's Prayer. He was so affected by the thought that he promised God if He would allow him to live to get away from the meeting he would never associate with these men in that way again. He burned his Knights Templar's uniform in the stove, he put his sword handle into the stove and burned off all that would burn, he took the blade and buried it in his back yard in the ground. He said it seemed to him that he did not want anything to remind him of that life of sin which he had lived when a lodge man.

NO REPENTANCE, NO CONFESSION, NO FAITH

Our Lord clearly declares that the entrance into the kingdom is through repentance and faith. If the reader will turn to the Ritual as found in this book, he will see that there is no mention of repentance anywhere. There is no call for confession of sin. Before the tabernacle as a worshipper approached he passed the altar of burnt offering, then the laver; then he passed into the holy place where he found on his left hand light and on his right hand bread, and before him the altar of incense. This is a clear revelation of the method in which men are saved. First, there must be the sacrifice for sin perceived and accepted. In this sin must be realized in some measure and acknowledged. This is repentance and confession, and then it is possible that the blood of Jesus should purge the sinner, repentant and acknowledging his fault. After pardon comes cleansing. The Holy Spirit cannot cleanse an unrepentant, unforgiven sinner. Such a person is not in a condition to be cleansed. He is polluted, unholy. After a sinner has been pardoned and washed, light will benefit him, food will sustain him and it will be possible for him to offer praise to God. Now, Knight Templarism, like all other Pagan religions, totally ignores the entrance into the Divine life. Men are taught to pray, to repeat the name of the Savior, even to speak of him as their Savior, without repentance or confession of sin. There is no such method of getting into the kingdom of God. Such a system shuts one up to the old folly of attempting salvation by works. This is the natural effort of the human heart, but it has never resulted in anything but failure; from the nature of the case it never can result in anything else. It can make hypocrites, but it cannot make Christians. It can make men profess to be good, but it cannot make them good. The reader ought to clearly comprehend this fundamental teaching of the Word of God. That we must obey or we are not friends of Jesus. We must obey or fail. And the first command is to repent and believe His Gospel.

We conclude this chapter by urging the reader to carefully consider again the scriptures which are read, and the lectures which are given in these last three degrees. How unspeakably horrible to think that even decent men repeat these words, unless they are sincere and humble believers in Jesus Christ, but when these Knights, so-called, are as a rule not even professing Christians, but men of the world, and very largely men whose habits do not commend them even as men, to think of such persons repeating such words, and again and again kneeling down to pretend to pray, is unspeakably horrible.

After the conclave which was held in Chicago years ago, a number of the newspapers spoke of the character of the gathering. I subjoin a few of the editorials which were written at that time.

NEWSPAPERS ON CONCLAVES

"To say that the subscribing merchants of the city are indignant over the manner in which the affairs of the Conclave have been conducted, is mildly to state a fact. Indignation is so strongly expressed that it amounts to a manifestation of positive anger and resentment. Many of them stigmatize the affair as an outrage, and while they are not willing to directly impeach any responsible person, do not hesitate to declaim against management so bad as to be culpable. The great majority of the unfortunate Knights themselves concur in this expression, believing that in one way or another they have met with extremely bad treatment during the three days they have been in Chicago. One irate merchant declared that he would not have gone to the trouble of decorating his buildings had he not supposed that he was to add thereby some grace to the magnificence of the procession. To get the emphatic idea of one of these gentlemen respecting the affair, the hardy explorer had better approach with some words of praise touching the conduct of the conclave."—*Chicago Inter Ocean*, Aug. 20.

Speaking of the enormous amount of liquors sold to the Knights, the Tribune of August 22 says: "One large establishment of Monroe street sold an average of over $1,000 in one day, for four days, over the counter, and $1,500 in one day in the wholesale department to Templars." This house is Chapin & Gore's. We are assured by a leading business man and a Mason that Vincent Lumbard Hurlbut, the Most Eminent Grand Commander of the order, spent a large amount of time at this place. The Tribune concludes as follows:

"In fine, it is shown that an enormous amount of Crusader beverage was sold in Chicago during the week just past. One prominent dealer estimated that a round million of dollars would not cover the amount spent for this alone. In this connection it is well to observe that the humorous order issued by the triennial authorities forbidding Knights to appear in places where T. L. was sold in their uniform, was taken in its exact spirit, and that every good Templar wore as much of his regalia as he could comfortably carry while making the rounds, particularly on the day of the procession.''

The *Chicago Times* of August 20 voiced public opinion in the following forcible style:

"There has not been from the beginning to the end of the series of conclave entertainments a single unqualified success. Failure, extortion, blundering, swindling have been the main features of everything which has taken place of an official nature and which had been arranged in advance. The grand parade was at once a partial failure and complete swindle on those portions of the city which have done the most to give the conclave a financial foundation. The exposition affair was a confidence game, pure and simple. It was not simply a confidence game, but it was a most disgraceful one—one in which there is not a single palliative feature. The competitive drill was still another operation which is a disgrace to every man who had anything to do with it in an official capacity. It was a swindle in that it asked commanderies to compete in one way and then at a later day forced them to compete in another way, and one for which they had not the time the prepare themselves. It was a most disgraceful affair in that there was no provision for water whereby visitors were obliged to pay for something to quench their thirst. It was still further a gross, inexcusable swindle in the fact that people who held tickets were bulldozed at the gates, and, to the number of thousands were compelled to pay for their admission to the grounds. There is no use in parading all the details of this affair, and inviting attention to those which are in the nature of complete or partial failures. It is much more easy to state the humiliating fact that not one of the promises of the triennial committee has been fulfilled."

Though the secular press spoke out thus boldly when backed by public opinion, some of the religious press analyzed the character of the order still more clearly:

"The Templars came here without any object commensurate with the time, trouble and expense of coming; they brought a great deal of money with them and left it here, largely in the saloons and theaters; they departed as they came, wearing their little caps with little crosses, and carrying their toy swords, leaving nobody here any wiser, any better, any happier for their visit. We asked several Masons, not Templars, what the object of the conclave was; none could tell. There did not seem to be any object save to make a grand display and to enjoy the hospitality of the city and a few days of revelry. Coming into the city one night on an Illinois Central train, the writer of this was enabled to look into the back doors of several of their tents pitched on the lake shore. The train was delayed along by the encampment for a long time, and ample opportunity was afforded for observation. The chief objects in all the tents seen were bottles of beer and brandy and wines, with jugs on jugs of "sour mash." The sole employment of the Christian Knights was found in surrounding the contents of the above-mentioned furniture, and in singing ribald songs. Now be it remembered that this is a religious order: they march under the sign of the cross and claim to do battle for the right."—*The Christian Instructor*, Aug. 26.

"What mean these emblems? There is the *red cross* upon every uniform. That is intended to signify *a soldier of the cross.* Everywhere also is the cross with the legend, "in hoc signo vinces," "by this sign conquer." Symbols and mottoes abound in lavish profusion, which speak of faith and hope and love. All point to the cross of Christ, and one would conclude from the outward signs that this order was devoted heart and soul to the maintenance of true religion. This would be all very well if those who flaunted them were real soldiers of Jesus Christ. Some are, but the majority are utterly indifferent. Some are infidels, some are licentious, some are tipplers, many are profane. The Knightly uniform was seen crowding the theaters, the ballroom and the saloons. All those places were covered with religious emblems. As we write we see the Knights crowding thickly a saloon across the street, and soldiers wearing the cross of the suffering Savior are standing at the bar drinking, swearing, honoring Satan rather than Christ. "The enemies of the cross of Christ" by thousands are wearing a badge that proclaims them the soldiers of the cross!

"What is the effect? It brings Christ and his suffering and his religion itself into contempt. All empty forms in the name of religion are blasphemous. Such empty, unmeaning, childish profession is calculated to lead the Templar himself, as well as others, to distrust all the professions of religion."—*The Evangelist*, Aug. 26.

"Such horrible incongruities as are seen in the display of the emblem of the cross over saloons and bagnios were never seen before in this country. 'Be faithful unto death' appears amid crosses and crowns over one of the most prosperous gin mills in the city. What a ghastly travesty that is! There is a jeer and a sneer in it that could only be equaled by the devil reading the sermon on the mount to a convocation of Belials and Molochs and Beelzebubs. 'For God, Man and Brotherhood' is the motto of another degrader of public morals. 'For God and the Right,' says still another corrupter of public virtues. We are told that a bagnio, with hideous levity, is spangled over with crosses and sacred mottoes. All this to some is a roaring farce—to some of the hundred thousand strangers in the city—more or less—they are baits and lures and snares. To all pure minds it is appalling blasphemy."—*The Interior*, Aug. 19.

If secular newspapers and Christian newspapers found this meeting to be as is described above, we ask once more, how unspeakably horrible that men capable of such things should be mouthing the Scriptures and repeating the prayers which are recorded in this book.

ARE YOU A KNIGHT TEMPLAR?

If so, I take a moment to make a personal appeal to you. I well understand how men become entangled in secret societies. They are usually ignorant of their character. All they know is that some friends are connected with them and that they have been told that if they should join they might secure certain advantages of one kind and another. The introduction is generally a loathsome, disenchanting service. Most men of good character are surprised and indignant at what they experience. In various ways they are urged to go forward and finally do so. Each degree is a step into the bog and each degree is an occasion for promises on the part of the lodge men that the future will show better things, and so men go on until some of them take the Templar degrees. Those of them who have read this book know that the facts stated in it are substantially true; that the ceremonies and obligations and lectures are substantially as herein recorded. It is to be hoped that by this time they are satisfied that the whole system is not from above, but from below, and that they ought at once to sever their connection with such an organization. There are tens of thousands of lodge men in this country at this hour who are in exactly this condition: they know they ought to abandon the organization. To do so requires humility, faith and an indomitable courage. The fear of what lodge men may do to one's business, to one's reputation, even to one's life keeps thousands of men in a perpetual slavery. Let every such brother, as he reads these words, remember that Jesus himself has said: "He that will save his life shall lose it," but he that will sacrifice his life for the honor of Jesus shall keep it unto life eternal.

CHAPTER XXVI

Secrets[*] of Thirteen Masonic Degrees Illustrated.

Note—As Freemasonry is one indivisible system, and as the signs of all the degrees below it must be given in the Opening and Closing Ceremonies of each degree, we, with these signs give the rest of the so called "Secrets" and a few Masonic quotations, which show the teachings and doctrines of Freemasonry.

PREPARATION FOR ENTERED APPRENTICE DEGREE.

The candidate having satisfactorily answered the questions given on pages 95-6 and paid the initiation fee, is prepared for initiation as follows:

The Deacons or Stewards strip him to his shirt and drawers, and his drawers must be exchanged for a pair furnished by the lodge which fasten with strings. The *left* leg of these is rolled up above the knee. If his shirt does not open in front it is turned around, and if there are metal buttons or studs on it they are removed.

The *left* sleeve of his shirt is rolled up above the elbow, and the *left* side of his shirt is tucked in; so that the left leg, left foot, left arm and left breast are bare. A slipper is put on his *right* foot, a hoodwink over his eyes, and a small rope called a cable tow is put once around his neck.

Candidate duly and truly prepared, Entered Apprentice Degree.

Note 382.—From "FREEMASONRY ILLUSTRATED."
"It has been well said that the emblems are the Masonic Secrets written out, conveying as they do—but only to the instructed eye—all the Esotery of the institution."—**Morris' Dictionary**, Art. Emblems—Symbols.

TAKING ENTERED APPRENTICE OBLIGATION.

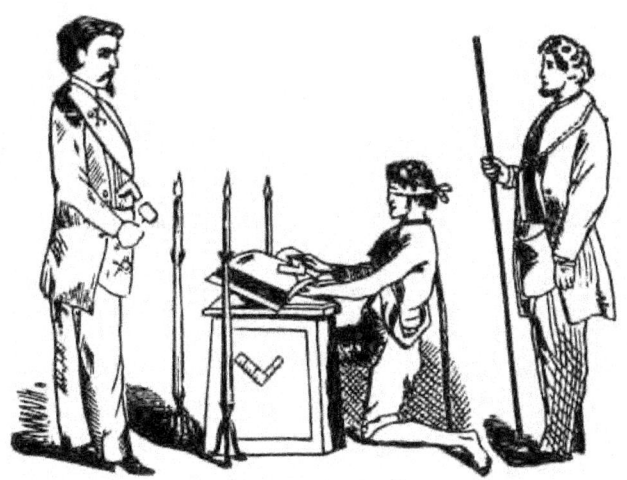

Candidate taking Entered Apprentice Obligation. See page 107.

"Every Mason is under an obligation to obey the laws of the lodge and the Grand Lodge. * * * It is the obligation which makes the Mason, and the difference between one Mason and another, consists simply in the fact that *one keeps his obligations better than another*.

"An obligation is an essential part of a degree."—*Morris's Dictionary, Art. Obligation.*

298   SHOCK OF ENLIGHTENMENT, FIRST DEGREE.

Shock of Enlightenment or Rite of Illumination, Entered Apprentice Degree

Due-Guard, Entered Apprentice.

DUE-GUARD OF AN ENTERED APPRENTICE.

Hold out left hand, with palm up, a little in front of the body, height of hips; next place right hand horizontally over the left, two or three inches above it. [See cut.]

ENTERED APPRENTICE SIGN, WORD AND GRIP.

SIGN OF AN ENTERED APPRENTICE.

Made from due-guard by dropping left hand to side, and at same time raise right arm, with hand still open, and draw hand quickly across the throat, the thumb being next to the throat, then hand drops to side. [See cut.]

Sign of Entered Apprentice.

ENTERED APPRENTICE SIGN WITHOUT DUE GUARD.

Draw open right hand across the throat, thumb next to throat.

Entered Apprentice Grip.

ENTERED APPRENTICE GRIP.

Grasp hands as in ordinary hand-shaking, and press ball of thumb hard against the knuckle-joint of each other's fore-finger.

ENTERED APPRENTICE WORD.

Boaz, which is the name of the grip. For mode of giving this "word" see page 113.

"THE WORKING TOOLS OF AN ENTERED APPRENTICE

Are the *Twenty-four Inch Gauge* and *Common Gavel*.

"THE TWENTY-FOUR INCH GAUGE

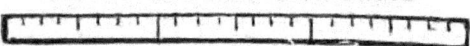

Is an instrument used by operative masons to measure and lay out their work; but we, as Free and Accepted Masons, are taught to make use of it for the more noble and glorious purpose of dividing our time. It being divided into twenty-four equal parts, is emblematical of the twenty-four hours of the day, which we are taught to divide into three equal parts; whereby are found eight hours for the service of God and a distressed worthy brother, eight for our usual vocations, and eight for refreshment and sleep."—*Mackey's Ritualist, page 38.*

"THE COMMON GAVEL

Is an instrument made use of by operative masons to break off the corners of rough stones, the better to fit them for the builder's use; but we, as Free and Accepted Masons, are taught to make use of it for the more noble and glorious purpose of divesting our hearts and consciences of all the vices and superfluities of life; thereby fitting our minds as living stones for that spiritual building, that house not made with hands, eternal in the heavens."—*Mackey's Ritualist, page 38.*

JEWELS OF A LODGE.

"A Lodge has six Jewels; three of these are immovable and three movable.

"The immovable jewels are the *Square, Level* and *Plumb.*

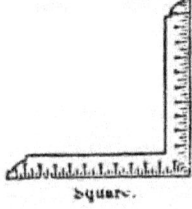
Square.

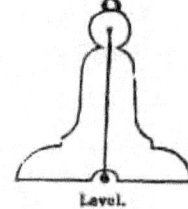
Level.

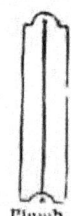
Plumb

JEWELS OF A LODGE.

"The *Square* inculcates morality; the *Level* equality; and the *Plumb*, rectitude of conduct.

"They are called immovable jewels, because they are always to be found in the East, West and South parts of the Lodge, being worn by the officers in those respective stations."—*Mackey's Ritualist, page* 57.

"THE MOVABLE JEWELS

Are the *Rough Ashlar*, the *Perfect Ashlar* and the *Trestle-Board*."

 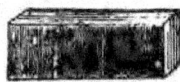 

Rough Ashlar. Perfect Ashlar. Trestle-Board.

"The rough ashlar is a stone as taken from the quarry in its rude and natural state.

"The perfect ashlar is a stone made ready by the hands of the workmen, to be adjusted by the working tools of the fellow craft.

"The trestle-board is for the master workman to draw his designs upon.

"By the rough ashlar we are reminded of our rude and imperfect state by nature; by the perfect ashlar, that state of perfection at which we hope to arrive by a virtuous education, our own endeavors, and the blessing of God; and by the trestle-board we are also reminded that, as the operative workman erects his temporal building agreeably to the rules and designs laid down by the master on his trestle-board, so should we, both operative and speculative, endeavor to erect our spiritual building agreeably to the rules and designs laid down by the Supreme Architect of the Universe, in the great books of nature and revelation, which are our spiritual, moral, and Masonic trestle-board."—*Mackey's Ritualist, page* 58.

THE POINT WITHIN A CIRCLE.

"Lodges were anciently dedicated to King Solomon, [who was said to be our first Most Excellent Grand Master] but Masons professing Christianity dedicate theirs to St. John the Baptist and St. John the Evangelist, who were two eminent patrons of Masonry; and since their time, there is represented, in every regular and well-governed lodge a certain point within a circle, the point representing an individual brother, the circle the boundary line of his conduct to God and man, beyond which he is never to suffer his passions, prejudices, or interest to betray him, on any occasion. This circle is embordered by two perpendicular parallel lines, representing those saints, who were perfect parallels in Christianity, as well as in Masonry; and upon the vertex rests the Holy Scriptures, which point out the whole duty of man. In going around this circle we necessarily touch upon these two lines, as well as upon the Holy Scriptures; and while a Mason keeps himself thus circumscribed, it is impossible that he should err."—*Sickels's Monitor, page 50.*

The Point within a Circle.

Preparation Fellow Craft Degree.

PREPARATION FOR FELLOW CRAFT DEGREE.

Candidate is prepared much the same as in the first degree. The *right* leg, *right* arm, *right* breast, and *right* foot being bare, a slipper on *left* foot and the cable tow twice around his naked right arm near shoulder.

A small white apron with bib turned up and he is "duly and truly prepared" to be made a Fellow Craft.

FELLOW CRAFT DUE-GUARD AND SIGN.

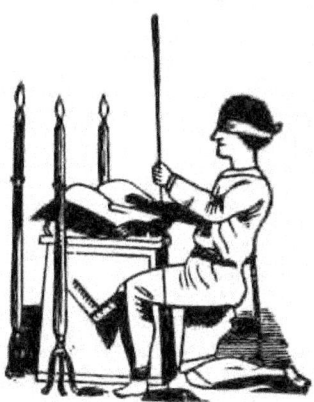

Candidate taking Fellow Craft Obligation.

"Increased privileges and honors thus encircling the profession of Fellow Craft, weightier and more numerous responsibilities are superadded.

Powerful obligations, impelling him to be secret obedient, honest and charitable, guide and restrain him. * * *

"He is subject to the discipline of his mother-lodge, and to all the penalties of Masonry."—*Morris's Dictionary*, Art. *Fellow Craft.*

Due-Guard, Fellow Craft.

DUE-GUARD OF A FELLOW CRAFT.

Hold out right hand, palm down, height of hips, and raise left hand to point perpendicularly upward, forearm forming a right angle with arm. [See cut.]

SIGN OF A FELLOW CRAFT.

Made from due-guard by dropping left hand carelessly to side while raising right hand to left breast, fingers a little crooked; then draw hand quickly across the breast; then drop hand to side. [See cut.]

Sign of a Fellow Craft.

304 FELLOW CRAFT GRIPS AND WORKING TOOLS.

Pass Grip of Fellow Craft

PASS GRIP OF A FELLOW CRAFT.
Grasp right hands as in ordinary hand shaking and press ball of thumb hard between knuckles of first and second fingers.

PASS OF A FELLOW CRAFT—*Shibboleth;* the name of the grip.

GRIP OF A FELLOW CRAFT.

Grasp right hands in the usual way and press thumb on knuckle joint of second finger.

"THE WORKING TOOLS OF A FELLOW CRAFT

Plumb.
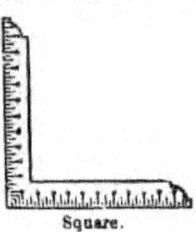
Square.
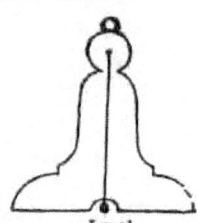
Level.

Are the *Plumb,* the *Square,* and the *Level.*

"The *Plumb* is an instrument made use of by operative masons to raise perpendiculars; the *Square,* to square their work; and the *Level,* to lay horizontals; but we, as Free and Accepted Masons, are taught to make use of them for more noble and glorious purposes; the plumb admonishes us to walk uprightly in our several stations before God and men, squaring our actions by the square of virtue, and remembering that we are traveling upon the level of time to that undiscovered country from whose bourne no traveler returns."-*Mackey's Rit. p. 73.*

MASTER MASON'S PREPARATION AND DUE-GUARD.

Preparation of Candidate Master Mason's Degree.

PREPARATION OF CANDIDATE, MASTER MASON'S DEGREE.

The candidate is stripped, as in previous degrees, but in this "*Sublime Degree*," both breasts, both arms both feet and legs are bare. He is hood-winked and the cable-tow is put three times around his body.

Candidate taking Master Mason's Obligation. See page 252.

DUE-GUARD OF A MASTER MASON.

Extend both hands, in front of the body, height of hips, palms down, thumbs nearly touching each other. [See cut.]

Due-Guard, Master Mason.

SIGN OF A MASTER MASON.

Made from due-guard, by dropping left hand and drawing right hand across the bowels to the right, thumb toward the body, height of hips. [See cut:]

Sign of a Master Mason.

Pass Grip of a Master Mason.

PASS GRIP OF A MASTER MASON.

Grasp hands naturally and press thumb between knuckles of second and third fingers.

STRONG GRIP OF A MASTER MASON OR LION'S PAW.

Hands joined as shown in cut, thumb and fingers pressing hard on hand and wrist of each other.

PASS OF A MASTER MASON *Tubal Cain;* name of grip

"THE COMPASSES Are peculiarly consecrated to this degree, because within their extreme points, when properly extended, are emblematically said to be inclosed the principal tenets of our profession, and hence the moral application of the Compasses, in the third degree, is to those precious jewels of a Master Mason, Friendship, Morality, and Brotherly Love."— *Mackey's Ritualist, page 110.*

"THE WORKING TOOLS OF A MASTER MASON, 807

Are all the implements of masonry indiscriminately, but more especially the *Trowel*.

"The *Trowel* is an instrument made use of by Operative Masons to spread the cement which unites a building into one common mass; but we, as Free and Accepted Masons, are taught to make use of it for the more noble and glorious purpose of spreading the cement of brotherly love and affection; that cement which unites us into one sacred band, or society of friends and brothers, among whom no contention, should ever exist, but that noble contention or rather emulation; of who can best work and best agree."—*Mackey's Rit. p. 111.*

THE TRAGEDY OF THE THIRD DEGREE.

PLAYING MURDER AND RESURRECTION IN TEN SCENES.

SCENE I.—PLAYING MURDER Assault by "*Judeia*" on the Candidate alias "Grand Master Hiram Abiff."

SCENE II: PLAYING MURDER. —"Jubela" draws 24 inch gauge across his throat.

SCENE III: PLAYING MURDER. —Assault by "Jubelo" on the Candidate.

SCENE IV: PLAYING MURDER.—"Jubelo" strikes him with the square on left breast.

SCENE V: PLAYING MURDER.—Assault by "Jubelum" on the Candidate.

310 PLAYING MURDER AND MOURNING.

SCENE VI: PLAYING MURDER.—"Jubelum" kills him with the Setting Maul &c.; tumbles him into the Canvas.

GRAND HAILING SIGN OF DISTRESS.

First Position.

Second Position.

Third Position.

SCENE VII: PLAYING DISTRESS.—Mourning for "our Grand Master Hiram Abiff."

Raise hands and arms as shown in first cut, and if in the ceremony of "raising" or in the dark, the words in brackets may be used, otherwise not. [O Lord.] Bring arms from first to second position, [My God,] bring arms to third position [is there no help for the widow's Son?] bring arms to side.

PLAYING MOURNING AND RESURRECTION.   311

In the dark, when in distress, the words are "O Lord, my God is there no help for the widows son?" In the ceremony of *"raising"* after the second attempt and failure to raise the body, first by the Entered Apprentice's Grip and then by the Fellow Craft's when this sign is given the words are, "O Lord my God! O Lord my God! O Lord my God! I fear the Master's word is forever lost."

SCENE VIII: PLAYING DISTRESS.—Procession Singing Dirge for "our Grand Master Hiram Abiff."

SCENE IX: PLAYING RESURRECTION—Praying at Mock Resurrection of Candidate alias "our Grand Master Hiram Abiff."

FIVE POINTS OF FELLOWSHIP.

Foot to foot, knee to knee, breast to breast, hand to back and cheek to cheek, or mouth to ear, when they whisper: *Mah-hah-bone*, which is the Master's word.

SCENE X: PLAYING RESURRECTION.—Candidate Raised on the Five Points of Fellowship.

EMBLEMS[*] OF THE MASTER MASON'S DEGREE.

"THE THREE STEPS"

Usually delineated upon the Master's carpet, are emblematical of the three principal stages of human life, viz: *youth, manhood, and age*. In youth as Entered Apprentices, we ought industriously to occupy our minds in the attainment of useful knowledge; in manhood, as Fellow Crafts, we should apply our knowledge to the discharge of our respective duties to God, our neighbor, and ourselves; that so in age, as Master Masons, we may enjoy the happy reflection consequent on a well-spent life, and die in the hope of a glorious immortality.

NOTE 383.—"Under the term Emblems, writers include those conveying both the esotery and exotery of Masonic knowledge."—*Morris's Dictionary*, Art. *Emblems*.

EMBLEMS MASTER MASON'S DEGREE. 313

"THE POT OF INCENSE

Is an emblem"* of a pure heart, which is always an acceptable sacrifice to the Deity; and as this glows with fervent heat, so should our hearts continually glow with gratitude to the great and beneficent Author of our existence, for the manifold blessings and comforts we enjoy.

"THE BEE HIVE

Is an emblem of industry, and recommends the practice of that virtue to all created beings, from the highest seraph in heaven to the lowest reptile of the dust [etc. See p. 307 of "Freemasonry Ill'd."

"THE BOOK OF CONSTITUTIONS GUARDED BY THE TYLER'S SWORD

Reminds us that we should be ever watchful and guarded in our thoughts, words and actions, particularly when before the enemies of Masonry; ever bearing in remembrance those truly Masonic virtues, silence and circumspection.

"THE SWORD POINTING TO A NAKED HEART

Demonstrates that justice will sooner or later overtake us; and although our thoughts, words and actions may be hidden from the eyes of man, yet that

NOTE 384—"Everything in the *esotery* of the society is written down, or engraved upon durable objects by Symbols. Each of these has a public and private meaning, the latter communicated only by suitable restrictions to proper persons. These Symbols form a large part of the universal language of Masonry."—*Morris's Dictionary, Art. Symbol*

314   EMBLEMS MASTER MASON'S DEGREE.
"ALL-SEEING EYE,

Whom the Sun Moon and Stars obey, and under whose watchful care even comets perform their stupendous revolutions, pervades the inmost recesses of the human heart, and will reward us according to our merits.

"THE ANCHOR AND ARK

Are emblems of a well-grounded *hope*, and a well-spent life. They are emblematical of that divine *ark*,[etc. See p. 309 of "Freemasonry Illustrated."]

"THE FORTY-SEVENTH PROBLEM OF EUCLID.

This was an invention of our ancient friend and brother, the great Pythagoras, who, in his travels through Asia, Africa and Europe, was initiated into the several orders of priesthood,[etc. See page 310.

"THE HOUR GLASS

Is an emblem of human life. Behold! how swiftly the sands run, and how rapidly our lives are drawing to a close!

"THE SCYTHE

Is an emblem of time, which cuts the brittle thread of life, and launches us into eternity. Behold! what havoc the scythe of time makes among the human race! If by chance we should escape." [etc. See p. 311.]
—*Sickels's Monitor, pages 113-119.*

EMBLEMS MASTER MASON'S DEGREE.

THE SETTING MAUL, SPADE AND COFFIN.

"The second class of emblems are not monitorial, and therefore their true interpretation can only be obtained within the tyled recesses of the lodge. They consist of the Setting Maul, the Spade, the Coffin, and the Sprig of Acacia. They afford subjects of serious and solemn reflection to the rational and contemplative mind."—*Mackey's Ritualist, page 131.*

FOURTH, OR MARK MASTER'S DEGREE.

[FIRST DEGREE OF THE CHAPTER.]

CRAFTSMEN FROM THE QUARRIES.

 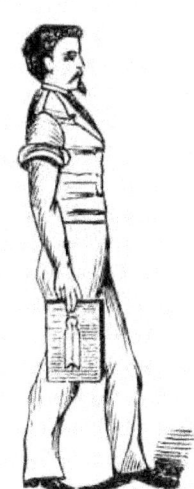 

Candidate. Junior Deacon. Senior Deacon.

PENALTY OF AN IMPOSTER.

Penalty of an Imposter, when detected in trying to collect wages not due.

Preparation or Mark Master's Degree. Stripped to his shirt and drawers and both breasts bare; hoodwinked and a cable-tow four times around his body.

Due-Guard Mark Master.

DUE-GUARD OF A MARK MASTER.

Third and fourth fingers of right hand closed; thumb and first and second fingers extended; position of carrying the keystone; then bring right hand up to right ear and move it back and forth as if brushing back a lock of hair, ear passing between thumb and finger each time. [See cut.] This refers to the penalty of having right ear smote off.

SIGN, MARK MASTER.

Made from due-guard by dropping right hand and arm to a horizontal position, extended in front on a line with the hips, and at same time raise left hand about the height of your chin, and bring it down edgewise on right wrist, as if to chop off right hand.

GRAND HAILING SIGN.

Close the third and fourth fingers of right hand, extending the thumb and second finger —the position in which the keystone is carried.

Sign, Mark Master.

Grand Hailing Sign of Distress, Mark Master.

HEAVE OVER, OR PRINCIPAL SIGN.

With a vigorous *slap* place back of *right* hand in palm of *left*, both being flat and held down near right hip, then swing them together over to *left* shoulder.

SIGN OF RECEIVING WAGES.

Hand and arm extended, third and fourth fingers closed, thumb and first fingers extended and spread as in cut.

Principal Sign.

Sign of Receiving Wages.

GRIPS AND WORKING TOOLS OF A MARK MASTER.

PASS GRIP OF A MARK MASTER.

Right hands grasped, as if to pull a person up a steep bank. thumbs touching at ends. [See cut.]

Pass Grip of Mark Master

REAL GRIP OF A MARK MASTER.

Little fingers locked, others closed, points of thumbs together as shown in cut.

Real Grip of a Mark Master.

WORD: *Siroc, or Mark Well.*

WORKING TOOLS OF A MARK MASTER.

"THE CHISEL

Morally demonstrates the advantages of discipline and education. The mind, like the diamond in its original state, is rude and unpolished, but as the effect of the chisel on the external coat soon presents to view the latent beauties of the diamond, so education discovers the latent virtues of the mind, and draws them forth to range the large field of matter and space, to display the summit of human knowledge, our duty to God and to man."

"THE MALLET

Morally teaches us to correct irregularities. and to reduce man to a proper level; so that, by quiet deportment he may, in the school of discipline, learn to be content. What the mallet is to the workman, enlightened reason is to the passion; it curbs ambition, it depresses envy, it moderates anger, and it encourages good

DUE-GUARD AND SIGN OF A PAST MASTER.   319

dispositions; whence arises among good Masons that comely order.

> "Which nothing earthly gives, or can destroy,
> The soul's calm sunshine, and the heartfelt joy."
> —*Mackey's Ritualist, page 286.*

THE MARK OF A MARK MASTER.

"In the passage from the second chapter of Revelations, which is read during the presentation of the keystone, it is most probable that by the white stone and the 'new name.' St. John referred to these tokens of alliance and friendship."—*Mackey's Rit. page 287.*

DUE-GUARD OF A PAST MASTER.

Fingers of right hand closed, end of thumb between closed lips, as if ready to split open the tongue with thumb nail. [See cut and penalty of obligation.]

SIGN OF A PAST MASTER.

Raise right hand to left shoulder, hand open, and draw it diagonally down across body to right hip, thus crossing the penalties of the first three degrees. [See cut.]

Step and Due-Guard of a Past Master.

Sign of a Past Master.

PREPARATION MOST EXCELLENT MASTER.

Grip of a Past Master.

GRIP OF A PAST MASTER.

Give Master Mason's grip, inside of right feet together, then whisper the " Word " *Giblim.* Next grasp left arms just above the wrist with right hands and right arms at elbow with left hands, saying as change is made, From a grip to a span.

PREPARATION OF CANDIDATE,
MOST EXCELLENT MASTER'S DEGREE.

Junior Deacon removes candidate's coat, and puts a cable-tow six times around his body. No hoodwink in this degree.

Preparation Most Excellent Master.

DUE-GUARD, SIGN AND GRIP, M. E. MASTER. 321

Due-Guard, or Penal Sign, Most Excellent Master.

Sign of Astonishment, Most Excellent Master

DUE-GUARD, OR PENAL SIGN, MOST EXCELLENT MASTER.

Hands on centre of breast, fingers just touching each other, and crooked, as if to tear open your breast, which is the penalty of this degree. [See cut.]

SIGN, OR SIGN OF ASTONISHMENT.

Hands and arms extended forwards and upwards, eyes rolled back, as shown in the cut.

GRIP, MOST EXCELLENT MASTER.

Grip, Most Excellent Master.

Grasp right hands, and with finger on under side and thumb on top press third finger near knuckle. [See cut.]

"It is this bringing of the ark into the temple with shouting and praise, and depositing 't in the holy spot where it was thenceforth to remain, that is commemorated by a portion of the ceremonies of the Most Excellent Master's degree —*Mackey's Ritualist*, page 328.

322 ROYAL ARCH CANDIDATES.

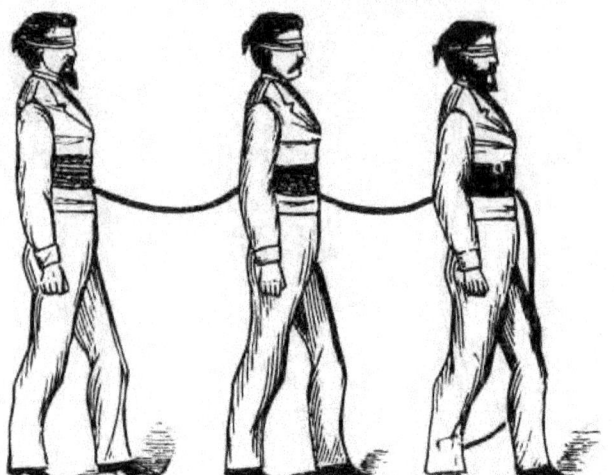

Royal Arch Candidates Duly and Truly Prepared.

Royal Arch Due Guard—1st Position.   Royal Arch Due-Guard—2d Position.

ROYAL ARCH DEGREE.

ROYAL ARCH DUE-GUARD.

Turning to the left and looking up, raise left hand and arm, as shown in cut, first position, palm of hand out; then bring up right hand, with a slight slap on back of left; then turn to the right, and raise right hand, and bring up left hand with a slap on right hand. [In some Chapters this is called the penal sign, as it is.]

Royal Arch Sign.

ROYAL ARCH SIGN.

Right hand held with edge against forehead, thumb next to forehead; then draw hand across to the right. This refers to the penalty of the degree—skull smote off.

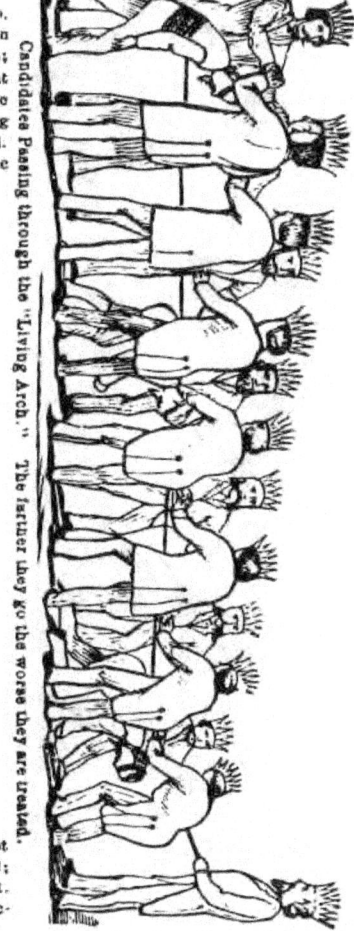

Candidates Passing through the "Living Arch." The farther they go the worse they are treated.

324   ROYAL ARCH DEGREE.

Candidates Passing over the "Rough and Rugged Road" from Babylon to Jerusalem.

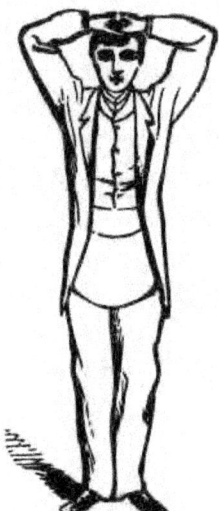

Royal Arch Grand Hailing Sign.

2d Position Grand Hailing Sign.

ROYAL ARCH DEGREE. 325

ROYAL ARCH G. HAILING SIGN.

Fingers interlaced and held over the head as shown in cut, first position; turning to the right bring hands down on thighs with a slight slap as if suffering severe pain in the back.

Sign of Grand Master First Veil.
Holding out a cane.

Sign of G. Master Second Veil.
Putting right hand into bosom.

Sign of Grand Master Third Veil.
Pouring out water as shown in cut.

WORDS OF G. M. FIRST VEIL.
Shem, Ham and Japheth.

WORDS OF G. M. SECOND VEIL.
Shem, Japheth and Adoniram.

WORDS OF G. M. THIRD VEIL.
Haggai, Joshua and Zerrubbabel.

SIGNET OF G. M. THIRD VEIL.
That of Zerrubbabel or Truth-

"THE WORKING TOOLS OF A ROYAL ARCH MASON.

Are the *Crow, Pickaxe* and *Spade.* The *Crow* is used by operative masons to raise things of great weight and bulk the *Pickaxe* to loosen the soil and prepare it for digging; and the *Spade* to remove rubbish. But the Royal Arch Mason is emblematically taught to use h em for more noble purposes. By them he is reminded that it is his sacred duty to lift from his mind the heavy weight of passions and prejudices which encumber his progress towards virtue, loosening the hold which long habits of sin and folly have had upon his disposition, and removing the rubbish of vice and ignorance, which prevents him from beholding that eternal foundation of truth and wisdom upon which he is to erect the spiritual and moral temple of his second life."—*Sickels's Monitor, Part* 2, *p.* 65.

SQUARES OF OUR THREE ANCIENT GRAND MASTERS.

"Freemasonry is throughout so connected a system that we are continually meeting in an inferior degree with something that is left to be explained in a higher. Such is the case with the *three squares of our ancient Grand Masters,* whose peculiar history can only be understood by those who have advanced to the degree of Select Master."—*Mackey's Rit. p.* 381.

"THE EQUILATERAL OR PERFECT TRIANGLE.

Is emblematical of the three essential attributes of Deity, namely: Omnipresence, Omniscience and Omnipotence, and as the equal sides or equal angles form but one TRIANGLE, so these three equal attributes constitute but one God. —*Sickel's Monitor, Part* 2, *page* 73.

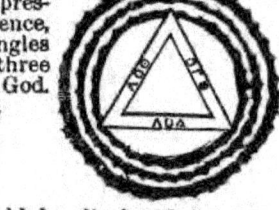

THE ROYAL ARCH BANNER,

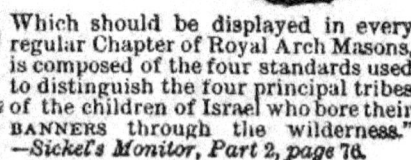

Which should be displayed in every regular Chapter of Royal Arch Masons, is composed of the four standards used to distinguish the four principal tribes of the children of Israel who bore their BANNERS through the wilderness." —*Sickel's Monitor, Part* 2, *page* 76.

328 GRAND OMNIFIC OR ROYAL ARCH WORD.

This must only be given by a group of three. Each with his right hand grasps the right wrist of the companion on the left, and with his left hand the left wrist of his companion on his right, throwing forward his right foot, hollow in front, his toe touching the heel of his companion on the right. This is called three times three, as there are three right hands, three left hands and three feet forming three triangles. They then repeat the verse given on page 500 of *Freemasonry Illustrated*.

They then balance three times three, with a short pause between each three, when they raise their right hands over their heads, as shown in cut, and the Grand Omnific Royal Arch word is given in low breath in syllables, as follows: The first one says *Jah*, second one *buh*, third one *lun;* then the second one says *Jah*, third one *buh*, and first one *lun;* then the third one says *Jah*, first one *buh*, second one *lun*.

Group of Three, Giving Grand Omnific Word.

The word *Je-ho-vah* is treated in the same way, and the word *G-o-d* is given in the same way but letter by letter, thus each of the three being repeated three times, varying each time as explained. In some Chapters only the word Je-ho-vah is given in this way, and in others the word Jah-Bel-On was formerly used.

Due-Guard.

DUE-GUARD OF A ROYAL MASTER.

Place forefinger of right hand on lips.

GRIP OF THE BROKEN TRIANGLE, OR ROYAL MASTER'S GRIP.

Royal Masters Grip.

Right hand hold of each other's right wrist, and left hand hold of each other's left wrist, raise arms as if to begin giving the Royal Arch Word, when left hands fall to side and right drop on to each other's shoulders, each looks down and the dialogue begins.

Thrice Illustrious Master—Alas!
Deputy Master—Poor Hiram!

[It takes three to give the Grand Omnific or Royal Arch Word as explained on pages 146 and 326.]

DUE-GUARD, OR FIRST SIGN OF A SELECT MASTER.

Arms held similar to second position in Master Mason's sign of distress, with hands clenched in allusion to the penalty of the obligation; to have both hands chopped off to the stump   See cut.

Due-Guard or 1st Sign.

SECOND SELECT MASTER'S SIGN.

2d S. M. Sign.

Crossing hands and arms as in engraving quickly draw the hands edgewise across the body, downwards, as though in the act of quartering your body; then hands drop to side. This refers to the penalty in obligation, to have the body quartered.

3d S. M. Sign.

THIRD SELECT MASTER'S SIGN.

Place the hands over eyes as shown in engraving, and quickly jerk arms downwards, as though tearing out your eyes and throwing them on the ground; then hands drop to side. This also refers to the penalty in obligation.

FOURTH SELECT MASTER'S SIGN.

1st position.   2d position.
4th Select Master's Sign.

Place left hand on upper part of forehead, palm down and right hand over it, heels together and body erect as in cut first position. Then take a long, *vigorous* step with right foot, throwing out hands and arms as in cut, second position.

SELECT MASTER'S DEGREE.

Other Select Master's Signs.

OTHER SELECT MASTER'S SIGNS.

Forefinger of left hand on upper lip, hand open, palm inward and forearm horizontal; say, SILENCE.

Right hand on bowels and, say, SECRECY.

Left forefinger to lips and right hand over eyes and say, SILENCE AND DARKNESS.

SELECT MASTER'S GRIP.

Left hand on candidate's right breast then grasp the right lapel of his coat just below the collar, saying, Rise, Izabud! be voluntarily deaf, dumb and blind to all you may hear and see in the ninth arch. This (the grip of the lapel of his coat) is the grip of a Select Master and the word is IZABUD or ISH SODI which signifies, Man of my choice, or Select Master.

First Sign, S. E. Master

DUE-GUARD OR FIRST SIGN, SUPER-EXCELLENT MASTER.

Cross arms, as shown in cut, fingers clinched, thumbs pointing upwards.

SECOND SIGN SUPER-EXCELLENT MASTER.

Right hand and elbow height of the eyes, two first fingers extended like a fork, thumb and other fingers clinched; then draw arm back, as shown in cut, and dart hand and arm forward horizontally. This alludes to the penalty of S. E. Master's obligation—eyes gouged out.

Second sign S. E. Master

GRAND HAILING SIGN OF DISTRESS OF A SUPER-EXCELLENT MASTER.

Right hand clinched, make sign of a Past Master with a zig zag motion, and alludes to a portion of the obligation, that of being bound in chains of brass. The word accompanying the last sign is NAHOD ZABOD BONE.

Grand Hailing Sign of S. E. Master.

PASS GRIP, SUPER-EXCELLENT MASTER.

Right hands grasped, as if to pull a person up a steep bank, thumbs touching at ends,

Pass grip, Super-Excellent Master.

This is same as Mark Master's grip.

WORD: *Siroc*, or *Mark Well*.

REAL GRIP, SUPER-EXCELLENT MASTER.

Same as pass grip, except grasping each other by both hands, arms crossed. See cut.

1st. (says) *Saul the first King of Israel.*

2nd. (says) *Zedekiah the last King of Judah.*

The two last sentences are called the "Word" or "Pass."

Real grip S. E. Master.

DRAW SWORDS.

First Motion. At the word "draw," grasp scabbard with left and sword with right hand, and draw sword about two inches.

Second Motion. At the word "swords," draw sword out, and throwing right hand in front, drop sword in hollow of elbow.

Third Motion. Bring right hand with hilt of sword to right thigh, elbow a little bent, sword perpendicular and held by thumb and forefinger. This is the position of

CARRY SWORDS.

As this is the usual position of holding a sword, the position is asssumed in executing the order to "Draw—swords," and resumed at the command "Recover," given after a salute or when a cross is formed.

Carry swords.

PRESENT SWORDS.

Sword being at "carry," at the word "present" grasp hilt firmly and at the word "swords" raise sword perpendicularly, guard or hilt height of shoulder, arm against the body. See cut.

After "Present—swords," the order "Carry—swords," is executed by extending the hand in front when sword drops in hollow of arm at elbow; then bring hand and hilt to right thigh, sword perpendicular.

Present swords

OPENING CEREMONIES.

SALUTE.

Bring sword to "present," then extend arm and let point of sword drop as shown in cut, hand on right thigh, back of hand up.

RETURN SWORDS.

First Motion. Bring swords to "present" and at same time grasp scabbard with left hand near the mouth.

Second Motion. Drop point of sword to the mouth of the scabbard and turning the head to the left raise the hand when the sword is pushed in, then, eyes front and hands at side.

Salute

FORM CROSS.

This command is given only when lines are formed facing inward, as for reception of Sovereign Master, or Eminent Commander, as he is called in the next degree, or for inspection and review.

Knights facing each other, each throws right foot forward about eighteen inches, throwing the weight of the body forward and right arm extended forward and and upward, when swords of opposite knights are crossed about eight inches from the point.

Form cross.

SWORD CUTS.

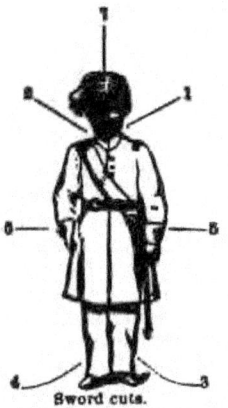

Sword cuts.

There are seven *regular* sword cuts, and when at such practice, the officer in command orders the cuts by the numbers.

The preliminary commands are, first: "*Prepare to guard!*" when sword is brought to the position of "present;" when the second preliminary command, "*Guard!*" is given, and each throws the right foot forward about eighteen inches and at same time extends right arm and cross swords with each other as in "form cross" except that swords are crossed about midway of the blade. Swords are held in this position till the order for the cuts is given.

CUT ONE is a downward cut from the right toward the neck, as shown in engraving, when sword is brought back to position of "prepare to guard," and *after each cut swords are brought to "prepare to guard."*

CUT TWO is same as cut one, except a *left* downward stroke toward the neck.

CUT THREE is made by a sweep of the sword around to the right and then up toward the legs as shown in engraving, and is called a '*right under cut.*"

CUT FOUR is the same as cut three, but from the left and called a "*left under cut.*"

CUT FIVE is a cut from the right toward the body at or near the waist.

CUT SIX is the same as cut five except from the left.

CUT SEVEN is a vertical cut toward the head and is called the "*head cut.*"

JEWISH PASS.

Master of Palace advances to Sovereign Master, brings his sword to "recover," when they give "the word *over* an arch of steel," as follows: They clash their swords together and then give cuts *one* and *four* [See page 132] as in regular sword practice, the blows being parried. Each then throws forward his left foot and grasps the other's right shoulder with his left hand, when a dialogue takes place.

Giving Jewish Pass.

Master of Palace—JUDAH.
Sovereign Master—BENJAMIN.
Master of Palace—BENJAMIN.
Sovereign Master—JUDAH.
(They resume their places.)

PERSIAN PASS.

Giving Persian Pass.

Sword practice as before, except that there are *four* regular cuts, *two, one, four* and *two* and the word is "given *under* an arch of steel."

Chancellor—TATNAI.
Sovereign Master—SHETHAR-BOZANI.
Chancellor—SHETHAR-BOZANI.
Sovereign Master—TATNAI.
(They resume their stations.)

RED CROSS WORD.

Giving Red Cross Word.

The knights opposite each other give cuts-*one*, *two* and *four*, then each draws back his sword in a quick, threatening manner as if to thrust it into his companion, each of the Second Division whispering, VERITAS, and the First answering, RIGHT.

RED CROSS GRAND SIGN, GRIP AND WORD.

Knights advance to each other; First Division gives cut *three* with swords; then each raises his left hand and places thumb and forefinger against his lips, the others spread open upward as if holding a horn to give a blast, and then with a graceful sweep form a semicircle around to the left, when hand falls to side. Then give cuts *one, four* and *two* with sword and throwing left foot forward interlace the fingers of left hands, when knights of First Division whisper to Second Division, LIBERATAS, and Second replies, The word is right. All the way through each knight of the First Division takes the knight opposite him in the Second Division.

Red Cross Sign.

Red Cross Grip.

338   KNIGHTS TEMPLAR DEGREE.

Table in the Chamber of Reflection.

Pilgrim Penitent.

Pilgrim Warrior.

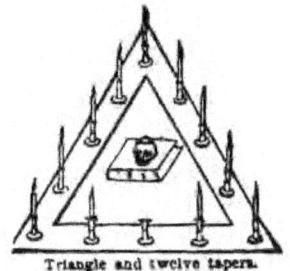
Triangle and twelve tapers.

KNIGHTS TEMPLAR DEGREE.   339

DUE-GUARD OF A KNIGHT TEMPLAR.

Thumb of right hand under the chin, as shown in cut, fingers closed in hand.

This alludes to the penalty of the obligation. Head placed on the highest spire in Christendom.

Due-Guard K. T.

Giving Persian Pass

PILGRIM WARRIOR'S PASS.

This is given in the same manner as the Persian pass.

Four sword cuts are given, the fourth being toward the neck, either cut No. 1 or 2, when the Pilgrim Warrior's pass, *Maher-shalal-hash-baz*, is given under an arch of steel. See cut.

PILGRIM PENITENT'S PASS.

Golgotha; given under an arch of steel. The same as the Pilgrim Warrior's pass.

Knights Templar Grip.

KNIGHTS TEMPLAR GRIP AND WORD.

Fingers of right hands and left hands interlaced and of course arms crossed, as shown in cut.

IMMACULATE WORD, *Immanuel*. (Spoken as arms are crossed.

KNIGHTS TEMPLAR DEGREE.

Enforcing fifth libation.

KNIGHTS TEMPLAR GRAND HAILING SIGN.

Right foot crossed over the left as shown in cut. Arms and hands extended and head inclined to the right. Then say, "*In hoc signo vinces,*" the motto of the order. It is pretended that Christ hung on the cross in this manner.

K. T. Grand Hailing Sign.

KNIGHT OF MALTA SIGN.

Both hands held out as if warming them; then quickly seize left hand near knuckle joint of little finger with thumb and forefinger of right hand, raising them in this position as high as the chin when they are jerked apart and hands and arms extended downward at an angle of forty-five degrees, fingers extended, palms down. This is supposed to represent Paul on the island of Melita, discovering a scorpion on his hand and jerking it off into the fire where he was warming.

Knight of Malta Sign.

KNIGHT OF MALTA DEGREE. 341

GRAND SIGN AND GRIP, KNIGHT OF MALTA.

Knight of Malta grand Sign and Grip.

Eminent Commander (to candidate)—Thomas, reach hither thy finger and feel the print of the nails. (They join right hands each forcing the forefinger into the palm of the other's hand.)

Eminent Commander—Reach hither thy hand and thrust it into my side. (Each extends his left hand and arm, thrusting it into the other's left side, right hands still joined.]

Eminent Commander—MY LORD.

Candidate (prompted)—AND MY GOD.

NOMENCLATURE AND CLASSIFICATION OF THE GRADES IN FREEMASONRY

SYMBOLIC GRADES

Conferred only in regular Lodges of Master Masons, duly constituted by Grand Lodges

1° Entered Apprentice
2° Fellowcraft
3° Master Mason

INEFFABLE GRADES

4° Secret Master
5° Perfect Master
6° Intimate Secretary
7° Provost and Judge
8° Intendant of the building
9° Master Elect of Nine
10° Master Elect of Fifteen
11° Sublime Master Elected
12° Grand Master Architect
13° Master of the Ninth Arch
14° Grand Elect Mason

Conferred in a Lodge of Perfection, 14°, duly constituted under authority of the Supreme Council of the 33°.

ANCIENT HISTORICAL AND TRADITIONAL GRADES

15° Knight of the East or Sword
16° Prince of Jerusalem

Conferred in a Council, Princes of Jerusalem, 16°

APOCALYPTIC AND CHRISTIAN GRADES

17° Knight of the East and West
18° Knight of Rose Croix de H-R-D-M

Conferred in a Chapter of Rose Croix de H-R-D-M, 18°

MODERN HISTORICAL, CHIVALRIC, AND PHILOSOPHICAL GRADES

19° Grand Pontiff
20° Master ad Vitam
21° Patriarch Noachite
22° Prince of Libanus
23° Chief of the Tabernacle
24° Prince of the Tabernacle
25° Knight of the Brazen Serpent
26° Prince of Mercy
27° Commander of the Temple
28° Knight of the Sun
29° Knight of St. Andrew
30° Grand Elect Kadosh or Knight of the White and Black Eagle
31° Grand Inspector Inquisitor Commander
32° Sublime Prince of the Royal Secret

Conferred in a Consistory, Sublime Princes of the Royal Secret, 32°

OFFICIAL GRADES

33° Sovereign Grand Inspector General

Conferred only by the SUPREME COUNCIL, 33°, and upon those who may be elected to receive it by that high body which assembles yearly.

OTHER MASONIC TITLES

A Dictionary of Freemasonry
Freemasonry and its Etiquette
Freemasonry at a Glance (Answers to 555 Questions)
Freemasonry Character Claims
Morals and Dogma of Freemasonry
Order of the Eastern Star
Revised Duncan's Ritual Vol. 1
Revised Duncan's Ritual Vol. 2
Revised Knight Templarism Illustrated
Scottish Rites Masonry Vol. 1
Scottish Rites Masonry Vol. 2
Secret Societies Illustrated
The History of Freemasonry
The Illustrated History of Freemasonry

MASONIC RELATED TITLES:

Freemasonry and Judaism
Freemasonry Interpreted
Freemasonry and the Vatican

WWW.LUSHENABKS.COM

www.ingramcontent.com/pod-product-compliance
Lightning Source LLC
Chambersburg PA
CBHW061954180426
43198CB00036B/809